Pioneer Cattleman in Montana

PIONEER CATTLEMAN IN MONTANA
The Story of the Circle C Ranch

By WALT COBURN

University of Oklahoma Press: Norman

Also by Walt Coburn

The Ringtailed Rannyhans (1927)
Mavericks (1929)
Barb Wire (1931)
Law Rides the Range (1935)
Sky Pilot Cowboy (1937)
Pardners of the Dim Trails (1951)
Beyond the Wide Missouri (1956)
Stirrup High (1957)

Library of Congress Catalog Card Number: 68–15691

ISBN: 978-0-8061-4208-1 (paper)

Copyright 1968 by the University of Oklahoma Press, Norman, Publishing Division of the University. Manufactured in the U.S.A. Paperback edition published 2011.

All rights reserved. No part of this publication may be reproduced, stored in a retrieval system, or transmitted, in any form or by any means, electronic, mechanical, photocopying, recording or otherwise—except as permitted in Section 107 or 108 of the United States Copyright Act—without the prior written permission of the University of Oklahoma Press.

To my father Robert Coburn
and all other pioneer cattlemen in Montana

Preface

ALONG ABOUT 1900, A. W. Bowen and Company, Chicago, published a book entitled *Progressive Men of the State of Montana*. This large volume consisting of 1,886 pages contains most of the names and steel-engraved photographs of the men who were the Montana pioneers, with brief outlines telling about each pioneer's birth and family and describing his particular role in the settlement of the frontier—whether he was a placer miner, banker, merchant, fur trader, or stockman.

The index lists 1,881 of these hardy pioneers, whose taproots were planted in Montana Territory and who opened that vast northern wilderness once claimed by the Plains Indians, the Sioux and Blackfeet and their tribal bands.

Those who followed the trail blazed by the Lewis and Clark expedition were a courageous and hardy breed of pioneer. Some came by steamboat up the Missouri River to the city of Fort Benton, the head of navigation, and some came by wagon train over the Oregon Trail. Others came with trail herds of longhorns from Texas. Some were prospectors who made overnight fortunes panning gold at Virginia City, Bannack, and Last Chance Gulch, now the city of Helena, the thriving capital of Montana.

There were hundreds of others who also came to Montana—plainsmen, scouts, mountain men, prospectors, cowpunchers, soldiers, missionaries, road agents, gamblers, outlaws, horse thieves, cattle rustlers, and adventurers of all sorts. And a special niche should be made in the hall of fame for the pioneer women whose splendid brand of courage and fortitude oftentimes surpassed the bravery of their pioneer husbands and fathers during the bloodspattered Indian wars. They endured countless dangers and untold hardships. Theirs were the unshed tears and the silent prayers for the protection of God which were answered countless times in many ways.

The hardy breed of pioneers braved the unknown dangers and hardships of an uncharted wilderness to make a safe homeland for the less courageous. Some of the pioneers perished in the struggle for the survival of the fittest, but others survived the years of untold hardship to conquer the wilderness and establish towns and villages.

The history of the pioneers of Montana has become legend; their unwritten saga, handed down for generations, has become a proud heritage treasured by their descendants. Far too little has ever been written about this vanished era, and countless stories that made up the warp and weave of the saga of the pioneers have been lost and forgotten.

This book was written in the hope of preserving a segment of the history of frontier Montana, and it is to the fond memory of the courageous pioneer that this story of Robert Coburn's Circle C outfit is dedicated.

Prescott, Arizona WALT COBURN
August 19, 1968

Contents

	Preface	*vii*
1.	The Island Mountains	3
2.	Meeting with Chief Joseph	8
3.	The Hard Winter of '86	15
4.	The Great Land Swindle	27
5.	The Lawless Range	36
6.	The Curry-Landusky Feud	53
7.	The Showdown	63
8.	The Violent Death of Johnny Curry	72
9.	The Wagner Train Robbery	82
10.	Ambush	111
11.	The Disappearance of Abe Gill	117
12.	The Circle C Cowhands	126
13.	The Pioneer Jerk-Line Freighters	145
14.	The Hungry Plight of the Indians	154
15.	The Allen Killing	163
16.	A New Foreman for the Circle C	175
17.	Trouble at the Circle C Roundup Camp	187
18.	Shipping Time at the Malta Stockyards	203
19.	Mutiny at the Circle C Ranch	210
20.	"One of Ourn"	215
21.	Tales of South America	221
22.	The Circle C Enters the Sheep Business	228

23. Bucking Range with the Sheep Outfits 236
24. A New Routine at the Circle C 245
25. Hiring the Sheepherders 254
26. The Little Yaqui Sheepherder and His Collie 263
27. Misadventures in a Tin Lizzie 269
28. Windup of the Old Circle C Outfit 280
    Appendices 290
    Index 331

Illustrations

Roping a Cow, by Charles M. Russell	*facing page*	132
Robert Coburn	*page*	10
Peace pipe and elk-tooth necklace		11
Granville Stuart		17
William M. (Will) Coburn		21
Robert J. (Bob) Coburn		22
Wallace D. Coburn		23
Walt Coburn		24
Harold Coburn		25
Halfway stage station at Hog Ranch		30
Stagecoach on Alkali Bridge		31
Landusky, Montana		47
Harvey Logan, alias Kid Curry		55
Jim Thornhill		59
The Wild Bunch		69
The Winters-Gill ranch		73
Charles A. Siringo		79
Part of the Circle C remuda		89
The Kid Curry hideaway		105
Dynamited express car		105
Abe Gill		113
Cowhands at the Circle C corrals		129
Letch Lemon, Circle C cowhand		129

Zortman, Montana	148
Twelve-horse freight team	149
Big Foot Sturman's jerk-line freight outfit	149
Robert Coburn's house	158
Bob Coburn with Assiniboin chief	158
Ration day at Fort Belknap Reservation	159
Fort Belknap Indian Reservation Agency	165
Horace Brewster	177
Jake Myers with his wife and daughter	178
Mess wagon and bed wagon	181
Circle C roundup camp	181
Branding calves at the Circle C corral	189
Charlie Stuart	195
Malta, Montana	205
Black Dog	217
Ruby Gulch gold mine mill	229
Jake Myers and Bob Coburn	256
Stagecoach leaving the Circle C Ranch	285
Log buildings at the Circle C	285
Blacksmith shop at the Circle C	286
Facsimile of the Half Breed Cart	312
Anonymous picture of emigrant train	313
Bill Phipp's bull team	314
Murray freight outfit	315
Hartmann's sixteen-horse freight outfit	316
Hartmann driving near Zortman	317
Hartmann's twelve-horse freight outfit	318
Teams at Alabama Hill	319
Ore haulers	320
Boiler hauling	321
Iron truck	322
Jerkline headgear, right side	324
Jerkline headgear, left side	325

Map: Little Rockies country of Montana *page* 5

Pioneer Cattleman in Montana

1.

The Island Mountains

IN THE NORTHEASTERN PART of Montana, perhaps twenty-five miles north of the Missouri River and approximately thirty miles south of Milk River, the Little Rockies rise abruptly from the high plateau of the Plains. From a distance, this small mountain range presented a magnificent panorama of beauty to the westbound traveler who crossed the vast wilderness of the Middle West and the Dakotas in the early 1800's.

On a late summer afternoon, when shimmering heat waves hovered across the rolling prairie, the purple silhouette of the ragged mountains against the faded blue horizon had the appearance of a mirage-like island rising abruptly from the sea, and the whole became a vast panorama of the breath-taking beauty of God's creation.

Long before the coming of the first white man, the Indians called them the Island Mountains. This vast wilderness had once been covered by water and petrified fossils of oysters, clams, and fish were preserved in clay banks that were washed and polished by time. Indian hunting parties found huge white-bleached bones of prehistoric animals half-buried in the broken badlands country on both sides of the wide Missouri River, which they called the Big Muddy.

Long before this area was settled, the Island Mountains and the surrounding high plains were the habitat of great herds of buffalos and large bands of pronghorn antelope which roamed with the buffalos. Whitetail and blacktail deer inhabited the foothills and mountain country, as well as mighty grizzlies, black bears, brown cinnamon bears, mountain lions, and timber wolves. Grouse were abundant in the mountains. Eagles nested in the high pinnacles, and hawks soared through the air. Magpies, blue jays, crows, and various song birds greeted the sunrise and warbled evening songs.

On the prairies great flocks of sage hens and prairie chickens abounded. Honker geese, mallards, and teal ducks nested in the cattails and tall swamp grass on the lakes and in the high willows along the many creeks. Great prairie-dog towns covered the flats, and badgers were plentiful. Prairie wolves, coyotes, and kit foxes prowled the night. Beavers built dams in every creek.

The Island Mountains and the surrounding prairie country were one vast Indian hunting ground, extending from the Missouri River on the south to the Milk River on the north. The prairie land to the east was limitless, and while the great Sioux (Nakota) Nation and the warlike Blackfeet battled for control of that vast empire, the Assiniboins, a Siouan tribe, fought the Gros Ventres for control of the Island Mountains and the prairie environs. Countless battles were won and lost and treaties over boundary lines made and broken.

Before the advent of all latter-day Indians, an ancient, unknown people inhabited the Island Mountains and the great plains country of Montana. The carvings they left on the walls of caves where they dwelt contain strange symbols which the oldest ancestors of present-day Indians could not understand. These ancient people were the cave dwellers, the long-ago ghost people of Indian legend.

Thus, long before the coming of the first white man, the Island Mountains had been held sacred. According to Indian belief, the caves that bore the cryptic symbols carved deep in sandstone and granite were ghost haunted. Inside the caves, medicine men fasted and prayed and offered gifts as they sat cross-legged on the floor of the cave contemplating the strange symbols carved on the rock walls. With stoical patience they talked to the Great Spirit, praying for some sign that would be the key to the meaning of the cryptic

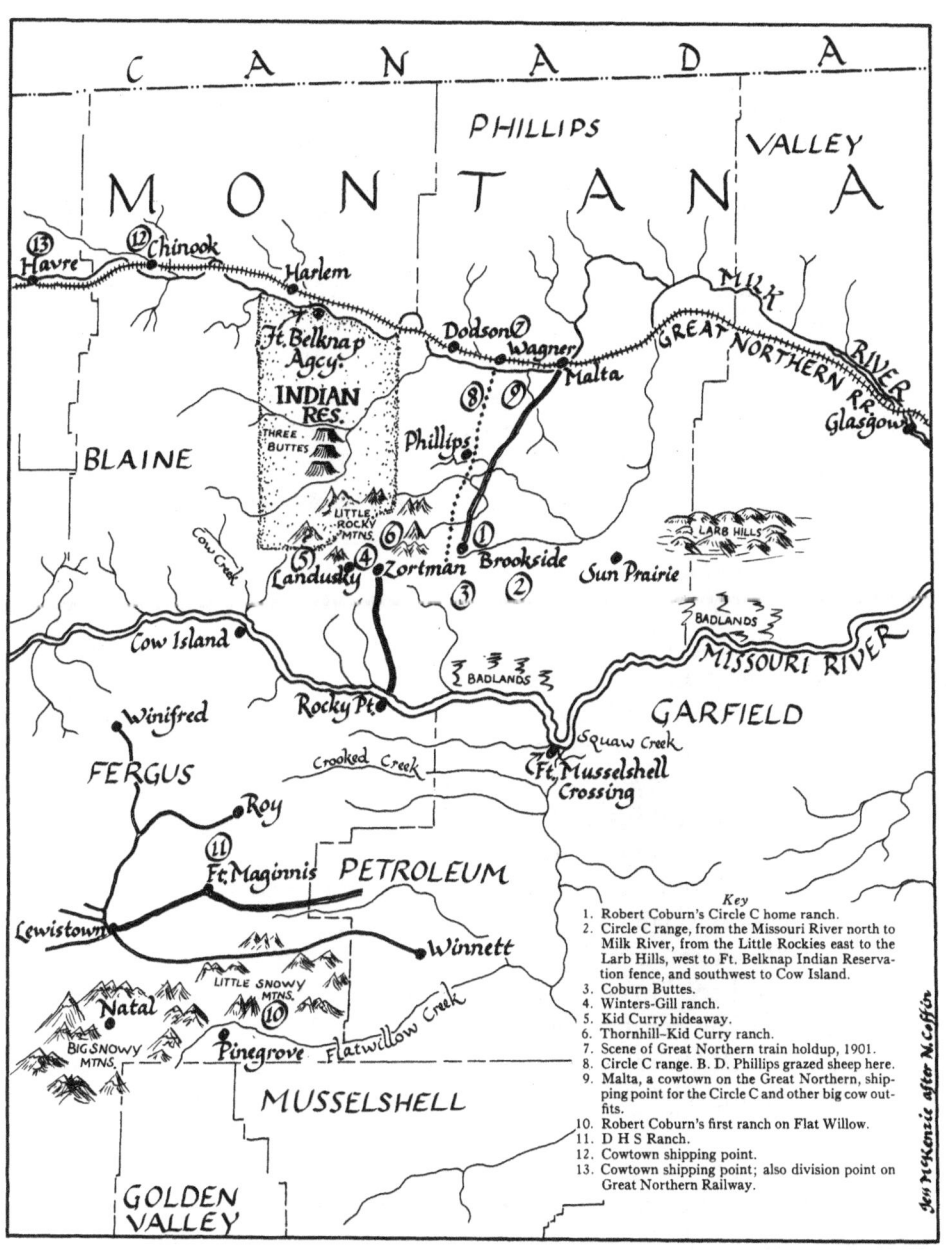

Little Rockies country of Montana

carvings, but to no avail. The secret meanings were forever hidden, and the Indians were wisely content in their lack of knowledge of the long-ago ghost people. And lest they might anger the evil spirits, the medicine men and tribal chiefs offered gifts to appease them.

When the Lewis and Clark exploration party in the year 1804 stopped at the Cow Island Crossing on the Missouri River, they sighted the distant mountain range to the north. In the mistaken belief it was the main range of the mighty Rockies, scouting parties were sent forth under the guidance of friendly Indians to explore further the Island Mountains, and the results of their findings were recorded in the journal of the expedition. In later years mountain men, such as Jim Bridger and Liver Eatin' Johnson, journeyed into this small mountain range that is now known as the Little Rockies.

By the time the town of Fort Benton was established as the head of navigation on the Missouri River, the Little Rockies were well known to the buckskin plainsmen. Fur-trading posts and military forts sprang up along the Missouri between Fort Benton and Fort Union. The gold rush stampede was in full swing at Virginia City, Bannack, and Last Chance Gulch, and the placer camps mushroomed into boom towns overnight.

The early pioneers of Montana Territory had come to stay. They built log cabins, raised families, and erected towns that soon became cities. Army posts were built, and the blood-spattered Indian wars were being fought the length and breadth of the vast wilderness throughout Montana Territory.

The American Fur Company had its taproots at Fort Benton, and the Whoop Up country that extended from Benton across the Canadian line became lawless. Fort Whoop Up was the first fur-trading post. Others sprang up along the Whoop Up Trail to compete with the mighty Hudson's Bay Company for the highly lucrative fur trade.

In the beginning, the American Fur trading posts and their offshoot whisky traders exchanged their rotgut whisky to the Indians for buffalo hides. The American trading posts in the Whoop Up country were known as "whisky forts," and the barter of rotgut

The Island Mountains

liquor for buffalo hides climaxed in the shameful Cypress Hill massacre across the Canadian border, when white whisky traders and wolfers massacred a band of Assiniboin Indians.

With the coming of the army and the establishment of military and fur-trading posts came the white buffalo hunters, many in the employ of the United States government. Whereas the Indians killed for meat and hides, the white buffalo hunters, such as the vainglorious U. S. scout, "Colonel" William F. Cody, better known as the showman "Buffalo Bill," so named for his prowess as a hunter, wantonly slaughtered the vast herds of buffalo for their hides only, leaving thousands of skinned buffalo carcasses to rot on the prairies. This wanton destruction by the white man, with the sanction and blessing of the "Great White Father" in Washington, resulted in almost total extinction of the American bison.

In the eyes of the Indian this wasteful, wanton slaughter of the shaggy, humped monarch of the Western prairies, the lifeblood of the Indian, was a black disgrace. Seen from the viewpoint of the great Indian chiefs, Sitting Bull of the Sioux, Chief Joseph of the Nez Percés, Geronimo of the Apaches, and other chiefs who put their mark to the white man's treaty, the slaughter of the great buffalo herds was typical of the white chiefs, who violated every treaty made with the Indians before the ink had dried on their signatures.

During the gold rush the first longhorn cattle herds from Texas came up the Old Chisholm Trail to Montana. Other trail herds of cattle were brought in over the Oregon Trail, and the first cattle ranches were established in the Deer Lodge valley and along the Rose Bud valley. Miles City was born, and cattle grazed in the Judith Basin and the Prickly Pear valley. The isolated ranches were in the heart of the Indian country.

The cattle industry in Montana Territory had come to stay. Men who had made small fortunes panning gold invested their sudden wealth in cattle, and took up government land as homesteads. Numbered among those pioneer cattlemen of Montana Territory was Robert Coburn, who owned and operated the Circle C outfit.

2.

Meeting with Chief Joseph

IN 1877, Robert Coburn had his ranch located on Flatwillow Creek south of the Missouri River in Montana Territory where he lived with his first wife, my oldest half-sister Jessie, and my oldest half-brother Will. With him at the time was his foreman, Horace Brewster. During that pioneer period in the area around the Judith Mountains the various cattle ranches were few and far apart, and the Circle C Ranch was no exception. It was remote and isolated, and the closest neighbor was the DHS (Davis-Hauser-Stuart) Ranch.

At daybreak on a memorable September day in 1877, a large Indian encampment suddenly appeared on a benchland overlooking the ranch with its one log cabin and pole horse corral. The Indians had come with stealthy quiet sometime during the night, and there in the light of the false dawn was a large circle of buffalo hide tipis. The blazeless glow of the many buffalo-chip campfires showed like red-coal eyes through the gray dawn a scant half mile away. Judging from the large number of lodges in the wide circle, Robert Coburn and Horace Brewster decided a whole tribe was on the move, a huge war party, the largest they had ever seen.

Coburn told Brewster to corral the horses. Then he gave his old friend and wagon boss the grimmest order Brewster ever had to take in his life—to go into the log cabin with his wife and children

Meeting with Chief Joseph

while he rode out alone to meet the two Indians who were riding towards the ranch from the encampment.

"God only knows what those Injuns are up to, Horace," said Coburn. "I'll do my best to dicker with them for horses if that is what they want. If they show fight, I'll die with a gun in my hand. If they kill me, I want you to kill my wife and children rather than let them fall into the hands of the Indians to be tortured and scalped." The two men shook hands in silence, then Robert Coburn rode out to meet two mounted Indians. He was armed with a Colt .45 pistol, and a carbine was in his saddle scabbard.

An Indian wearing the ceremonial dress of a chief was riding in the lead, and the other Indian, a young man about eighteen, rode a short distance behind. The chief's tall figure was clothed in fringed, beaded, buckskin shirt and leggings. A war bonnet fashioned of bristled horsehair and dyed in many bright colors was tied to his forelock. His black hair was plaited in two heavy braids that hung down in front of each shoulder. Red powdered dust was rubbed into his high cheekbones and forehead. Sitting tall and erect on his Appaloosa horse, he posed a strikingly handsome figure of a warrior as he rode with his right arm lifted, his palm outward in a sign of peace.

The three men reined up a short distance apart, and the leader spoke in his native tongue, the younger Indian translating slowly.

"Tell the white man that I am Chief Joseph of the Nez Percés. Ask the white man to get off his horse. I am here to smoke with him, to have a medicine talk."

Robert Coburn saw that both Indians were unarmed as they dismounted. When he got off his horse, Chief Joseph spread a tanned buffalo hide on the ground, and they all sat down. Joseph opened the drawstrings of a worn buckskin pouch that was decorated with beadwork, and took from it a ceremonial pipe of dark red pipestone. The long stem was in two separate pieces that joined together by a short length of hollow willow stick. He filled the bowl with a mixture of trade tobacco and kinnikinnick and lit it with a sulphur match. Holding the pipe in both hands, he puffed smoke,

Robert Coburn, age about 70.

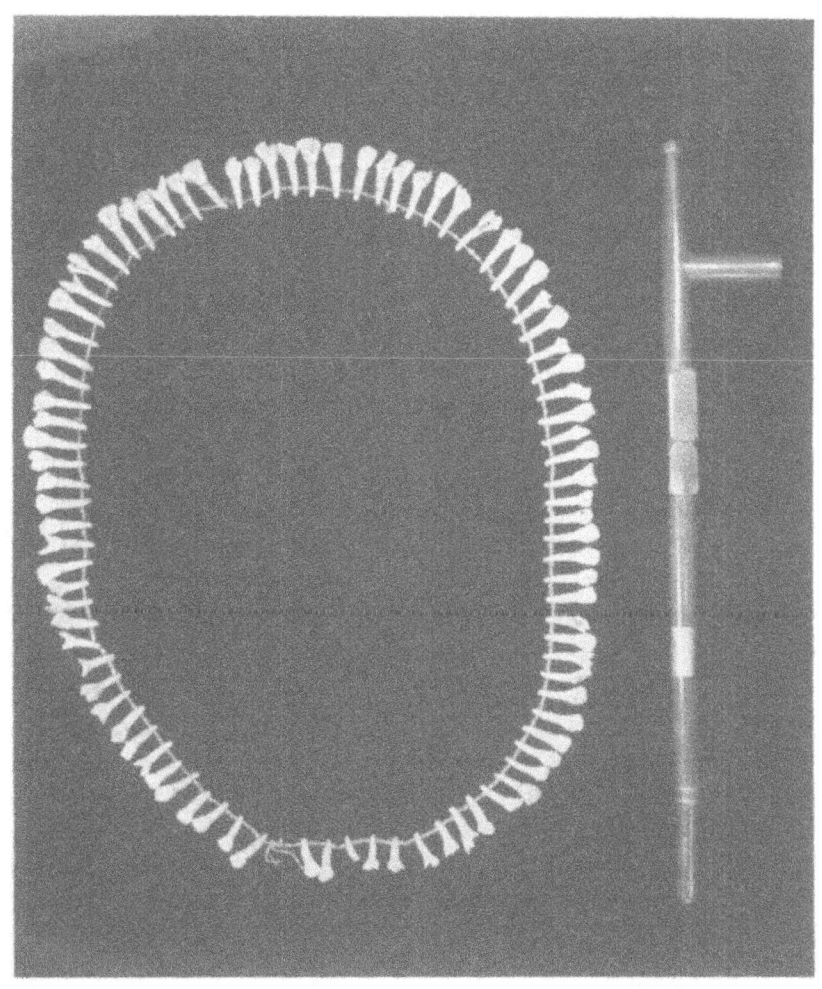

Peace pipe and elk-tooth necklace
Chief Joseph gave to Robert Coburn.

then handed it, stem foremost, across to Coburn, who took a few long drags and blew the pungent smoke from his mouth. Then he handed the pipe back to Joseph who carefully laid it down on the buffalo hide.

Then Joseph talked to the interpreter, and his hands moved in the sign language, and the younger Indian repeated the message aloud.

"Tell the white man that Chief Joseph and his Nez Percé people are not at war with the white settlers. We are on our way to Canada to seek the protection of the great white grandmother who rules the land to the north. There we will be safe from the many soldiers who are trailing us. We will live in peace there where there are many buffalo. We have fought with the soldiers. We have lost many brave warriors. We are sick and tired of fighting. My people are hungry. We have sighted no buffalo in many days. All I ask you for is meat to fill the empty bellies of my people."

One particular thing that impressed Robert Coburn at the time was that Chief Joseph spoke only in his native Nez Percé tongue and let the young Indian, who had apparently gone to some mission school, do the translating. Yet Coburn had the feeling that the Nez Percé chief had a knowledge of the white man's language although there was nothing revealed in the proud expression on his intelligent face. Perhaps in the opaque black of his eyes there was a certain look of understanding and great wisdom without enmity or arrogance. It was a look of appeal, a man-to-man look that sought for understanding regardless of race. Coburn said the powerful magnetism of the Indian was plainly revealed. He was a born leader, with the wisdom of a medicine man and warrior, sincere and honest in his belief.

Coburn told Joseph he was welcome to kill as many beef steers as he needed for meat for his warriors, women, and children. Then they shook hands.

Joseph was wearing a long necklace of elk teeth. He took it off and placed the necklace around my father's neck. Then he untied the many-colored horsehair war bonnet and handed it to my father.

Meeting with Chief Joseph

Then he again filled the ceremonial pipe, and when they had smoked, he left the ashes in the bowl and presented it with the other gifts. They got to their feet and again shook hands. Then they mounted and rode away in opposite directions. That day the Indians gorged themselves on fresh beef.

During that long, endless night inside the log cabin, with barred door and shuttered windows, Robert Coburn, his wife and two children, and Horace Brewster waited for daybreak. The two men stood armed guard, peering through the narrow, slitted portholes they had gouged out between the mud daubing of the logs.

At long last there was enough daylight to see the distance to the Nez Percé encampment. There was no hostile movement, and no trace of the tipis remained. The Indians had departed during the night as quietly as they had come.

It is recorded in the annals of Montana history that the memorable Nez Percé battle with the soldiers in the Bear Paw Mountains which was fought for five days and ended on October 5, 1877, was the most courageous battle against overwhelming odds that Chief Joseph's warriors ever fought and lost. It was possibly the bravest battle in the history of the bloody Indian wars.

History records Chief Joseph's memorable speech to his Nez Percé people the day he surrendered to General Miles:

> *Hear me, my chiefs,*
> *My heart is sick and sad,*
> *From where the sun now stands*
> *I will fight no more forever.*

Word of the battle in the Bear Paws between Chief Joseph and his Nez Percé warriors and the combined forces of General Howard and General Miles drifted back to Robert Coburn at his ranch in Judith Basin. For him it was sad news that Chief Joseph failed to reach the safety he sought for his people across the Canadian border, for he knew that the Indians wanted only friendship and peace.

During the following years I heard my father tell and retell the story of his brief meeting with Chief Joseph, and I still have in my possession the elk-tooth necklace and the pipestone peace pipe that once belonged to Chief Joseph. The horsehair war bonnet was given to Jessie Coburn Maddox, who was the small daughter with my father on that memorable day.

3.

The Hard Winter of '86

IN THE YEAR 1886, Robert Coburn purchased from Granville Stuart the DHS Ranch on Beaver Creek in the long shadow of the Little Rockies, Stuart, a lifelong friend, was part owner of the famous Davis-Hauser-Stuart cattle outfit, whose headquarters ranch was at Gilt Edge, adjacent to Fort McGinnis in the Judith Mountains and Judith Basin country. Coburn traded his ranch on Flatwillow as part of the deal for the new ranch on Beaver Creek.

On an early summer day, as Coburn and Stuart rode the boundary lines and closed the deal for the ranch on Beaver Creek, Coburn remarked that he had found the ranch he was looking for and called it a "cattleman's paradise."

To the north, east, and south was an endless stretch of rolling prairie land as far as the human eye could see. To the west were the Little Rockies. Just south of Beaver Creek were two large timbered buttes that joined the south end of the main range of the Little Rockies by long, scrub-pine gulches and ridges and lesser buttes in a rough L shape. The two buttes were a part of the ranch and became known as the Coburn Buttes.

The north-south survey line of the Fort Belknap Reservation cut through the brushy saddle between the east and west buttes, and the east-west reservation line took in the lower part of the east butte, and extended west to the Little Rockies. In later years, when the Fort Belknap Indian Reservation was fenced in, the home ranch of the Circle C was about two miles east of the reservation gate.

The Little Rockies were an ideal winter range. The timbered, brushy foothills afforded shelter, whereas the rolling prairies, while an ideal summer range, afforded little or no shelter from the icy north winds that brought the killing blizzards down from Canada.

The year 1886 was like a black brand burned deep in the heart and memory of every old-time cattleman in Montana and the entire northwestern range. The disastrous winter of 1886–87 was a gut shot that hit every stockgrower. For the smaller cowman it proved fatal. Only the larger cow outfits survived, and for the most part their recovery was slow. To the best of my knowledge, the Circle C outfit suffered about a 50 per cent loss, but Robert Coburn still maintained that his new location on Beaver Creek was a cowman's paradise.

I have often wondered how the old-time stockmen got refinanced and restocked their range after the loss of stock during the hard winters and long dry summers. Wallace Kingsbury, pioneer son of A. W. Kingsbury, cattleman and sheepman who came to Montana Territory in 1864, told me he believes that the bankers had implicit faith in the honesty of the early-day stockmen and knew that no one was more capable of running the ranches than the ranchers themselves. The cattlemen had made fortunes in livestock in past years and would again. The cost per head of livestock was low, as were wages and operating costs. The bankers had money to loan to stockmen in whom they had faith and whom past experience had proven honest, hard working, and anxious to succeed. General stores also furnished groceries and needed ranch supplies on an annual payment policy. The word of any Montana cattleman worthy of that title was as good as a banker's bond.

During the hard winter of 1886–87, the rationed hay was running short and there was barely enough to feed the horses. The big steers were left to rustle for themselves in the mountains. Because of the low price of cattle and the comparatively high price

Granville Stuart on his seventy-fifth birthday, 1909.
Montana Historical Society

and scarcity of hay during the eighties, it was cheaper to let the cattle die than feed them. They roamed over such a large range that it was impossible to furnish them hay. The hay that was put up in the summer was used to feed the working cow horses and, in a few instances, to feed cattle at winter line camps.

Granville Stuart remarked after that hard winter that he would never own another head of stock he couldn't feed. But I believe he still retained his share in the DHS (Davis-Hauser-Stuart) outfit until it was disposed of at a much later date.

The year of 1886 was also a heartbreaking year for the Assiniboin and Gros Ventre Indians on the Fort Belknap Reservation, which had been established the year before, in 1885, adjoining the Circle C Ranch. For some remote reason known only to the United States Indian Department, the Assiniboins and their lifelong enemies, the Gros Ventres, were rounded up like animals by the soldiers and thrown together on the same reservation, doomed for generations to remain within its limited confines. Both Indian tribes managed somehow to get along without undue blood letting, thus putting to shame the blundering stupidity of their white man captors.

Under the supervision of an Indian agent, Indian police of both tribes were issued regulation brass-buttoned blue coats and were armed with policemen's clubs to maintain peace and order. This was a foolish attempt to impose the white man's way on the Indians. It remained for the old men of each tribe, the tribal chiefs and medicine men, to meet in intertribal council to smoke the peace pipe and hold long medicine talks.

I have no way of knowing whether or not Robert Coburn was fully aware of the potential danger of living next to the Fort Belknap Indian Reservation which held two enemy tribes. At heart he was a man of peaceful nature, born without the knowledge of fear, and his many years of association with the Indians created a mutual feeling of understanding.

During the hard winter of 1886–87, the old men of the Assiniboins and Gros Ventres came to the Circle C Ranch to talk to Robert Coburn. Chief Black Dog of the Assiniboins acted as spokesman for the others, and a young full blood who had gone to school acted as interpreter.

"My people are starving," Black Dog said. "The white man has killed the buffalo. We have no meat to fill our empty bellies. The women and children are dying from hunger."

"I have no hay to feed my cattle," Coburn replied. "I have turned the steers loose to rustle. When you see a steer humped up and dying, you have my permission to kill it and divide the meat. Kill only the ones that are weak from starvation."

Thus Black Dog, Iron Horse, Long Knife, Watch-His-Walking, Eyes-in-the-Water, Takes-the-Shield, Has-the-Whip, White Horse, and many others, and their women and children survived the long winter by eating lean meat from Circle C steers that perhaps would have died anyway. During the years to come, those old men repaid that debt of gratitude whenever they had the chance.

From the year 1886 until the Circle C outfit was sold to the Matador Land and Cattle Company in 1916, Robert Coburn never had trouble with the Assiniboins and Gros Ventres. But there were a few squaw men on the Fort Belknap Reservation who from time to time caused plenty of trouble—serious trouble that climaxed when the leader of the trouble-making squaw-man faction was shot and killed in the log office at the Circle C home ranch.[1]

During those years from 1886 to 1916, Robert Coburn had a government permit to graze a certain number of cattle on the reservation. His cattle were turned loose with the ID (Indian Department) cattle, and, with the exception of the few squaw men who stole calves and butchered Half Circle C (the Coburn cattle brand) beef, there was little trouble. Most of the squaw men were honest and staunch friends of the outfit. Their half-blood sons, along with a number of full bloods, worked for the Circle C during the roundups and haying season.

During the years Robert Coburn owned the Circle C Ranch, there never was a hungry Indian who did not get fed. Coburn gave standing orders to the ranch cook to feed any and all Indians who visited the ranch, and seldom a day passed, summer or winter,

[1] See chapter 15.

without one or two Indians showing up. This policy dated back to the day in 1877 when Coburn met and talked with Chief Joseph of the Nez Percés.

During the hard winter of 1886–87, after the long awaited chinook winds had released the cow country from winter bondage, there came an event that was almost as welcome as the delayed chinook wind. The St. Paul, Minneapolis and Manitoba Railroad owned by Jim Hill came west from Bismarck, North Dakota, by way of the Milk River valley to Havre to join rails with the Montana Central from Great Falls, Helena, and Butte. (In 1889 they combined with other holdings to become the Great Northern Railroad.)

Stockyards were hastily built at various cow towns. Malta, Glasgow, Havre, Fort Benton, and Chinook became the shipping points for the cow outfits adjacent to the towns. But because of summer drought and the hard winter and the low price of cattle on the eastern market, the trainloads of big four-year-old beef steers loaded at those towns to be shipped to the Union Stockyards at Chicago were comparatively few and far between.

The summer drought had caused a poor crop of wild hay, inadequate for the large number of cattle on the range. The first heavy snow came in late November, and the drifts stayed until an early, premature chinook wind in January melted the snowdrifts. In the ensuing warm days green grass sprouted, but a cold wind from the north changed the slushy snow into ice, and what grass there was for feed lay under the ice. The starving cattle drifted and piled up in the cutbank coulees, humped up on the windswept prairies, and froze to death in their tracks.

The hard winter of 1886–87 was depicted in a painting by a young cowboy artist, Charles M. Russell, who was a horse wrangler and sometime nighthawk for the Stadler-Kaufman outfit near Utica in the Judith Basin. Russell sketched an old, droop-horned, Texas cow, hump-backed in the snow, rump to the cold north wind, the glaze of death in its sunken eyes, and its bushy tail snapped off by three gaunt prairie wolves that were stalking the dying cow. It was a grim, stark sketch made on the white cover of a shoe box,

William M. (Will) Coburn

Robert J. (Bob) Coburn

Wallace D. Coburn

Walt Coburn

Harold Coburn

but that realistic portrait of a starving, spotted cow was destined to launch the fabulous career of Russell, whose master's touch portrayed the cowpuncher and his life during the pioneer days of free range in the territory of Montana.

About 1906, when I was in high school at Great Falls, my father took me to Helena for a meeting of the Montana Stockgrowers Association. A memorable highlight occurred in the crowded lobby of the Placer Hotel, when Louis Kaufman related the story of the Russell painting and reminisced about that hard winter, lamenting the loss of his five thousand head of cattle and the then famous Russell sketch, *The Last Of The Five Thousand* or *Waiting For The Chinook,* which he had foolishly given away. Other old-time cattlemen, mellowed by good whisky, swapped tall tales about the hard winter of 1886–87, paying no mind to the bald-faced kid who sat in the lobby of the hotel with the uniformed bellhops. Had I known there would come a time in later years when I would try in vain to recall those stories related by gray-bearded old-timers, I would have paid more attention.

My youngest half-brother, Wallace Coburn, who was fifteen years my senior, took me to supper at the famous Montana Club, where I got a little tipsy on beer served in chilled steins. A goodly group of drinking cronies was gathered there, including Johnny Ritch and Frank Linderman, both well-known Montana citizens, who added salty spice to the tall tales they swapped. I was the only kid among the convivial gathering, but whenever or wherever I went with Wallace (and we traveled now and then into forbidden places where teenagers were barred at the door), I was always made welcome as Wallace's kid brother.

That was a memorable evening, never to be forgotten. The years of my boyhood and youth in Montana are the most treasured of all and therefore easy to remember as I look back on those final years that marked the passing of the cow country and open range. The big outfits I knew in my youth remain only as a memory.

4.

The Great Land Swindle

BEFORE PROCEEDING WITH THE STORY of the Circle C Ranch, there are two misconceptions about Montana cattlemen which should be cleared up. First, the despised title of "cattle baron" was wrongly applied to Robert Coburn and other Montana cattlemen. Secondly, their treatment of the homesteader who invaded the country with the coming of the railroad was not unjustified.

Since my point of view might be considered biased, I am borrowing a little thunder from my old friend, Bob Fletcher, who recorded the history of the cattle industry in Montana. In a dispatch dated March 19, 1889, the Miles City correspondent to the *Montana Livestock Journal* wrote:

> Our cattlemen . . . are a singularly retiring and modest class of people who have been foisted into an undesirable notoriety by the sensational press of the East which has painted them with an artist's brush, though in lurid colors, in the guise of feudal barons who, having appropriated the western range by most questionable methods, proceeded to parcel the grazing grounds out among themselves to the exclusion of all other people and the extinction of all other rights but theirs.
> It is true that, comparatively speaking, a few men and a few cattle occupy the vast ranges of Custer County over which, though we are reputed to be the banner cow country of the Territory, one may travel for hundreds of miles and never see as many cattle as would supply

one tenth of the demand of the Chicago market on a brisk day. The idea of there being any traits in common with our mild-mannered cowmen and the blood-thirsty and acquisitive barons of the medieval ages is simply preposterous.

The cattlemen occupy the ranges now because there is no one who cares to dispute the occupancy with them, but not because it could not be done successfully. The history of all range countries will undoubtedly be repeated here. The cattlemen, who are the true pioneers, come first in the majority of cases, disputing their holdings with the Indians and suffering much more by their predatory and hostile instincts than the outside world has any knowledge of. Following him comes the speculative squatter who plants himself near some spring or water course merely for the purpose of being bought out, and "ranches" in a hand-to-mouth way until the desired end is attained.

Then comes the bona fide settler whose intent is to make a home and, although he may, in isolated instances, interfere with rights and privileges that his range neighbor had previously enjoyed without let or hindrance, he meets with no persecution. On the contrary, if he sets earnestly or intellectually to work to improve his condition, he finds in his neighbor, the range cattleman, a purchaser for much or all his surplus crop of hay and grain besides getting many an odd day's work around the ranch or on the roundups. Thus their relations become mutually agreeable and their interest rarely confliction.[1]

In 1889, the year the above article appeared in the *Montana Livestock Journal,* Chouteau County included Blaine, Hill, and Phillips counties, and Fort Benton was the county seat. Chouteau County was indeed a vast empire, its prairie range extending from the north bank of the Missouri River to the Canadian border. This unfenced empire with its free range was the grazing ground of the cattlemen who comprised the Shonkin Stock Association, headed by M. E. Milner's Square outfit, the Bear Paw Pool, the Circle Diamond, the Circle C, and other smaller outfits who sent their reps to work with the various big roundups. A few years later the Northern Montana Roundup Association was formed.

It was here in the free range country in later years that the so-called "Empire Builder," Jim Hill, with his large-scale adver-

---

[1] *Free Grass to Fences* (New York, University Publishers, 1960), 112–15.

The Great Land Swindle

tising campaign in the Middle West and the East, lured thousands of gullible people to take up homesteads on free government land. Jim Hill had built the Great Northern. He had to make it pay, and he put on a propaganda drive to fill up the empty plains of Montana, as well as his empty boxcars.

Lured by the "pie in the sky" bait of free land with title in three years, the homesteaders invaded Montana during the first years of the 1900's. The homesteaders were known by various uncomplimentary names, such as scissorbills, dry-land farmers, honyockers, sodbusters, squatters, and nesters. They came by the trainloads to Montana via the Great Northern Railroad.

The railroad made it possible to ship Montana cattle to eastern markets, although the cattlemen often were highly taxed by the exorbitant rates. But in spite of the high freight rates, the Empire Builder, who had been hailed as something of a hero and his railway a boon to the stockmen, turned traitor to the cattle industry of Montana by perpetrating a great disservice to the cattlemen whose friendship he once had held above all things. The name of Jim Hill became a dirty word throughout the Montana cow country.

The first indication that the Circle C outfit had of the unwelcome homestead invasion was a string of so-called day-coach passenger cars and freight and stock cars containing farm implements and work teams sitting on the stockyards' siding at Malta, with men and their wives and children camped nearby.

Land offices were opened with tacked-up wall maps and rolled blueprints. The surveyors and land promoters in search of the fast buck waited with buckboards and top buggies, ready to take the swarm of eager homesteaders out to locate their land. Land promoters sprang up like mushrooms overnight. The large Great Northern freight warehouses and wide plank platforms were piled high as haystacks with rolls of barbwire, kegs of staples, stacks of cedar fence posts, wire stretchers, and post-hole diggers.

Ruel Horner, the stage driver, pulled in one evening at the Circle C Ranch, which boasted a third-class post office called Brookside, and told Jake Myers the bad news. He said that, due to heavy rain the night before, Hard Luck Smith's jerk-line freight wagons, piled high with fence posts, barbwire, and kegs of staples, was bogged down to the hubs and axles in the sticky gumbo clay of Phillips Lane at the Hog Ranch stage station.

According to Ruel Horner, Hard Luck Smith had postponed taking his regular freight load of cased bottled beer and barrels of whisky destined for the saloon keepers at Zortman and Landusky in the Little Rockies in order to take advantage of the more lucrative trade of the land locaters who had doubled the usual freight rates established among the jerk-line freighters.

"Hard Luck was bogged down to a fare-thee-well," the stage driver said. "Ol' Hard Luck had to drop trail and haul one wagon out at a time, leaving the stacks of barbwire in the gumbo beside the road. Hard Luck was sore as a boil because the Hartmann boys had picked up the load of beer and whisky and got their freight wagons through the Red Lane before the cloudbuster came, and Big Foot Sturman and his boys had picked up another load of whisky at Dodson the day before.

Halfway station at Hog Ranch.

Courtesy of Dave Nichols, Malta, Montana

The Great Land Swindle

"There was four of them land locaters waitin' for Hard Luck at the Hog Ranch, rollin' poker dice for the drinks at the saloon. They had rolled-up blueprints in their coat pockets, with transits and surveyor's telescopes in their rigs. A bunch of scissorbills were camped at the Hog Ranch with tents set up along the crick, their wagons waiting to pick up Hard Luck's load of barbwire and fence posts."

While Ruel Horner told the story, Jake Myers, the Circle C foreman, walked the floor whistling an off-key hungry tune through his teeth, with a set, mirthless grin on his weathered face that sprouted a three-day growth of black, wiry stubble.

"Better wake up and hear the birdies sing, Jake," Horner advised. "I listened to some of the talk, and those land sharks are aimin' to locate them squatters on every high benchland between Wild Horse and the Big Warm, plumb to Beaver Crick. You'll wake up some mornin' and find them camped all around the Circle C Ranch. Don't say I didn't warn you."

Stagecoach on Alkali Bridge near Malta. Robert Coburn and son Harold on driver's seat. Standing from left to right are Sam and Luke Deniff, gamblers, saloonkeepers, and ranchers, and Little Tommy Carter, prospector and mine owner. The other man may be a deputy sheriff from Landusky.

What Jake Myers had not told the stage driver was that for the past week or two Charlie Beard, part-time justice of the peace at Zortman and Landusky and a licensed surveyor who for years had done the surveying for the Circle C, had been in the field with blueprint map and transit and his two-man chain crew, locating all the Circle C cowpunchers on the choice bottomlands along the creeks with various springs and water sources within a twenty-five-mile radius on all sides of the home ranch.

I was a member of the chain crew, as was Frank Howe, top hand and straw boss under Jake Myers. We had traveled by horseback from one homestead location to the next, and the half-dozen Circle C cowpunchers, including Al Taylor the ranch cook, armed with legal survey location papers, had already filed their homestead claims at the land office.

Charlie Beard had located me at a marshy spring between the home ranch and the reservation fence that bordered the east side of my homestead. The established stage road from the ranch to the reservation gate bisected the south end of my claim, which had been filed at the state land office a week earlier.

In due time the required acreage was plowed, tilled, and seeded on these claims. Log cabins were built and springs dug out and boxed in with wide planks. And, in accordance with the law, we lived in those log cabins for the required period in order to prove continual residence. The continual residence and immediate improvements of the land were the main requirements for getting title to the land.

The get-rich-quick, fly-by-night land locaters, who were unworthy of the dignified title of realtors or real estate brokers, were busier than the proverbial bird dogs. Their two-by-four offices were stacked with Jim Hill's pamphlets, handbills, and agricultural brochures containing advice to the dry-land farmers.

Those fast-buck land locaters were a dime a dozen. They were fast-talking salesmen, ruthless in their disregard for the cattleman's fenced-in hay pastures. They cut the barbwire fences on deeded land in their hasty greed to locate some pilgrim homeseeker on patented land belonging to the cowman. Or they would

The Great Land Swindle

locate some sucker on an arid benchland, miles distant from the nearest creek or available water, where the dry-land farmer would dig dry wells in hopes of finding water and then be forced to haul it in barrels for miles for domestic purposes.

Those land locaters were like so many buzzards. Once they located some homesteader on the bald prairie, a high benchland, or an alkali flat, where only greasewood or sagebrush could survive, and once they collected their fee, they hastily departed to fetch the next sucker, leaving the dry-land farmer and his family to their fate. Those human beggars never looked back to view the sorry plight of the homeseeker who was staking his life's savings, all he had in the world to lose, in a summer's drought, and was facing a long, bitter-cold, snowbound winter.

The consensus of opinion throughout the cow country was that Jim Hill, the Empire Builder, had successfully perpetrated a gigantic land swindle by preying on gullible people from the Middle West—Minnesota, Wisconsin, and Ohio—and as far east as the New England states. Among them were store clerks, college professors, city dwellers of all manner and description, and health seekers, as well as farmers. They were men and women of moderate means, with no more than a few hundred dollars set aside for a rainy day. Those luckless people were destined to pray long and fervently but in vain for the rains that did not come, while their planted grain, up a few inches, dried and withered in the hot prairie winds.

Those homesteaders watched their life's savings slowly trickle away like sand down a prairie-dog hole. There was forever something they had to buy, such as barbwire and fence posts to fence in their plowed and seeded land to protect their crops from drifting cattle. They needed work teams, plows, and harrows, as well as new layers of tar paper for their board shacks for protection against the winter storms and wood for the little sheet-iron cookstoves to keep the shacks warm. There was grub to buy and there were doctor bills to pay. And at the end of the summer's drought that meant no crops and after the long winter of enforced illness when the money played out and none came in, many of the farmers

Pioneer Cattleman in Montana

used the last of their life's savings to go back home. Those who had no money were trapped in a strange land. Their hopes vanished and their prayers unanswered, they cursed the name of Jim Hill.

But in their pitiful condition, I know of no cattleman who ever mistreated the unfortunate homesteaders. The Circle C outfit gave them employment from time to time, and during the months when work was scarce, their credit was good on the company books for food and warm clothing. The homesteaders worked during haying season and hauled cordwood from the timbered Little Rockies to the ranch during the winter, and some worked as carpenters. One of the homesteaders, who had been a bookkeeper in St. Paul where Jim Hill lived in a palatial home, was hired as a bookkeeper at the ranch, where he was employed until the Circle C sold out.

For the most part, life was no more than a hand-to-mouth existence for the drouthed-out homesteader. Eventually most of them managed to earn enough money to return to wherever they came from, sadder but much wiser. Few stayed the necessary three years to get title to the land, and those who were located in fertile valleys with available water were a lucky minority. In most cases the abandoned homesteader lands reverted to the government.

Soon the deserted homestead lands became an eyesore. The tarpaper shacks were deserted, and the neglected plowed ground became overgrown with tumbleweeds. Barbwire fences fell down, and work teams were turned loose on the range to rustle. The neglected shacks of the hopeful home-seekers remained as tragic monuments to their heart-breaking defeat. The bleak north wind drove snow through broken windowpanes and open doorways, where the doors creaked dismally on broken rusted hinges. There might be a once whitewashed picket fence that kept prowling wolves and coyote packs away from a lonely grave, where perhaps a small child was buried in a pinewood box lined with a mother's threadbare dress.

In time the deserted homesteads also became a menace. The neglected fences with snarled tangles of barbwire on the ground were dangerous to livestock, stray cattle, horses, and bands of sheep. Finally crews of ranch hands hauled the wire away, dug up the fence posts, and filled the holes. For a few years the plowed land yielded bumper crops of Russian thistle which threatened to cause prairie fires until it was harvested into stacks and burned by ranch crews who controlled the fires. It was a long time before the plowed land of the once grassy range was again sodded with native grass.

Meanwhile the work horses left behind by the dry-land farmers became a nuisance. The mares foaled colts sired by sorry studs that should have been gelded, and those small bunches of roaming horses ate the valuable grass meant to fatten the range cattle and bands of sheep.

The machine era had arrived, and tractors and pickup trucks replaced the work teams. Automobiles took the place of buggy teams, and there was little demand for saddle horses. So the increasing bunches of so-called "wild" horses were rounded up and driven to the nearest stockyards where they were sold to slaughter houses, canneries, and zoos for meat to feed animals. This was the fate of many a faithful work horse the homesteader left behind to rustle on the Montana prairie. Perhaps it was a merciful end to many a good and faithful horse that otherwise might have starved or frozen to death.

The man who had worked the horses, hitched to plow and harrow and wagon, and who had a man's fondness for these gentle animals had to face a bitter choice: either destroy his horses or turn them loose to shift for themselves. No doubt influenced by the pleading tears of wife and kids and his own tenderheartedness, the homesteader made his difficult decision. In many cases it was the final decision forced on the saddened, disillusioned, embittered homesteader as he turned his back on the barren ground that had become the graveyard of cherished dreams.

5.

The Lawless Range

COUNTLESS WORDS HAVE BEEN WRITTEN by latter-day historians concerning the lawless cow country in the Little Rockies and its environs in the 1880's. With the exception of pioneers such as Granville Stuart and especially Johnny Ritch, who lived in and around the Little Rockies for considerable years, modern-day historians never set foot in the Little Rockies and the badlands country north of the Missouri River during the so-called lawless period. They acquired their knowledge second-hand, gleaned it from the newspaper articles in the *Great Falls Tribune* written by Johnny Ritch, the man who was there. They also listened to stories told by old-timers, but some of those old cowhands, called windjammers in the cow country, had a habit of telling it scary to a pilgrim. Johnny Ritch wrote about their story-telling in his account of the killing of Pike Landusky by Kid Curry.

> I recall in particular that there were two men in Jake's saloon [where the killing took place] whom no one seemed to know. They must have been transients in town. I think, however, their names must have been "Legion" for I've talked, personally, to more than 100 men as the years have gone by who told me they saw it all—were eye witnesses. I couldn't dispute any of them as I didn't know the names of the two strangers.[1]

[1] *Great Falls Tribune,* January 20, 1935. For the entire article, see Appendix A.

The Lawless Range

Later, in 1894, Wyoming stockmen started to clean up on rustlers, many of whom came into Montana. Johnny Ritch described the outlaws in his article:

> These were gunmen. They were gunmen of sorts; the kind that had a Colt's .45 slung to each hip and tied down to the leg with a buckskin thong so there wouldn't be any accidents when they went to make the draw. Most of them were deadly sudden. Some of the lesser lights among them had only one notch on their gun; others had two, three, four; Long Henry had six. . . . It was not long before Landusky became a favorite resort of these knights of the long rope and the quick draw.[2]

The Circle C Ranch was only a few hours horseback ride from Landusky. The lawless badlands between the Missouri River and the Little Rockies, as far east as the Larb Hills, were included in the Circle C range, from the Cow Island Crossing on the Missouri east and downstream to the old Fort Musselshell Crossing, with the Rocky Point Crossing in between. The Missouri River was the southern boundary and the Milk River the northern boundary. There was no denying that this was indeed a lawless range in 1886. It was a cattleman's paradise, but by that same token the stomping ground for cattle rustlers and horse thieves.

During the early 1880's the cattle rustlers and horse thieves had rapidly increased in numbers throughout Montana Territory. The lawless fraternity was well organized. The leaders of its many gangs were top cowhands and ruthless gunslingers. They handpicked their members for their ability as cowhands and gunmen, their guts and outlaw cunning, and their determination to play their tough string out. They had to be willing to die with their boots on and a smoking gun in their hand if it came to a showdown.

The horse-thief trail became a well-established route. Horses stolen in Wyoming were sold in Montana, and Montana horses were sold in Dakota or were drifted north across the Canadian border. Horses stolen in Canada were sold in Montana, and Dakota horses were sold in Montana or drifted across the Wyoming border.

[2] *Ibid.*

Each horse-thief gang had one or two brand artists who were experts at altering a brand by using a wet gunnysack or blanket to blot a brand, by hair-picking a brand with tweezers, or by various other methods. They boasted that overnight they could alter any brand, including the Royal Canadian VR brand, to look like the original. And they did.

The menace of cattle rustling and horse-thief operations had become so grave in 1883 that the Montana stockmen finally persuaded the territorial legislature to introduce a bill for the inspection of all brands and registration of all cattle and horses. They also called for other means for safeguarding livestock driven out of Montana, but the bill failed to pass. The stockmen blamed the failure on the antagonistic attitude of Governor John S. Crosby, who was described by Joseph K. Howard in his account of the meeting of the Montana Stockgrowers Association:

> Governor Crosby, a New Yorker, who according to [Granville] Stuart was . . . "A delightful person to meet socially [but] . . . had spent most of his life on the staff of various generals of the army and in Europe and was entirely out of harmony with his surroundings in Montana and unfamiliar with the needs of the Territory."
>
> The clamor at the meeting of the Montana Stockgrowers Association in the spring of 1884 was for direct action. Stuart warned that the outlaws were intelligent and ruthless and their badland strongholds were fortresses. He and some other cool heads counseled caution and succeeded in preventing an outright declaration by the Association in favor of lynch law. In view of what occurred later this action by Stuart, who was one of the chief sufferers from the ruthless depredations, undoubtedly was intended merely to keep the association itself "in the clear." This association included in its membership Theodore Roosevelt, ranching in North Dakota; Russell B. Harrison, son of a subsequent President of the United States; and the Marquis de Mores, French nobleman who established a packing plant at Medora, North Dakota. Roosevelt and the Marquis, said Stuart, were all for "cleaning the rustlers out."[3]

With the denial of legal protection from cattle rustlers and

[3] *Montana: High, Wide, and Handsome* (New Haven, Yale University Press, 1943), 126.

The Lawless Range

horse thieves, the cattlemen had to take it upon themselves to do something about the situation. After the spring roundup in the Judith Basin, a group of cattlemen and their foremen met at the DHS Ranch near Gilt Edge.

At that time Robert Coburn had his ranch on Flatwillow Creek in the Judith Basin country. His foreman, Horace Brewster, represented him at that meeting at the DHS headquarters ranch. Spokesman for the group was Granville Stuart, one of the owners of the Davis-Hauser-Stuart outfit and the president in 1883 of the Council Cattlemen who had sponsored the bill that was vetoed by Governor Crosby. The meeting of the irate stockmen in the Judith Basin country was held in strict and necessary secrecy, and no minutes were recorded when Stuart organized the Judith Basin vigilantes.

The cattlemen had gathered considerable information concerning the names of the leaders of the well-organized horse-thief gangs and their members, as well as their methods of operation and the location of their hideouts and corrals in the badlands where stolen horses were kept while their brands were altered.

One badlands rendezvous at the Rocky Point Crossing on the Missouri River was a small trading post that formerly had been a hangout for wolfers and whisky traders. The trading post boasted a small saloon and a hotel that served meals. Rocky Point had enjoyed a tough reputation during the seventies, at the height of the river steamboat era, and in the early eighties it was used by the horse-thief gangs.

Another more favored horse-thief hangout in the badlands country was at Bates' Point, located about fifteen miles downstream from the old Fort Musselshell Crossing on the wide, muddy Missouri. Bates' Point became the horse-thief headquarters for young Jack Stringer, better known as Stringer Jack, one-time buffalo hunter. Stringer was a tall, handsome, reckless gunslinger, and his gang consisted of hand-picked gunslinging cowhands, each man dangerous in his own right.

In the meeting at the DHS Ranch, the stockmen chose a man named Floppin' Bill Cantrell as their range stock detective who would head the vigilantes. Cantrell, whose father had been one of Quantrill's Guerillas during the Civil War, came from the hills of Arkansas. He came west from the Dakotas, married an Assiniboin woman, and became a woodyard owner near Fort Peck. The flopping motion of his arms when he swung an ax had earned him the name of "Floppin' Bill." Soon Cantrell's business expanded to include trapping and wolfing with Pike Landusky, and he became acquainted with most of the scoundrels in the area. The reason why Cantrell took up with the cattlemen rather than the rustlers is unknown, but it is doubtful that he was motivated by a sense of ethics. It is more likely that he saw a better chance for profit in the position with the cattlemen's organization.

Thus Floppin' Bill Cantrell became Montana's first stock detective, and regardless of his motivation in accepting the job, he executed his assignments with thoroughness and dispatch. Bob Fletcher described the results of his association with the Judith Basin vigilantes:

> As a result of the affiliation of Floppin' Bill and the stockgrowers who had met at the DHS, a self-appointed vigilance committee called on Stringer Jack's gang that summer (at Bates' Point) and found Old Man James, his two sons, Frank Hansen, Bill Williams, Stringer Jack, Paddy Rose, Swift Bill, Dixie Burr, Orvil Edwards and Si Nickerson at home. There are many speculative tales and conflicting accounts of what followed. Omitting sanguinary details, in a short time most of the gentlemen named could be referred to in the past tense, their spirits having been wafted to the Sand Hills on a cloud of gunsmoke. Their survivors inclined to be taciturn and the others could not be interviewed except through the unreliable medium of a ouiji board. There was considerable public and private comment, pro and con concerning both the principles and principals behind the affair. Dixie Burr was the son of a highly respected pioneer and the nephew of another. There were well known citizens in the posse. That summer, a chartered train picked up another band of avengers and their horses at a secluded siding near Miles City. It stopped at intervals between Billings and Medora. The train crew waited until the passengers had returned from missions to the hinterland. Nemesis rode with them

The Lawless Range

packing a hair rope. It is alleged that the tally credited to this and similar forays totaled sixty-three. Rustling subsided for awhile.

It might be argued that this drastic action lacked legality and so was not to be condoned, but it did make clear the need for central, respected, regulatory authority, properly equipped to enforce its mandates, especially in the eastern portion of the Territory.[4]

Shortly after the cleanup of cattle rustlers and horse thieves at Bates' Point, Granville Stuart's vigilantes quietly disbanded. The Miles City stockmen, who patterned their methods after Stuart's vigilantes, had also attained the goal of ridding their area of lawless predators of livestock. The cattle rustlers and horse thieves who somehow had managed to escape punishment quit the country for a climate that better suited their clothes. And for the time being, there was no longer any lawless element on either side of the Missouri in the vicinity of Rocky Point and the old Fort Musselshell Crossing. The Montana stockgrowers were duly grateful to Granville Stuart, the one pioneer stockman who had the courage of his convictions. Those who branded Stuart's vigilantes as "stranglers" were men on the other side of the fence, men whose sympathies lay on the side of the cattle rustler and horse thief. Proof of the success of Stuart's vigilante activities was the more than three hundred stolen horses recovered.

In 1886, when Robert Coburn purchased the DHS Ranch in the Little Rockies from Granville Stuart, cattle rustlers and horse thieves were as scarce as hen's teeth in the badlands country. The memory of the dreaded vigilantes still lingered throughout that part of the cow country and remained the main topic of conversation in bunkhouses and roundup camps. But it was a safe bet that those cowhands who swapped stories had taken little part in ridding the country of rustlers, because all the members of Stuart's vigilantes had taken an oath of secrecy. It was not until many years later, if ever, that any of them divulged any part of their activities.

Nevertheless, the badlands along both sides of the Missouri still offered safe refuge for any man on the dodge. In 1892,

[4] *Free Grass to Fences*, 65–66.

when the Johnson County Range War in Wyoming finally broke out in sudden gunfire after a long period of smoldering, those who sought safety in flight drifted into Montana, and the badlands along the Missouri south of the Little Rockies offered a measure of security.

Some of these men were lawless renegades. Others were more or less law-abiding citizens, small rancher nesters who had located on Wyoming land claimed by the big outfits. The Wyoming nesters had been branded as outlaws, and the price placed on their heads attracted bounty hunters like Tom Horn and his kind. Rather than be shot down in a bushwhacker's gun trap with a rock for a pillow, most of the nesters chose to leave Wyoming between sundown and sunrise and cross into Montana. More than a few of those embittered men took to the outlaw trail, while others took up squatters' right in Montana and became law-abiding citizens. Some of the Wyoming cowpunchers hired out as cowhands to the big Montana outfits. Almost all of them changed their names when they crossed the boundary line, but since most of them were all-round cowhands, no questions were asked when they hired out. Almost every big cow outfit in Montana had its quota of cowpunchers exiled by the Johnson County war in Wyoming.

Once more the badlands along the Missouri became the hideout for cattle rustlers and horse thieves. Gun-toting cowpunchers would ride boldly into the mining town of Landusky in the Little Rockies to buck their horses down the street and empty six-shooters in the air, ride into saloons, and raise hell in general. "Cowboys in town" was the signal for women and kids to stay indoors while the celebration lasted.

In 1895 the Northern Montana Roundup Association, a new organization, merged with the Shonkin Stock Association, which had headquarters at Fort Benton. M. E. Milner of the Milner Square on Shonkin Creek near Fort Benton, who had been sort of ramrodding the Shonkin organization from its beginning in 1881, had fostered the idea of a merger. There were several important reasons for the closer knit organization of the stockmen whose ranges were in the northern part of the state.

The Lawless Range

In the first place, it was a long distance for the northern cattlemen to travel to attend the meetings of the Montana Stockgrowers Association at Miles City, and failure to attend each meeting put the northern stockmen out of touch with what went on, and they had no vote in vital matters that came up for discussion.

Since Jim Hill had extended his St. Paul, Minneapolis and Manitoba Railroad from Bismarck, North Dakota, to Havre to meet the Montana Central in 1887, several big cow outfits had moved into the Milk River country to take advantage of the open range that extended to the Canadian border. That stretch of Milk River country became better known as the "High Line." When Milner strongly suggested the merger of the Montana Roundup Association and the already strongly established Shonkin Stock Association, to which many of the big outfits in the High Line country already belonged, his suggestion was met with hearty approval.

At the first meeting held at Chinook in 1895, forty prominent stockmen signed up as charter members of the newly merged Northern Montana Roundup Association. The second meeting held at Chinook in 1896 was attended by more than seventy-five members and double that number of invited guests, including the ever present railroad officials, commission men from the Union Stockyards at Chicago and St. Paul, and the meat-packing companies.

The Northern Montana Roundup Association was off to a running start and was destined to stay in the running, for the combined wealth and aggressive spirit of the so-called "Northerners" added needed strength to the organization. A strong executive committee, chosen by popular vote, included the following ranchers who belonged to the association:

J. T. Harrison, John Survant, Colin Hunter, L. E. Kaufman, C. W. Price, Tom Clary, Sam Miller, Con Kohrs, John Lepdey, Henry Sieber, Will Coburn, M. E. Milner, W. K. Flowerree, A. W. Kingsbury, and Tom Handon.

As things turned out there was little change in the personnel of that committee during the existence of the Association. They did the work and the membership at large approved their actions and policies. They battled the railroad as a matter of course, but their main activity was the suppression of rustling. They were once defined as a "large, well equipped and excellently organized detective bureau."

It boded ill for any rustler who attracted their attention.[5]

Due to the aggressive activities of the Northern Montana Roundup Association and its able stock inspectors and range detectives, cattle rustling and horse stealing was cut down to a minimum. The Deer Lodge penitentiary held its quota of gun-toting gents who had swung a hungry loop and were now making horsehair bridles to be raffled off in saloons for tobacco money.

During that period the stockmen and miners in the Little Rockies region held a meeting at Rock Creek in June, 1894, and gave the mining camp in the heart of the Little Rockies the name of Landusky in honor of the hard-bitten, tough character, Pike Landusky, wolfer, whisky trader, buffalo hunter, cowman, and sometimes prospector. Baptized in the name of Powell Landusky, he gained the nickname "Pike" from his drunken boast that he came from Pike County, Missouri, and could whip any man who ever walked on two legs. As a rule he lived up to his bragging. Pike Landusky was tough as a boot, and the town of Landusky, named in his honor, was destined to become the toughest little cow town and mining camp in Montana.

If Pike Landusky ever killed a white man, he kept it a buried secret. But he enjoyed the reputation of being an "Injun hater," and he never kept track of the Indians he killed and scalped. But when Pike whipped a white man in a rough and tumble fight with no holds barred, fought with fists and boots, his luckless opponent never forgot the terrific beating that took the fight out of him.

During Johnny Ritch's sojourn in Landusky and the Little Rockies, he became well acquainted with Pike Landusky, and the following is his description of the notorious character:

> He was young when he reached Last Chance and became famous as one of the hard men and a tip top rough and tumble fighter before he had been there a year. He cleaned up on so many tough

[5] Fletcher, *Free Grass to Fences*, 123.

men around Last Chance that most of them conceded he was bad medicine.

Tall, rangy, with a frame like a cruiser of the first class and arms of extraordinary length, he had all the good things for a fighter as a beginning. These, and his prodigious strength and endurance made him a formidable antagonist for any man. Besides, fear was not part of his makeup. He was a battler by nature. . . . A man of such unusual physical powers would naturally become widely known and Pike's fame reached far and to many borders.

Pike hadn't very attractive features when I first knew him. He might have been good looking at one time but a Blackfoot Indian had scrambled his facial exteriors all up with a buffalo gun in 1860 so it was hard to tell just how good looking he might have been. . . .

I do not think Pike ever killed a white man; he just beat them with his hands so they didn't fight anymore. His hatred for Indians was a mania—and no man knows how many he killed. He held no particular aversion for any tribe; to him they were all just Indians and he hated them all.[6]

Pike Landusky was a battle-scarred old fighting cock, and while he lived, he ruled his town with an iron hand, putting fear into any man who had the foolhardy whisky guts to cross him. It was Pike's boast that he could lick any man in the Little Rockies, and even when he was getting along in years, he lived up to his bragging. One day another tough character known as Jew Jake drifted into the town of Landusky. He went under the name of Jake Harris, which probably was his legal name, but around Landusky and the Little Rockies country he was known as Jew Jake, and he was tough in his own right. A few years prior to Jew Jake's arrival at Landusky, he was involved in a shooting scrape with the town marshal at Great Falls. According to rumor, the ruckus took place on the wide plank platform at the Great Northern depot. During the gun fight Jew Jake supposedly fell from the raised platform onto the tracks just as a train was pulling in, and one leg was severed at the knee by the incoming train. Jew Jake had a wooden pegleg and traveled on crutches when he came to Landusky.

[6] *Great Falls Tribune*, January 20, 1935. For the entire article, see Appendix A.

No sooner had Jew Jake arrived in town than he and Landusky became good friends. Pike built him a log cabin saloon with a sort of general merchandise store in a large room at the rear. The store had a long counter where a man could buy canned goods and tobacco and overalls, gloves, work shirts, underwear, and socks.

When Jew Jake tended bar, he used only one crutch in order to keep his gun hand ready to reach for the No. 8 sawed-off shotgun he kept handy under the bar. At other times he used the sawed-off shotgun for a crutch.

As soon as Jew Jake was established in his saloon and store known as Jew Jake's saloon, he sent to Anaconda for one of his tough gunman cronies who went by the name of Hogan. Hogan was a small, frail-looking, wiry man, said to be tubercular, who had a reputation as a gunslinger. Hogan tended bar and waited on customers at the store when Jew Jake was off duty.

The town of Landusky boasted a second- or third-class post office. Pike Landusky was the postmaster, and Jew Jake was his assistant postmaster. The post-office books, ledgers, and stamp supply were kept at the rear store end of the saloon. The mail came by stagecoach from the town of Harlem on the Great Northern Railroad. The large canvas sack that contained the first-class mail was a padlocked pouch. The key that unlocked the padlock was fastened to the store counter by a short length of small dog chain.

When the four- or six-horse Concord stage pulled in and halted in front of Jew Jake's saloon, the stage driver tossed the mail sacks out while the passengers disembarked. Then without leaving his seat the driver headed for the barn. As a rule Jew Jake or Hogan came out and picked up the mail sacks, but if they were busy tending bar and waiting on store customers, one of the men lined up at the bar would pick up the mail sacks and dump them on the store counter or on the poker table.

If Pike Landusky happened to be in the saloon, he proceeded to fulfill his postmaster duties, but usually Jew Jake tended the mail. It was his habit to unlock the first-class pouch, empty the letters on the big, round, poker table, and leave them there for

The Lawless Range

those who expected letters to paw through. To add to the general confusion, the contents of the second-class mail sack were also dumped on the same table.

It was the duty of the postmaster to keep a simple set of books and see that the stamp used to cancel the postage on letters was kept up to date. But there were many times when Pike or Jew Jake forgot to change the dates. The postage stamps were kept in an open cigar box at the end of the counter. Letters to be mailed were deposited in an open box that once had contained dried prunes, according to the lettering on the box end. The two canvas-backed ledgers lay on a high shelf above the stacked merchandise, but the pages were devoid of any entry. Layers of dust, cobwebs, and fly specks spoke of long neglect. Neither Postmaster Pike Landusky nor his assistant, who signed the name Jake Harris, had taken time out of their checkered careers to take up bookkeeping of any sort.

In short, the post office at Landusky was a self-operating, co-

Landusky, Montana, July 4, 1909.

operating system, run with the inebriated assistance of various and sundry citizens and transients.

No doubt there were a few regular newspaper subscribers who had valid reasons for objecting to this rather slipshod method of mail distribution. If they were not present when Jew Jake dumped the contents of the second-class mail sack on the card table, they were usually out of luck. The custom was first come, first served, and some news-hungry gent, ignoring whose name was printed on the wrapper of a tightly rolled newspaper, might slit the cover with thumbnail or jackknife and catch up with the latest news, then proceed to discard the newspaper or pass it on to the next avid reader. If the subscriber was some rancher, for instance, who got to town once a week, he was lucky if he found his copy of the *Great Falls Tribune,* the *Havre Plain Dealer,* the *Fort Benton Record,* the *Helena Independent* or *Daily Herald,* the *Butte Miner,* or the *Montana Livestock Journal.*

The saddle and boot catalogs addressed to certain individuals were considered public domain, as were the Montgomery Ward and Sears, Roebuck catalogs, known as sheepherder's bibles. The pink-paper copies of the illustrated *Police Gazette* were highly prized and more often than not became treasured possessions of their lucky claimants, to be read and reread in some bunkhouse or hoarded in some miner's cabin. And those unable to read could look at the pictures of burlesque queens or prize fighters and wrestlers.

The letters dumped out unceremoniously on the poker table from the first-class pouch were another matter. A certain value of personal property was attached to them, and very few, if any, letters were ever tampered with or stolen. When letters went unclaimed for a certain length of time, Jew Jake put them in a cigar box he kept on the back bar where they stayed indefinitely.

Seldom a week passed when the first-class mail did not include some reward dodger addressed to the postmaster with instructions to post it on a bulletin board on the walls for public viewing. Jew Jake, Pike Landusky, and the tubercular Hogan perused those notices with avid curiosity and discussed each at length. When the merits and demerits of the outlaw with a price on his head were thoroughly hashed out, a lighted match consigned the reward notice to gray ashes even though the wanted man might be a bitter enemy.

Naturally there were times when some irate newspaper or periodical subscriber who failed to get his mail on time was sorely tempted to lodge a protest. But few men had the temerity to voice their objections aloud. This was Pike Landusky's domain, and Jew Jake with his sawed-off shotgun stood ready and eager to back Pike's play.

One chilly day in November when there was snow on the ground, the stagecoach arrived in early afternoon. Among the passengers who alighted and entered the portals of Jew Jake's saloon was an unobtrusive, quiet-mannered man. Judging from his clothes, he was a city dude. He wore a business suit of salt-and-pepper weave, a white shirt with starched collar and black string bow tie, and polished, black, elastic-sided Congress gaiters.

Instead of lining up at the bar, the stranger removed his fur-lined overcoat and walked over to the large potbellied stove set in a sandbox in the center of the long room. As he stood with his back to the stove, he watched Jew Jake limp out from behind the bar on one crutch and pick up the mail sacks the stage driver had tossed through the open door with an experienced aim that landed them in the middle of the pine-board plank floor.

The stranger betrayed only a mild curiosity as he watched Jew Jake empty the contents of the second-class mail sack on the large, round, poker table, then unlock the first-class pouch and, shoving the newspapers and packages aside, upend it, letting the letters shower down like fluttering shot birds to land hit and miss on the table.

"Mail's delivered!" Jew Jake bellowed. "Come an' git 'er." He balanced his crutch and headed for the store counter, his free hand lugging the empty mail sacks. As he limped past the stove, the stranger spoke in a quiet voice, his tone mildly deceptive.

"Is that your habitual method of distributing the mail?" the stranger asked, pointing towards the group of men gathered around the table, talking and joshing as they pawed through rolled newspapers, packages, and letters.

"Hell, yes," Jew Jake answered as he eyed the stranger from head to foot with cold suspicion as if caught off guard by the foolish question. "First come, first served," he added for good measure. "You got any better notion, keep it to yourself, stranger. When I need any help around here, I'll hire me a swamper."

The stranger removed a flat wallet from the inside pocket of his suit and flipped it open to reveal a nickel-plated, shield-shaped badge pinned to the leather.

"A goddamned Pinkerton," Jew Jake spat out like a dirty word. "I mighta knowed it." He purposely spoke in a loud voice to warn any man present who might be on the dodge from the law. A sudden hushed silence followed his words.

"Postal inspector," the stranger answered with a thin smile that was wholly lacking in humor. His quiet voice was both faintly caustic and a little contemptuous, and there was a cold look in his sharp, pale blue eyes.

A hard twinkle showed in Jew Jake's bloodshot eyes as he heaved an exaggerated sigh of relief.

"Relax boys," Jew Jake put on a one-sided grin. "For a minute that tin badge had me fooled. He ain't no damned Pinkerton." Then he narrowed his eyes at the dude stranger and said, "I mind the time a cowpuncher showed up here wearin' a tin star that had Chicken Inspector on it—had an alum root in his vest pocket he chawed on—asked where the whore houses were located." Jew Jake scratched his head and put a puzzled look on his whiskered face. "Never heard tell of no postal inspector," he said solemnly as he eyed the stranger's derby hat.

The men who were crowded around the littered card table exchanged meaning looks and faint grins. It looked as though Jew Jake was getting ready to give this city dude some kind of rough initiation.

"The job of postal inspector," the stranger said in a bitter tone, "is to check the post offices in his territory. I find the name of Powell Landusky on the records as being the postmaster here at the town of Landusky. Are you by any chance Powell Landusky?"

"Powell Landusky," Jew Jake mumbled as he shook his head slowly in thoughtful denial. "Never heard tell of no Powell Landusky. This town was named after Pike Landusky, and Pike's a warthog, drunk or sober—hell on wheels. Pike owns this town, lock, stock, and barrel. The Little Rockies is his stompin' ground. Pike Landusky is bad medicine. Take my advice and walk slow and speak easy if you aim to leave town in one piece, mister."

"I'll make a note of it," the stranger answered, smiling thinly. "And to whom am I indebted for this sage advice and timely warning?"

"Come again, stranger." Jew Jake growled suspiciously,

"In words of one syllable," the postal inspector said crisply, "who are you? And in what official capacity are you entitled to handle, or mishandle I should say, the United States mail?"

"Now we're gettin' down to cases," Jew Jake replied grimly. "I'm signed up by Pike Landusky as assistant postmaster. The name's Jake Harris. I own this saloon and store. My friends call me Jew Jake. Strangers call me mister. What kin I do for you, stranger?"

"Acting in the capacity of postal inspector," the inspector said quietly, flashing the badge under Jew Jake's nose, "I'm here to examine the post-office books. And for your special enlightenment this badge carries the same authority as that of a United States deputy marshal, *Mister* Jake Harris!"

Anger seared Jew Jake's eyes as he whirled on his steel-collared pegleg. With the aid of one crutch, he moved behind the bar with a long, crow-hopping gait, pausing long enough to help himself to a quick drink and pick up the sawed-off shotgun. Then, using the shotgun as a crutch, he hopped over to the store counter. He reached up to the top shelf with his free hand and brought down two dust-covered, canvas-bound ledgers. With these in hand, he headed past the potbellied stove, where the inspector stood in silent wonderment, and flung open the saloon door. Standing framed in the open doorway, he threw the ledgers out into the snow-covered street. Leaving the door standing open, he took a backward step, and pointing to the door with the sawed-off shotgun, he bellowed like a bull pawing dirt.

"There's your goddamned post office, mister. It's bin nothin' but a nuisance from the start! Now git the hell outa my place while I got a tail holt on my temper!" Jew Jake spun around and crowhopped back behind the bar.

The inspector had a strained, pale look on his face. He put on his overcoat and went out the door, banging it shut behind him.

"Belly up to the bar, gents!" he heard Jew Jake shout. "Drinks on the house!"

Loud laughter from the crowd in the saloon followed the postal inspector as he picked up the ledgers out of the snow and headed towards the hotel. He had become angry and frustrated, and as he walked, he muttered threats through his clenched teeth.

Later on in the shank of the evening, Pike Landusky and a chosen delegation of allegedly sober citizens (by Little Rockies standards) paid the indignant postal inspector a formal visit at the hotel, in order to smooth the gentleman's ruffled feathers. In the due course of the evening, they somehow accomplished their mission. It was later rumored that a sealed quart of twelve-year-old whisky had a mellowing influence on the inspector. At any rate, the following day, while Jew Jake was sleeping off his drunk, a carpenter was hired to install a pigeonhole arrangement to hold the mail. The postal inspector brought the books up to date before he left on the morning stage bound for Harlem. A man with bookkeeping knowledge was hired as assistant postmaster, and for a time the Landusky post office was handled in a proper manner or a reasonable facsimile. But whatever the inspector wrote in his official report remained a secret between him and Uncle Sam.

For the time being the subscribers to the various newspapers and periodicals received their mail intact. But none of the old-timers in the vicinity of the Little Rockies can recall any reward dodgers of wanted criminals ever being posted on the walls of Jew Jake's saloon, which housed the United States post office.

6.

The Curry-Landusky Feud

IN THE SUMMER OF 1894, when the town of Landusky was officially recorded at the land office at Fort Benton, the three Curry brothers, Harvey, Johnny, and Loney, and their side partner Jim Thornhill, who had "drifted in from nowhere," were already located with a sizable herd of cattle and horses in the Little Rockies country of northeastern Montana.

All three of the Curry brothers had black hair and were good looking, and there was such a marked resemblance among them that even a stranger could tell at first glance they were brothers. Kid Curry was about thirty years old when he first came to Montana. Johnny was about twenty-eight and Loney about twenty-six. Their partner Jim Thornhill was about Kid Curry's age, give or take a few years. Even then, the oldest of the Curry boys, Harvey, was called the Kid. In later years he was destined to become the most dangerous outlaw of Butch Cassidy's Wild Bunch.

In those days no questions were asked or answered concerning a man's true identity—where he came from or what had happened along his back trail. Kid Curry's real name was not revealed until several years after his quick-triggered gun began blazing along the outlaw trail. Reward dodgers, which listed his crimes and the amount of bounty offered for his capture dead or alive, identified him as Harvey Logan, alias Kid Curry.

The three Curry boys and Jim Thornhill raised cattle and horses on a ranch located about five miles south of the town of Landusky in the vicinity of what became known as Thornhill Butte. The cattle brand was 4T (connected) on the left ribs, and the horse brand was 7UP (connected) on the left thigh. They were all top hands, including Johnny Curry who had one arm amputated at the elbow because of a gunfight he was in sometime prior to his coming to the Little Rockies.

Jim Thornhill, before buying the ranch, had worked for the DHS, the Circle Bar, and Circle C outfits, and at various times during the years all three Curry boys and Thornhill had worked for the Circle C and repped with the Circle C wagon on the roundups. They were easy to get along with, and they tended to their own business and got along first rate with their neighbors, including Pike Landusky.

Loney Curry played the fiddle at dances and ran a saloon at Harlem. He was well liked, and his saloon was the hangout for cowpunchers when they came to town from neighboring ranches. When the big outfits shipped their beef steers to the Chicago markets from the Harlem stockyards, the cowhands made Loney Curry's saloon their headquarters until the wagon boss rounded them up and sent them back to camp.

In other words, Kid Curry and his two brothers and Jim Thornhill were all well liked, and if they raised hell in Landusky and Zortman, neighboring mining camps and cow towns, or in Harlem, Chinook, and Malta, the shipping points on the Great Northern Railroad, they had plenty company. It was the custom for the cowhands to buck their horses down the street and ride into the saloons for their first drink before they put their horses up at the feed and livery barn. When they got ready to pull out for the roundup camp or head back for the ranch, their pockets empty, they shot at the stars as a farewell gesture before they went back to their jobs on the ranch or some isolated winter line camp.

The Curry boys and Jim Thornhill never discussed where they were born and raised or where they came from when they showed up in Montana, and they were reluctant to brag about what had happened along their back trail when in their cups, but their atti-

Harvey Logan, alias Kid Curry.

Union Pacific Railroad Museum Collection

tude of minding their own business was considered a natural state of affairs. Any man's past was strictly his own business those days, and nobody but a fool nosed into other people's affairs or asked personal questions. It was an unwritten law in the strict code of the frontier West, and any man with a lick of horse sense lived up to the code of the cow country. It was taken for granted they were what they were, hard-working cowhands and ranchers. If they were inclined to be clannish, that was only natural. After all, they had come to the Little Rockies together, punched cows with the same big outfits, and pooled their interests in raising livestock.

Things rocked along that way for quite a few years, up until the time big Pike Landusky stirred up a hornet's nest.

Pike Landusky had married a widow, Mrs. Julia Dessery, the mother of four grown daughters. Two of the daughters were married, and the other two lived at the Landusky ranch with Pike and their mother. In those days unmarried girls were scarce in that part of the cow country, and the widow's two daughters, who had taken the name of their stepfather and were known as the "Landusky girls," were much sought after and highly popular. Every cowpuncher in that part of the country had a woman-hungry loop built. Nearly every day some cowhand shaved his whiskers and scrubbed up, dressed in the prevailing height of cowboy fashion, and showed up at the Landusky place.

It was natural that all three of the Curry boys, who were neighbors to Pike Landusky, were among the more ardent swains who entered this free-for-all contest. Among the brothers it was a good-natured rivalry, and by the same token it was much the same kind of a deal between the two girls. The girls' mother took it all in stride and made the Curry boys welcome at the ranch.

Meanwhile Pike Landusky, who claimed in no uncertain manner to be the toughest man to whip in the Little Rockies, was viewing the goings on between the Curry boys and his stepdaughters with a jaundiced eye, nursing a growing suspicion that gradually became hatred for the Currys. He knew that Loney Curry was meeting one of his stepdaughters at some hidden rendezvous when she rode off alone from the ranch after dark on her private horse.

The Curry-Landusky Feud

While Pike was on one of his drunks at Jew Jake's saloon, he heard the whispered rumor that Loney Curry was "laying up" with one of his stepdaughters, and he began to call Loney a whoremaster and said that Kid Curry was a brand artist. Pike spilled his whisky talk across the bar into the listening ears of Jew Jake, and the talk spread beyond the confines of the saloon until the rumor was common knowledge at Landusky and throughout the Little Rockies cow country.

The ugly, malicious gossip, like the proverbial snowball rolling downhill, grew in volume with each telling. And as the feud between Pike Landusky and the Curry boys increased in tensity each day, the tough town of Landusky and its environs became divided. Pike had his following of tough characters among the miners and his drinking cronies, and the Curry boys had the backing of Jim Thornhill and the surrounding cowmen and cowhands. The Little Rockies cow country sat back and waited for the inevitable showdown. Landusky became a powder keg with the fuse attached. One tiny spark could set off a charge that would blow things to hell and gone.

Then one day without warning the sheriff from Fort Benton came to Landusky and arrested Kid Curry and his brother Loney on a trumped-up cattle-rustling and brand-changing charge made by rancher Jim Winters. After their arrest the sheriff deputized Pike Landusky and left the two prisoners in Landusky's "protective custody."

With their handcuffed hands fastened behind their backs and both feet tied together, Kid Curry and Loney were at the mercy of their sworn enemy. For long weeks on end Pike Landusky had nursed his grudge for the Curry boys, keeping the smoldering coals of hatred alive with forty-rod whisky. The two Curry brothers had challenged the almighty prowess of Pike Landusky, and by the trickery of fate Pike had them manacled and helpless, because the law had made him a special deputy sheriff.

Thirty years later, in 1924, Jim Thornhill and I made a two week camping trip to the Grand Canyon in Arizona. I had known him since I was a pistol kid, and he treated me like one of his own three sons. Jim Thornhill had sold his outfit at Thornhill Butte in Montana to the B. D. Phillips cattle and sheep outfit about the same time the Circle C sold to the Matadors. He and his family had moved to Globe where they had a small Arizona spread.

Sometimes we sat around a little campfire after supper, but more often we sat on a rimrock overlooking the Grand Canyon, where moonlight dusted the red cliffs with a coating of silver. On cloudless nights the stars seemed to come within reach, and the little night sounds and the faint breeze stirring in the ancient gnarled cypress and scrub piñons were the only sounds in a vast silence that hung over the Big Coulee, as Thornhill called it. Miles below flowed the mighty Colorado, and perhaps it was the eternal silence of the grandeur before us that prompted the aging Thornhill to talk, to uncover his back trail and speak of long dead ashes of lone campfires he had so painstakingly covered along the outlaw trail.

While we camped together, Jim Thornhill related to me the details Kid Curry had told him about Pike Landusky's abuse of his handcuffed prisoners. If any man in the Little Rockies knew what caused the feud in the beginning and on down the line, it was Kid Curry's ranch partner Jim Thornhill. He was there from start to finish.

Thornhill said that when the sheriff of Chouteau County slipped in from Fort Benton to arrest the Curry brothers and turn them over to Pike Landusky to keep on ice, none of the Currys' friends knew anything about it. The damage had already been done before Thornhill discovered what had happened.

Pike had the Kid and Loney where he wanted them. Thornhill said their hands were handcuffed behind their backs. The Kid's feet were hobbled by leg irons, and Loney's feet were hogtied. While they lay helpless on the floor, Pike worked them over with his fists until their faces looked like chopped meat. Then he stomped on them and kicked them around until he got tired. Pike was working on a quart of whisky and enjoying his job. He was chewing tobacco and kept spitting the juice in their faces and

Jim Thornhill, 1924, at the Grand Canyon.

calling them all the filthy fighting names he could lay tongue to. Then he opened the big blade of his jackknife and said he was going to geld the pair of them. He would teach them not to come around his stepdaughters.

Kid Curry told Pike that he had better kill them both while he had the chance, because no man could abuse them like he had and live to brag about it, and if he used the knife like he threatened to do, he would be the first man hanged in the two-bit mining camp of Landusky.

"If you got the tough rep you brag about, Pike," Kid Curry said, "you'll turn us loose right now, and it'll be strictly between me and you. When the sign is right, I'll give you the damnedest workin' over a man ever got and lived to tell about. You brag you're the toughest man in Montana, but you don't have the guts to live up to your tough rep."

Pike shut the blade of his knife and put it in his pocket. He said he was turning his prisoners over to the sheriff when he showed up—that chances were they would do a stretch in the Deer Lodge pen making horsehair bridles. Meanwhile he would bear in mind the Kid's threat to beat the hell out of him.

"From here on out, Kid," Pike said, "it's between me and you. This is big country but too small to hold both Pike Landusky and Kid Curry. I'll be ready for you any time, any place, you feel like crowdin' your luck, Kid."

When the sheriff returned, he took charge of the prisoners. He had already served a bench warrant on Jim Thornhill on the same brand-changing, cattle-rustling charge made by rancher Jim Winters. He took the three men to Fort Benton to stand trial.

The Circle C outfit posted bail for the three prisoners, who were then set free. Since they were hard pressed for cash at the time, they put up what cattle they had in their 4T brand as collateral to the Circle C. And thus matters stood for the time being. Jim Thornhill and the two Curry brothers were back ranching in the Little Rockies.

With the coming of Christmas, the Curry-Landusky feud was pushed aside. The town council of Landusky sent word to the

The Curry-Landusky Feud

nearby ranchers to attend a big town meeting in order to plan a large community dance for Christmas Eve and a banquet to end all banquets for Christmas Day. All hostilities were suspended as the town folk and neighboring ranchers discussed plans for the dance and Christmas dinner, and needless to say the forty-rod whisky flowed freely and loosened the tongues of the enthusiastic speechmakers.

Johnny Curry donated the new barn at his ranch for the dance hall. Loney Curry volunteered his services as fiddler, and some rancher, mellowed by the potent forty-rod, donated the use of his wife's organ that until then had played only hymns. The saloon-keepers promised to furnish the liquid refreshments, which completed the arrangements for the dance.

Next the Christmas dinner had to be arranged. Warren Berry said that such mundane bill-of-fare as turkey was out of the question, that an oyster banquet would really put the isolated mining camp and cow town of Landusky on the map for all time. His enlightened suggestion met with unanimous approval. Oysters it would be.

"Tie-Up" George, the best roundup cook in that part of the cow country, was chosen as chef and given strict orders not to get drunk until after the oysters were ready to serve. Johnny Ritch placed his new log cabin and new cookstove at "Tie-Up" George's disposal. "Lousy," the stage driver, was delegated to order the oysters. Not the canned variety, Johnny Ritch and Warren Berry carefully explained to Lousy, but fresh oysters with the shells on, packed in barrels of ice.

It was highly doubtful that Lousy had ever eaten so much as a canned oyster in his life, but orders were orders and he did his best when he got to Harlem. He sent a lengthy telegram ordering the raw oysters in the shell to the station agent at Minneapolis, where he was sure oysters came from. In due time the barrels of oysters arrived at Harlem, and Lousy loaded them aboard his Concord stage. The express bill was greater than the price of the oysters, but what the hell. The hat had been passed at the town meeting and everyone had donated freely.

Pioneer Cattleman in Montana

Cowpunchers spread the news of the Christmas celebration to be held at Landusky throughout the badlands as far as Rocky Point and the old Fort Musselshell Crossing.

Horsebackers, buckboards, dead X wagons, spring wagons, and top buggies came to Landusky, until more than a hundred people gathered at the Christmas Eve dance and banquet. It was said that there was enough grub on hand to feed an army. In order to maintain law and order in the spirit of the season, all six-shooters were left with the bartenders at the saloons. Never before in the history of Landusky had such a large gathering of people ever been assembled. The typical frontier celebration lasted for two days and nights, while they ate and drank and danced to their hearts' content.

The big jamboree lasted until the morning of December 27. The ranchers and their families wearily departed, and the hungover town came back to normal. The unarmed truce between Pike Landusky and the Curry brothers had ended, and the bitter feud was resumed with increased tension. It seemed as though the brief pause in hostilities had magnified the hatred between Pike and Kid Curry, and every man in town was somehow aware that a showdown was rapidly approaching.

7.

The Showdown

SNOW HAD FALLEN during the two days and nights when peace had prevailed in Landusky. It was about ten o'clock in the morning of the twenty-seventh day of December, 1894. The low overcast sky was the color of gun lead, and the chill in the air had a tendency to herd the drinking men to the various saloons to belly up to the bar and partake of the "hair of the dog."

Those who wanted no part of the Pike Landusky–Kid Curry feud shunned Jew Jake's saloon as if a quarantine sign had been tacked on the closed door. The one and only main street of Landusky was empty; no saddle horses were tied up at any of the hitching posts. The town had the deserted look of a dismal ghost town.

Although it was not prearranged that Jew Jake's saloon and store would be the site of the showdown, the fact that it was Pike Landusky's hangout made it the likely place. There Pike would have the backing of the one-legged proprietor, the consumptive gunman Hogan, and one or more of his tough gunslinger cronies.

Johnny and Loney Curry had remained in town while Jim Thornhill and Kid Curry went to the ranch in a spring wagon. On the way back to town, according to the story Jim Thornhill told me, Kid Curry told his partner, "No sonofabitch on earth can do what Pike done to me and Loney and get away with it."

Kid Curry went on to explain that the showdown would take

place at Jew Jake's, on Pike's own stomping ground. He said he would beat the living hell out of Pike with his fists, but if Pike reached for his gun at the start, he aimed to beat him to the draw.

Jim Thornhill warned the Kid about Pike's prowess as a fist fighter and that once the fight started, it would be a rough-and-tumble, no-holds-barred brawl, because Pike had bragged he would kill the Kid with his bare hands.

Kid Curry told Thornhill that Pike had made the same threat to his face the night of the dance at Johnny's barn and the Kid had told Pike he would give him the same treatment. "That goes as she lays, Jimmer," the Kid said. "Mebbe when the play comes up, I'll manage to get the bulge. All I want you to do when the ruckus starts is to keep Jew Jake off my back and see that Hogan doesn't shoot me."

"I'll be there regardless, Kid, and so will Loney and Johnny," Thornhill told him. "Between the three of us we'll tend to Jew Jake and Hogan, and that goes double for the rest of Pike's gun-slingin' cronies."

"There's one thing more, Jimmer," Kid Curry said. "Either me or Pike will wind up dead. That's the deal we made at the dance. I'll see Pike in hell before I'll holler enough. If Pike claws for his gun, I aim to beat him to it. It could wind up in one hell of a free-for-all shootin' match."

Before they left the ranch that morning, Jim Thornhill had tried to talk the Kid out of the notion.

"It was Pike started it, Jimmer, when he hollered for the law to help him," Kid Curry said. "A tough sonofabitch like him callin' in the law. It was Pike who ribbed the sheriff into nabbin' me and Loney and turnin' us over to him roped, throwed, and hogtied. That's when Pike Landusky broke his pick with every cowman and cowhand in the country. It's no dice, Jimmer. Pike started the ball rollin'. It's up to him to play his tough hand out. He jumped the wrong man when he tackled Kid Curry, and I aim to prove it between now and sundown."

When they reached town, Loney and Johnny Curry were waiting for them, and they held a brief medicine talk at the feed and livery

The Showdown

barn before they split up. It was agreed that Johnny would stand guard outside the saloon.

When Jim Thornhill and Loney Curry entered Jew Jake's place, Pike and one of his tough followers were lined up at the bar. Jim and Loney passed by them without speaking and went on to the store where Hogan was standing behind the counter. Jim bought a paper bag full of apples and ate one while they sized up the half-dozen men lined up at the bar. The way Jim and Loney figured the odds, if it came to a showdown, it was anybody's guess. There was a half-blood cowpuncher, Joe Contway, they had worked with on the roundups, and chances were he would want no part of any gun ruckus and would head for the door. Another cowhand, George Allis, would also probably slip out at the first sign of trouble. Tommy Carter, a prospector, was a drinking companion of Pike's and they had prospected together. But it was a tossup whether or not Carter would back Pike in a tight. The two other men were strangers and would bear watching.

Both men took particular notice of Jew Jake, who was tending bar. He was using his sawed-off shotgun for a crutch, a sure sign he expected trouble. The big man with Pike was packing a six-shooter, and the way he was downing his drinks looked as if he was using whisky to give him courage enough to back Pike if necessary.

About then Kid Curry came in the front door alone, kicked the door shut behind him, then walked across the plank floor to where Pike Landusky and his companion were standing at the bar. Pike, who was wearing a fur-lined overcoat, had just poured himself a drink when the Kid came in.

According to Jim Thornhill, Pike had seen Kid Curry enter but pretended he had not noticed his sworn enemy. Pike had a bottle of whisky in one hand and a filled shot glass in the other hand. Thornhill figured Pike was prepared to throw the whisky in his glass into the Kid's eyes and hit him over the head with the bottle. He was a seasoned barroom fighter and knew every trick.

That was exactly how Kid Curry also had it figured. Suddenly he slapped his open hand down on Pike's shoulder, with enough force to loosen his grip on the bottle, which fell on the bar and spilled the whisky in the shot glass. As Pike whirled around, Kid Curry swung a haymaker with all his 165 pounds behind it. The blow landed on Pike's jaw and sent him reeling backwards.

The instant the two combatants went down in a tangle of arms and legs, Jim Thornhill and Loney Curry went into action. With their six-shooters in their hands they covered Hogan and Jew Jake. Thornhill told Hogan to throw away his gun—that the fight was between Pike and the Kid and no concern of his. The hired gunman did as he was told.

While Loney Curry kept the two strangers covered, Jim Thornhill told Jew Jake that if he intended to use the shotgun, he should do so or else drop it. Jim said Jew Jake dropped the shotgun as if it were a hot branding iron. Then Thornhill warned the crowd that the fight was between Pike and Kid Curry and that any man who tried to interfere would live only long enough to regret it.

It was a brutal, ruthless fight, but not as one-sided as most chroniclers of the bloody fracas have reported. Pike Landusky at fifty was still a powerful man, and he fought with every ounce of his strength. If he had not been handicapped by the bulky fur-lined overcoat, the outcome of the fight might have been different. The first blow to the jaw was not a knockout punch by a long shot, and there were a couple of times when Pike was on top of the heap. But Kid Curry was younger and more active, and although the older seasoned battler outweighed him by fifty pounds, the Kid was able to squirm out from under and straddle his antagonist. It was a silent battle for the most part, and both men knew it would be fought to the death. Once when Pike was on top, he tried to gouge the Kid's eye out with his thumb and almost succeeded before the Kid twisted his head away and rolled the big man off.

Kid Curry sat astraddle Pike and hammered at his face with both fists until, according to Jim Thornhill, Pike hollered for somebody to pull the Kid off. Then Tommy Carter tried to persuade Thornhill and Loney Curry to stop the fight.

"You've watched Pike beat the brains out of a lot of good men,

The Showdown

Carter," Jim told him. "Pike's gettin' a dose of his own medicine. Keep the hell outa this, Tommy."

Loney Curry added, "That goes double for the rest of you." The cowpunchers, Contway and Allis, said something about having seen enough and went out the door.

"Lemme up, Kid," Pike finally pleaded, according to Thornhill. "I got a-plenty."

Kid Curry slowly rose to his feet. He was blood spattered and his gouged eye was swollen almost shut, and he watched the battered Pike as he slowly got to his feet.

As Pike got his balance by spreading his legs a little, he reached into his overcoat pocket. Kid Curry later said he figured Pike was reaching for a handkerchief to wipe the blood from his face. Instead his hand came out holding a new automatic pistol pointed at the Kid. But when Pike squeezed the trigger, the gun failed to shoot for some reason. If it had fired, Kid Curry would have been a dead man, because although Pike was battered and beaten, his gun hand was steady, and he could not have missed at close range.

Then Kid Curry reached for his six-shooter, a Frontier model single-action Colt .45. The Kid thumbed back the hammer and pulled the trigger twice, and the heavy slugs thudded into Pike's body. He fired a third time but missed as Pike fell.

The moment the shooting started, the crowd headed for both doors. Jew Jake, without benefit of crutch, hopped out the back door with his hands up, hollering, "Don't shoot! Don't shoot!" and plunged headlong into a drifted pile of snow. Thornhill said Jew Jake was the most frightened man he had ever seen. Jim told him to quit hollering—he wasn't worth the powder to blow him to hell.

Jim Thornhill, Kid Curry and Loney stood bunched together with their guns in their hands until Johnny Curry showed up with the spring wagon. Then they left the saloon, piled into the wagon, and headed for the ranch.

That night at the ranch Jim Thornhill and the Curry brothers had a medicine talk. Kid Curry said he was pulling out, because he did not intend to stand trial for killing Pike Landusky. He told Thornhill that he and his brothers were headed for the Hole-in-the-Wall country and that he would sell him his share of the ranch, including cattle and horses. Since Thornhill did not have the cash to pay his partner, he sold their cattle to the Circle C and gave the money to Kid Curry later at the Hideaway near Thornhill Butte.

Any cowhand who for some reason or other made a mistake that forced him to quit the country usually headed for the outlaw country to throw in with the Hole-in-the-Wall gang or the Wild Bunch.

Butch Cassidy's Wild Bunch called themselves the Train Robbers' Syndicate, and their members were carefully hand-picked. They were the elite among the outlaws and looked down their noses at the horse-thief gangs and two-bit cattle rustlers. They were high-stake gamblers who risked their lives and freedom in every venture. From their point of view, the railroad companies and banks were rich and could well afford the loss of a few thousand dollars.

Butch Cassidy's Wild Bunch rode high, wide, and handsome along the outlaw trail from Mexico to Canada and blazed a trail of glory from Robbers' Roost in Utah to Kid Curry's Hideaway in the badlands of the Missouri, just south of the Little Rockies. After a train or bank robbery, the gang divided their loot which they later squandered in the small cow towns where they were welcome. Sometimes when one of them went broke, he would hire out under a false name to a cattle outfit, or tend bar, or open a saloon for a while, until some Pinkerton range detective followed his trail and nosed him out.

When some member of the Wild Bunch hired out as a cowhand to some big outfit, the wagon boss or the owner of the spread usually knew who he really was. But instead of turning informer to claim the bounty offered on the reward dodgers, they would keep the outlaw's identity a secret and even warn him if they suspected a detective on his trail.

Most written accounts that describe the killing of Pike Landusky have branded Kid Curry a murderer. And William Pinkerton stated that the Kid was one of the worst of the badmen, that he did not

The Showdown

have a single redeeming feature. But there were many who disagreed. Butch Cassidy once told Jim Thornton that Kid Curry had more courage than any other man he had ever known, and if he ever had only one choice of all the outlaws to back him in a showdown, he would choose Kid Curry. More than once Kid Curry risked his life to save a companion.

One winter when Kid Curry worked for the Circle C, my half-brother, Bob Coburn, had a serious accident. During a blizzard, when Bob was several miles from the home ranch, the horse he was riding stepped into a badger hole and broke a foreleg. In the fall Bob was pinned down by the crippled horse and lay unconscious from a head injury and a broken jaw. Kid Curry found him, shot the crippled horse, tied Bob to his saddle, and brought him to the ranch. Then Curry rode to town in the blizzard to fetch the

The Wild Bunch. Left to right, standing, are Tod Carver and Harvey Logan, alias Kid Curry; sitting, Harry Longabaugh, alias the Sundance Kid, Ben Kilpatrick, and George Parker, alias Butch Cassidy.

doctor. When the doctor, who was drunk, refused to go out in the blizzard on a forty-mile ride, Kid Curry got a buckboard and team and gave the inebriated physician his choice: either he went or filled a grave in boot hill. Sometime during the night's snowstorm, Kid Curry drove into the ranch with a sobered-up doctor.

Another time Kid Curry managed somehow to save Jim Thornhill's life when the two of them were swimming a bunch of cattle across the Missouri River at the Rocky Point Crossing. It was during the fall roundup when they were repping for the Circle C with the DHS wagon. They were shoving a bunch of Circle C cattle, gathered on the roundup, to the north side of the river when Thornhill's horse quit in the broad middle of the swift current. Thornhill couldn't swim a lick. Kid Curry swam his horse alongside and managed to pull the half-drowned Thornhill across his saddle and told him to hang onto the horn. Then the Kid grabbed hold of a steer's tail and they both managed to get ashore. When Jim Thornhill told me the story, he remarked that "the hell of it was the Kid couldn't swim a lick either."

Kid Curry claimed he never killed a man who did not deserve killing. Jim Thornhill told me that Pike Landusky was the first man Kid Curry ever killed, but perhaps it is a little farfetched to deduce that the killing of Pike Landusky launched Kid Curry's spectacular outlaw career with the Hole-in-the-Wall gang and the Wild Bunch.

Needless to say, Kid Curry never stood trial for the killing of Pike Landusky. Therefore it is debatable whether he would have been convicted of murder and hanged. Most of the cowpunchers who were well acquainted with both men and knew the circumstances that led to the killing agreed that Kid Curry did not murder Pike Landusky. They viewed the killing as the outcome of a brutal saloon brawl that ended in a shooting scrape.

When Kid Curry and his brothers quit the country and headed for the Hole in the Wall, Jim Thornhill was left alone at his ranch at Thornhill Butte to face any of Pike Landusky's friends who might seek to avenge his death.

But in time it became apparent that none of Pike's tough friends

The Showdown

was going to pick up the dead man's hand. Perhaps something in Thornhill's quiet manner, his apparent indifference to any danger, held his enemies at a safe distance. Or perhaps the silent threat of reprisal by Kid Curry if any harm befell big Jim Thornhill kept them away. Furthermore, Thornhill had many cowpuncher friends who were outspoken in their staunch and loyal friendship for the cowman who made a habit of minding his own business.

8.

The Violent Death of Johnny Curry

MOST OF THE CITIZENS OF LANDUSKY agreed that Jim Winters, who had filed the cattle-rustling charge against the Curry brothers and Jim Thornhill, should have left that part of the country after Kid Curry killed Pike Landusky and took to the outlaw trail.

Instead, Winters bought the Dan Tressler ranch near Landusky in spite of the fact that there had been a water-rights dispute involving the Curry brothers, particularly Johnny Curry, who claimed ownership of the ranch. On what grounds Johnny based his claim remains a mystery.

Any other man sizing up the situation would have decided that discretion was the better part of valor and quietly departed from the Little Rockies country. But Jim Winters was fearless to the point of being foolhardy. He was a stubborn man who stuck staunchly to the courage of his convictions. The law was on his side, in spite of the fact that the only law was gun law.

While it was a known fact that Kid Curry had taken to the outlaw trail and was a member of the Hole-in-the-Wall gang, his brothers Loney and the one-armed Johnny were still in the Little Rockies. On more than one occasion Johnny and Loney Curry warned Jim Winters to vacate the Dan Tressler ranch and quit the country. Winters refused, claiming he had bought the ranch and he did not intend to be run off or bluffed out by the Currys.

The Violent Death of Johnny Curry

It had been Jim Winters' custom to keep his window blinds pulled down or covered with a double gunnysack and his door bolted. About nine o'clock one night, when he was getting ready to go to bed, Winters heard the sound of horse's hoofs. He blew out the lamp, and reached for his double-barreled shotgun that was loaded with buckshot. Crouched beside his bunk, he heard the sound of Johnny Curry's voice in the dark cold night.

"Winters, you sonofabitch, I'm warnin' you for the last time. I'm giving you ten days to quit the country!" Then the rider loped off into the night.

Ten days later Johnny Curry came back in broad daylight. About ten o'clock on the morning of February 1, 1896, he rode up to the Winters ranch on a big roan bronc. He was a good bronc rider, and because he was one-armed, he kept his bridle reins tied so he could drop them across the horn of the saddle, leaving his gun hand free.

No doubt Jim Winters had been on the lookout for Johnny. He

The Winters-Gill ranch

was ready with a loaded double-barreled shotgun propped against the log wall near the door on the inside.

"Open the door, Winters, and step outside," Johnny Curry called out as he reined up twenty feet from the cabin door.

Winters cautiously opened the door part way.

"I thought I told you to quit this ranch," Curry said as he pulled his six-shooter, thumbed back the hammer, and pulled the trigger.

The abrupt movement spooked the bronc. The bullet missed Winters' head by a scant margin and struck the door sill. At the sound of the gunshot the bronc sank its head and began pitching in a tight circle, and Johnny Curry had trouble sitting tight in the saddle without the use of the bridle reins.

Meanwhile Winters grabbed his shotgun. He was a crack shot, and at that short distance Johnny Curry, forking a pitching bronc, was an easy moving target. Winters' charge of buckshot hit Johnny in the chest and belly.

"Whoa! Whoa!" the wounded rider hollered to his horse as he fired his gun, again missing.

Winters squeezed his second trigger and the charge hit Johnny's left side, tearing into his chest. The mortally wounded man had a death grip on his gun, and with a last dying effort he pulled the trigger, but the .45 slug again hit the ground.

The bronc, stung by buckshot, squealed and pitched high. When its feet hit the ground, Johnny Curry fell off and lay motionless in a widening pool of blood. Freed of its rider, the roan bronc broke into a run, the empty stirrups popping against its sides. As the last echoes of the gun blasts died away, the one-armed Johnny Curry, his body riddled by buckshot, died as he had lived, with his boots on and a smoking six-shooter in his hand.

Jim Winters must have realized the tight he was now in. Although, as far as he could tell, Johnny Curry had come alone, Winters must have known it would be only a short time before the Curry gang would learn of the killing. Loney Curry was in the Little Rockies, and perhaps Kid Curry was at his Hideaway

The Violent Death of Johnny Curry

or at the Jim Thornhill ranch. Jim Winters knew he had to leave right away. His only bet was to seek the protection of the law.

Winters lost no time saddling his horse. He left the ranch on a high lope, carrying a Winchester .30-.30 carbine across his saddle. He took the shortest route possible through the broken foothills. The fear of pursuit by the Curry brothers and their friends pushed him on, for he knew full well that the killing of Johnny Curry, even in self-defense, would bring them down on him. He crowded his stout cow horse to the limit, and when he reached Brown's place on the Fort Belknap Reservation, his horse was broken-winded. Brown was a squaw man married to a full-blood Indian woman.

By the time he reached the Brown place, Winters was convinced that the Curry gang was hunting him, and his only desperate thought was to hide out there. He penciled a note on a scrap of brown wrapping paper which said, "Jim Winters shot Johnny Curry in self-defense at the old Dan Tressler place. I'm holed up at the Brown ranch on the reservation. The Curry gang has the place surrounded. I want to surrender to the law. Fetch a sheriff's posse here at once." The message was delivered by a half-blood to R. W. Garland, a merchant at Malta, who owned a ranch nearby. Garland in turn wired the sheriff at Chinook.

Jim Winters must have suffered the same mixed emotions of a condemned man during the long hours of waiting for the coming of the sheriff's posse. Occasionally a rider or a small group of horsebackers could be seen in the distance from the log cabin where he was hiding, and to the anxious Winters it must have seemed as though the riders were Kid Curry and Loney and their friends. Needless to say, he was a most willing and eager prisoner, anxious to place himself in the protective custody of the law.[1]

Considerable excitement and anxiety was caused in the towns along the Great Northern Railroad by the report that flew over the wires to the effect that Johnny Curry had been shot and killed

---

[1] For a newspaper account in *The Daily River Press*, February 5, 1896, see Appendix A.

by Jim Winters and that Winters was surrounded in a cabin at the Brown place. The sheriff's office at Chinook received the following telegram signed by R. W. Garland from Malta: "James Winters shot John Curry. Winters is at Brown's ranch and wishes to give himself up. Going after him, you will need a posse." Although that was all that was known, it was enough to start all kinds of rumors and conjectures in the area.

A newspaper article in the *Chinook Opinion*, dated February 6, 1896, stated that the only eyewitness to the shooting was W. W. Lankin. This was probably Wash Lampkin who had worked off and on for the Circle C outfit for many years. He was a quiet-mannered, good-natured, top all-round cowhand, who stayed clear of trouble. Like many other cowpunchers in that part of the country, he took no sides in any gun argument involving the Curry gang.

Wash Lampkin could have been working for Jim Winters at the time of the shooting scrape, but it is a sure bet he took no part whatever in the ruckus. According to his testimony at Winters' trial, Johnny Curry was alone that bleak February morning when his attempt to run Jim Winters off the disputed Dan Tressler ranch ended in his death.

At Fort Benton, the county seat, Jim Winters was tried and acquitted on the grounds of self-defense. Meanwhile, the deputized members of the sheriff's posse kept themselves hidden around Landusky and the Little Rockies, but Loney Curry had quit the country by then. If Kid Curry had been around when Johnny was killed, he vanished from sight. When the dust settled and the coast was clear, Winters returned to the ranch.

Jim Winters had killed Johnny Curry in self-defense and was acquitted by the law without delay or argument. In the eyes of his friends, Winters was something of a hero. But his friends discussed it among themselves in small groups, because the walls of saloons had ears and the rustling of the leaves along the outlaw trail carried the news. No man dared to voice an opinion in public places.

Jim Winters had "cut the big gut," as the saying went, when he killed Johnny Curry; with that shotgun blast he had signed his

The Violent Death of Johnny Curry

own death warrant. Everyone knew that someday when the sign was right, Kid Curry or Loney Curry would come back to avenge the death of their brother. Jim Winters was a marked man, and no one was more aware of the fact than Winters himself. But he ignored the warnings of his friends to sell out and quit the country, and declared he would hang and rattle before he would leave. People who knew him said he was a stubborn man with plenty of nerve and no horse sense, and even his enemies had a certain respect for his determination.

Even if Winters had wanted to sell out, he would not have found any buyers for the disputed ranch. No man would have risked buying the old Dan Tressler place as long as the Curry boys had some real or fancied claim to it.

Winters somehow managed to keep at least one cowhand working for him, and any cowpuncher riding the grub line was welcome at his ranch. His fear of living alone was understandable under the circumstances, and keeping a companion was a matter of precaution rather than cowardice. Jim Winters never rode without one of his hired hands with him. If he paid fighting wages, it was strictly between him and his men. After a year or two passed without Kid Curry or Loney Curry showing up, Winters relaxed a little. The Little Rockies country got word that the two Currys had joined Flatnose George Curry's Hole-in-the-Wall gang and that the gang had joined forces with Butch Cassidy's Wild Bunch.

When the Union Pacific train was held up on June 2, 1899, at Wilcox, Wyoming, the newspapers reported that the Pinkerton detectives had identified one of the train robbers as Harvey Logan, alias Kid Curry. Again on July 11, 1899, when a train on the Colorado and Southern Railroad was held up at Folsom, New Mexico, the newspapers reported that Kid Curry was one of the robbers.

There was no mention of Loney Curry in the reports of either train robbery, but Harvey Logan, alias Kid Curry, now rode the outlaw trail with a price on his head. When the reward dodgers were tacked up in the post offices at Malta, Chinook, Harlem, Landusky, and Zortman, those who had known Kid Curry and his brothers learned that their real name was Logan, but even then and long after they were known throughout Montana as the Curry boys.

Sometime after the Wilcox and Folsom train robberies Kid Curry and Loney returned to Dodson, Missouri, to visit their aunt, Mrs. Lee, who had raised the three orphaned Logan brothers. Her son, Bob Lee, had come to Montana under the alias of Bob Curry, and he and Loney had run a saloon at Harlem. While the Kid and Loney were in Dodson, they made the mistake of trying to pass some of the incomplete currency from the Wilcox, Wyoming, train robbery. The Pinkerton Detective Agency found out and at night surrounded the cabin where Kid Curry and Loney were staying. The detectives opened fire to smoke out the two outlaws, and Loney was shot and killed. Kid Curry ran the gauntlet of gunfire and escaped under the cover of darkness and somehow managed to rejoin the Wild Bunch.

After Loney Curry had been killed in February, 1900, the Pinkertons sent Charlie Siringo, one of their top cowboy detectives, to the Little Rockies to locate Kid Curry. Siringo, under the alias of Charles Carter, supposedly a drifting cowpuncher, hired out to Jim Thornhill. He took advantage of Thornhill's unsuspecting hospitality to try to gather information about the Kid. During his six-month stay in the Little Rockies, Siringo visited the Jim Winters place on several occasions. He wrote about the death of Jim Winters and his search for Kid Curry.

> I had a good chance to get information about the Wild Bunch from Jim T. [Thornhill], but he would never give a hint as to where Kid Curry was, though I found out enough to convince me they kept up a correspondence through the post office in the prosperous town of Chinook, on the railroad, not far from Harlin [Harlem], but under what name I couldn't tell. He informed me that his mail addressed to Landusky was watched when it left the railroad station at Harlin.
>
> In talking Jim T. showed a very bitter spirit against the Dickersons [Pinkertons] for the killing of his friend, Loney Logan [Curry], and for sending Bob Lee, alias Bob Curry, to the pen. Our Agency had lately captured and convicted Bob Lee for his connection in the Silox [Wilcox], Wyoming, U.P. train holdup. He was caught in Cripple

Charles A. Siringo, Pinkerton detective.
Union Pacific Railroad Museum Collection

Creek, Colorado, and convicted and sentenced to the pen for ten years in Cheyenne, Wyoming.

Jim T. assured me that Loney's brother Kid Curry would soon get even with the U.P. Railroad Company and the Dickersons by robbing another U.P train; that the "Kid" was then in the south making preparations for a deal of that kind. . . .

I received orders by mail to meet [U.S. Marshal] Joe La Fors in Denver, to go with him to Old Mexico in search of Flat Nose George Curry (no relative of Kid Curry). We decided that Kid Curry, Jim T's partner, would steer clear of the Little Rockies where everybody knew him, but in this we were mistaken, for not long after I left he slipped back and killed Ranchman Winters, who had killed his brother Johnny. Winters was a prosperous stock raiser and he had told me that he expected to be waylaid and killed by Kid Curry.

In the latter part of August, I slipped out of the country. Arriving in Denver, Colorado (after an absence of over a month), I found the particulars of a late train holdup on the U.P. railroad at Tipton, Wyoming (8 o'clock on the evening of August 29, 1900). . . .

Hence I concluded that Jim T. knew what he was talking about.[2]

During the four years since Jim Winters had killed Johnny Curry in February, 1896, until the Pinkertons killed Loney Curry at Dodson, Missouri, in February, 1900, Winters had stayed on at the old Dan Tressler place in spite of the constant threat of sudden death. He used to say, "A man lives until the day he dies. When my number's up, I'll cash in my chips. I'm ahead of the game if I never see another sunrise."

When news of Loney Curry's death reached Landusky, Jim Winters took it in his stride and said, "Them Pinkertons done paid off that fiddlin' sonofabitch in his own kinda money. If they'd killed the Kid while they had him dead to rights in that cabin, they'd have somethin' to brag about. But they let the Kid slip away somehow in the dark with a sorry posse surroundin' the cabin." But in spite of his apparent unconcern over the failure of the Pinkerton operatives to kill or capture Kid Curry, Winters was a worried man.

Meanwhile he had taken in a partner in his ranch holdings. His

[2] *A Cowboy Detective* (Chicago, W. B. Conkey Company, 1912), 335–36, 338.

The Violent Death of Johnny Curry

partner was a man by the name of Abe Gill, an eastern dude who had come West to be a cowboy and cattleman. He was a tall, well-built, handsome man, a college graduate and member of a wealthy family. His jet-black hair and olive complexion supposedly resulted from a trace of Cuban blood.

Just why a man of Abe Gill's cultural and family background decided to settle in the tough Little Rockies country around Landusky, Montana, remains a mystery. Still more puzzling is the fact that he bought a partnership with Jim Winters in the old Dan Tressler ranch, which was a blood-stained, disputed land. Gill seemed to be infatuated with the idea of becoming a part of the Wild West as pictured in Frederic Remington's paintings, and he copied the Remington cowpuncher garb in his own dress. Perhaps the pilgrim from back East discounted the danger involved in his partnership with the controversial Jim Winters and wanted to bask in the glory of being the partner of the man who had killed the brother of Kid Curry. Regardless of his reasons, the innocent pilgrim soon became involved in the dangerous feud between Jim Winters and the Kid Curry outlaw gang.

9.

The Wagner Train Robbery

THE SUMMER MONTHS AT THE RANCH were the slack period for the cowpunchers. The spring calf roundup was over by the middle of June, and the fall beef roundup didn't start until the last week in August. During those slack summer months the haying season was in full swing, and any old-time Montana cowhand worthy of the name would quit his job if he were put to work in the hay field, drawing the line at being downgraded as a hay hand.

So the regular cowpunchers drew their wages when the spring roundup was over, saddled their private horses, loaded their beds on a second horse, and headed for town to blow in their hard-earned money. When their credit ran out at the saloons, they saddled up and rode the grub line, drifting from one ranch to another, staying overnight or a day or two, earning their grub by helping out with barn chores and odd jobs, then drifting on before they wore out their welcome. It was a sort of summer vacation. Like tumbleweeds, they drifted free and easy wherever the breeze carried them until the beef roundup started in the fall and they returned to their regular jobs.

During the slack summer months the bronc rider broke out his string of green broncs, usually on a contract of ten dollars a head.

At the windup of the spring calf roundup, the Circle C outfit returned to the home ranch. The bed wagon and mess wagon, with

The Wagner Train Robbery

their four-horse teams driven by the cook and nighthawk, pulled into the ranch in a cloud of dust. The wagon pilot rode in the lead and the bunch of cowpunchers, including the reps from ten or a dozen other outfits, rode in groups with the wagons. The horse wrangler trailed the remuda behind the wagons.

The nighthawk pulled the bed wagon alongside the bunkhouse while a couple of cowpunchers unloaded the bedrolls. Then he drove to the warehouse where he and some cowhands unhooked and unharnessed the team. The horse collars and harness were left temporarily on the raised wagon tongue, braced by the upended neckyoke, and later stored in the warehouse. The four horses were turned loose in the lower remuda pasture.

The cook drove the mess wagon to the front of the warehouse, unharnessed the four-horse team, and turned them loose in the pasture. The cowpunchers unsaddled at the log barn and turned their horses loose.

By afternoon the two wagons were unloaded. The mess wagon's stove, mess tent, and surplus grub were placed in the storehouse. The bed wagon's tent and tent poles, rope corral and Y-shaped wooden braces, and iron corral stakes in worn gunnysacks were piled in the storehouse. The branding irons, kegs of horseshoes, and shoeing equipment were left in the wagon.

Then the two wagons were taken to the blacksmith shop below the barn where the blacksmith would make any needed wagon repairs and inspect the score or more branding irons, discarding the burned-out stamp irons and replacing them with new hand-forged irons.

That afternoon was a busy one for the bookkeeper, because every cowpuncher in the outfit, including the reps, needed new clothes from the store commissary—socks, underwear, shirts, Levis, black silk neckerchiefs, bandanna handkerchiefs, and smoking and chewing tobacco.

The cowhands changed clothes in the bunkhouse, and discarded their dirty clothes in a big pile at the far corner of the room. Most of them took a bar of yellow laundry soap, waded out into Beaver Creek behind the bunkhouse, squatted in the warm water, and lathered from head to toe. Then they shaved off their stubble of wiry beard, and the few who were handy with barber shears and hand clippers did a land-office business for free. If any cowhand wanted a fancy haircut, the ranch cook, Al Taylor, took over. He had bought a second-hand barber chair and set it up in a corner of the mess hall, where he kept barber scissors, clippers, and a set of razors with hone and strop, as well as a shaving mug, bay-rum hair tonic, and talcum powder.

Later on in the day Indian women from the nearby Fort Belknap Indian Reservation would come to the ranch to gather the dirty discarded clothing which they divided. After laundering, the clothes for their men were often as good as new.

That night the wagon boss and bookkeeper were busy figuring up the wages of each cowhand and deducting the cost of the new clothes and tobacco on the time book.

The following day every cowpuncher in the outfit was busy. The horse wrangler corraled the remuda, and the reps roped out their strings of ten horses each. After loading their beds on pack horses, they saddled up and departed, hazing their horses ahead of them as they headed for their home ranches, forty, fifty, or even a hundred miles away.

After the reps pulled out, the Circle C cowhands roped out their strings of ten mounts each, one at a time. After leading the horses outside the corral, they used long-handled horse pliers to remove the shoes from every horse until the entire remuda of more than two hundred were unshod. They remained barefoot until they were shod again for the fall beef roundup. But the ten horses in the wagon boss's string were kept shod, and Will, Bob, and Wallace Coburn kept two or three shod horses to ride during the summer. Robert Coburn kept his favorite cow horse, Reader, shod for riding around the ranch.

Some of the horses in the remuda went barefoot the year round, because their hoofs were hard as flint and required only trimming and rasping down for broken edges. In this prairie country the unshod horses, like the Indian ponies that had never worn shoes, seldom pulled up lame.

The Wagner Train Robbery

The only shod horses in the remuda were the horse wrangler's string. Usually Jack Davis, the nighthawk, took charge of the remuda in the summer months. Every horse in his string of ten were big, long-legged, ridge runners that could pack a man all day. They were hand-picked by Davis, who was a mighty good judge of horseflesh. A nighthawk needed a fast, sure-footed horse in order to keep his remuda together on a stormy night when thunder crashed and chain lightning popped. Some horses could see better at night than others, and Jack Davis liked to brag a little on his night horses that were fast-moving, sure-footed, and had plenty of endurance and good eyesight.

Altogether there were about fifty saddle horses from the remuda kept up during the summer months, as well as a dozen to fifteen work teams that were used during the haying season. The work horses were kept in the lower pasture and wrangled each morning before breakfast in order to give the teamsters time to harness the work teams before the breakfast bell rang.

It was my job to wrangle the lower pasture, and the summer of 1901 was a memorable one for me, because for the first time the bookkeeper recorded my name on the time book as a forty-a-month cowhand. My twelfth birthday was due in October, so June 10, the day my name went on the time book, was a red-letter day that marked my full status as a cowpuncher. However, that status included many menial ranch chores, lowly jobs that no self-respecting cowhand would be asked to do. Such was the lot of a bald-faced kid on a big cow outfit, but I had no kick coming. I was drawing cowpuncher wages, which wasn't hard for a twelve-year-old button to take.

Jack Davis, the nighthawk, stayed on that summer to take over the remuda that was kept at night in the pasture at the Coburn Buttes. As soon as early breakfast was over, he would saddle up his wrangling horse, and with his lunch and a quart bottle of coffee wrapped in his slicker behind the saddle cantle, he would take the horses out of the pasture to graze in open country south of the ranch and the twin buttes. He would be gone all day, and it would be late twilight when he drifted the remuda back into the pasture and ate a late supper.

Pioneer Cattleman in Montana

I spent most of that summer riding fence and doing odd jobs around the ranch. Sometimes I rode with my father and Horace Brewster, the ranch foreman, on a long day's ride, looking through the widely scattered range cattle within a twenty-five-mile radius. Other times I would go out with Jack Davis, and at the end of ten days, thanks to his infinite patience and knowledge of the horses in the remuda, I could pick out any horse by his individual color, markings, and general conformation, and call him by name. Davis taught me to listen closely to the sound of each horse bell strapped around the necks of a dozen or more bunch quitters, because each bell had a slightly different tone. Each bunch quitter had an individual habit of sneaking away. Some would wander down long draws or cut coulees or bush up in a coulee where the buck brush grew high enough to hide a small bunch of horses. During fly time other belled bunch quitters would head for the pinnywankles (or high ridges) to stand with their cronies, head to tail, and switch the horseflies and deerflies off one another. Jack Davis claimed horses were like a bunch of humans, each with individual characteristics. Some were wild, some ornery, some lazy, some gentle, some smart, some dumb.

There were four wire gates that led into the large remuda pasture. The main north gate was across Beaver Creek from the Circle C Ranch buildings, and the north fence extended from the reservation fence east for about ten miles following Beaver Creek. The gate on the east side was located at the wagon road leading to the Veseth place on Beaver Creek along the old roundup trail to Sun Prairies and the Larb Hills. The gate on the south side spanned a seldom-traveled road that led through the hilly antelope country across Fourchette and Beauchamp creeks and down through the badlands to the Rocky Point Crossing on the Missouri River. This was the old freight road used now by the roundup wagons. A branch road at the Beauchamp line camp forked southeast to the old Fort Musselshell Crossing on the Missouri. Other dim trails branched at the head of the brakes leading to Rock Creek, Seven Mile, and C.K. Creek winter line camps.

The vast stretch of land was a combination of fences that met

The Wagner Train Robbery

the badlands. There was an old obscure Indian trail from the south gate that forked in a southwest direction to the Cow Island Crossing on the Missouri. A wagon pilot who knew the country and had a keen eye to follow the dim trail could ride ahead of the roundup wagons, but it took a cowhand who knew that broken country like the palm of his hand to get the job done. A green hand could run into trouble in the cut coulees and rough short chops where no wagon could travel.

The west gate was part of the reservation fence. It was located at the foot of the east Coburn Butte in a coulee below the timber line. This wire gate was seldom used, and because it led directly to the Fort Belknap Reservation, it was fastened by a chain and padlock. One key on a leather marker was kept in the office at the home ranch. Another key was cached under a boulder inside the pasture, a hundred yards from the fence. This was a private gate used only by the Circle C outfit to move cattle back and forth from the pasture onto the reservation.

The west gate was purposely located in a strategic spot, because the southeast corner of the reservation fence was less than a hundred yards south of the gate. Just beyond the fence was a good spring, a log cabin, and an old thatched-roof log cattle shed with haystacks fenced in by barbwire. It was once used by the DHS outfit as an adjacent line camp and was now owned by the Circle C. In the low saddle the grass grew stirrup high on both sides of the fence, and our outfit cut hay in the little meadow park. On the Indian side of the fence the tall rank grass had never been cut. There was a sandstone rimrock surrounding the basin-like meadow which formed a natural cliff barricade around the basin-park that was about a quarter-mile in diameter.

Time had been when this was a large Indian encampment. The half-buried, ancient tipi rocks, now hidden under the thick high bunch grass, could be found in a great circle close to the high outcropping. Jack Davis had told me that close to the rimrock top there was a cave hidden by scrub brush. He said you had to get down on all fours to get into the narrow slit in the rock, but, once inside, the cave was big enough for a dozen men to stand up in. Farther back there was a big hole, and if you dropped a rock into it, you could hear the water splash a hundred feet or more below.

From the mouth of the cave, Jack Davis said, a man could see to hell and gone in all directions. Jack promised he would take me up to the hidden cave, but he never got around to it because he pulled out the first of July to run a matched race with his black quarter-horse mare at Lewistown. I got the job of handling the remuda until he got back to the ranch.

By the third of July the Circle C home ranch looked like a ghost ranch, as though the black plague had wiped out everybody except Al Taylor, the cook, Pete Olson, the big Swede who did the irrigating and milked the cows, and me.

My father and Will had gone to Great Falls, where Will had rented a house for his family and where my mother and sisters lived. Wallace was in Helena to compete in the state rifle, shotgun, and pistol contest held there each year. Horace Brewster, the ranch foreman, had gone to the Fort Belknap agency to see Major Logan, the Indian agent, about renewing the Circle C permit to run cattle on the reservation. Frank Howe and the other cowhands had pulled out for town to celebrate the Fourth. Charlie Brewster, who was breaking out a string of broncs, had saddled up and headed for Chinook to enter the Fourth of July bronc-riding contest. Tim Maloney, who had the hay contract that year, had gone to Malta to hire a crew of hay hands. Even the bookkeeper, Mac McClennan, had taken the stage to Malta to go on one of his "periodicals" that lasted a week or ten days.

Bob Coburn was left in charge of the ranch, and he had saddled up his black gelding, Midnight, and pulled out for the Ruby Gulch Mine. Before he left, he gave me my orders. I was to shove the remuda out the west gate and graze them on the reservation. In case I lost a few head of horses, they would still be inside the reservation fence, Bob said, as if he didn't have too much confidence in me as a horse wrangler. When sundown came, I was to bunch the remuda, shove them back into the big pasture, and get a count on the horses.

Right after an early-morning breakfast on July 3, I saddled

The Wagner Train Robbery

my cow pony, Snowflake, and wrangled the pasture, with my lunch wrapped up in my yellow slicker tied behind my saddle. I unlocked the west gate and propped it open against the fence, and got a tally on the horses as they drifted through on their own accord. One of the first cardinal rules of a good horse wrangler is never to crowd horses through the gateway of a barbwire fence in order to avoid a horse knocking down a hipbone on a gatepost or getting a wire cut. When the last of the horses ambled through, I got down and fastened the gate with the chain and padlocked it, then hid the key under the rock.

It was easy pickings for a horse wrangler with the scattered remuda grazing on good feed and water in that park-like basin. There was enough breeze to keep away the horseflies, deerflies and mosquitoes. All a wrangler had to do was to ride up on the rimrock ledge where he could sight all the horses, then get down and sit in the shade of a scrub pine. If any bunch quitter got the notion of pulling out, the sound of his bell betrayed him, and I could ride

Part of the Circle C remuda, 1906.

89

down to head him and his cronies off. The big circle of shelving rimrock was like a mile-wide corral.

Every half an hour or so, sun time, I would get a range count on the remuda. I sure wasn't taking any chances on spilling any horses. When the sun was noon high, I rode up on the rimrock lookout and got off and ate my lunch while Snowflake grazed. The Indian camps below looked deserted. All the Indians had gone to the Lodge Pole subagency, taking their families and dogs and tipis along.

Near sundown I got a last tally on the remuda. For the past hour or so I had been waiting for Jim Thornhill or his two sons, Man and Bill, to come to pick up the horses they needed. Sometimes after the spring calf roundup the Thornhills, riding Circle C horses, would take a pack outfit down into the badlands to brand any calves missed on the roundup. Because it was hard for a roundup to get a clean work of the badlands, Jim Thornhill's little pack outfit would brand any calves they found in whatever brand was on their mammies. For his trouble Jim Thornhill was entitled to brand any maverick in his own iron. He let Man and Bill rope the mavericks, and in addition to the 7UP Thornhill brand, the boys would put a slash brand on the thigh to mark the calf for their own. If it was a bull calf they branded and cut, they would get the money for the four-year-old beef steer when it was shipped in the fall. If it was a heifer calf they had marked with their tally brand, they were entitled to all its calves.

When the remuda was gathered, I unlocked the padlock and put the key back under the rock. I had just about decided nobody from the Thornhill place was coming when I sighted four horsebackers. They were riding in pairs about a hundred yards apart. When they got close enough to sight the remuda, the two pairs of riders joined, and one of the horsebackers loped on ahead to where I sat my horse.

When he rode close enough, I saw a Winchester carbine across his saddle. A two-week growth of black whiskers covered his face. He had a cartridge belt buckled on and a holstered six-shooter tied down across his thigh. A sewed-up boot top with the long leather boot straps slit fitted over his saddle horn, and it was filled with .30-.30 cartridges for his saddle gun.

He bared his white teeth in a whiskered grin as he pulled up and called me by name and said, "Jim Thornhill says you know how to keep your mouth shut." He shoved the Winchester into its saddle scabbard.

"Yes, sir," I said.

"Me 'n my pardners need a change of horses. We're borrowin' the loan of some. You got any shod ones in the bunch?" he asked.

I pointed out the ten horses in Jack Davis' string.

"Remember, kid, if anybody asks you if you seen four horsebackers, you ain't seen hide ner hair of me and my pardners. You don't know nothin'." His grin widened.

"I'll keep my mouth shut," I promised, my kid voice sounding shaky.

"That's the ticket. The Circle C horses we borrow will be back in your remuda inside of a week. We're not two-bit horse thieves."

Then he told me to ride my white cow pony up on a nearby high pinnywankle and keep my eye peeled. If I sighted any horsebackers coming, I was to ride around in a tight circle, then hightail it for home in a high lope. He also told me that if any henyard posse showed up at the ranch asking questions, not to give them the time of day. He cautioned me again to keep my mouth shut and dummy up like a locoed sheepherder.

"Nobody'll get anything out of me," I promised. "You got my word on it." Then he held out his hand and we shook on it.

I rode Snowflake up on the high ridge and sat there as a lookout. I wasn't exactly scared, just all keyed up and excited. I could feel my pulse beat in my throat, because I knew who the black-whiskered man was. I had seen reward dodgers tacked up in the post offices and on telegraph poles giving his name as Harvey Logan, alias Kid Curry, with his description and the amount of the reward offered for his capture dead or alive. I knew full well without being told that the other three whiskered outlaws were members of the Wild Bunch and that the heavy-set gent with the yellow whiskers was Butch Cassidy.

Pioneer Cattleman in Montana

Every ranch kid in the Little Rockies cow country knew all there was to know about Kid Curry and the Curry gang, and we all tried to pattern our cowboy ways after Kid Curry. The Thornhill kids were the only ones who actually knew Kid Curry, because the Kid was formerly Jim Thornhill's partner in the ranching business. The oldest Thornhill boy, Harvey, known as Man, had been named for Harvey Logan. But the Thornhill boys never bragged about it and kept their mouths shut.

I had always dreamed kid dreams about someday joining the Wild Bunch, and here I was acting as lookout for the outlaws as they took turns roping out the shod horses I had pointed out. And I was the only kid in the country, except the Thornhill brothers, who had ever shaken the gun hand of Kid Curry. A sheriff or any other man would have to beat me to death before I would squeal on him and his three partners.

After the outlaws had saddled fresh horses and mounted, Kid Curry motioned with his hat for me to come down. I watched the four of them ride off at a high trot, and they were long gone when I opened the wire gate and drifted the remuda into the big pasture. The only telltale sign they had been there were the four 7UP (Thornhill) sweat-covered horses they had left behind.

I figured that Kid Curry and his companions would locate some remote spot to cross the reservation fence by cutting the five wires and splicing them back after they had gone through. Then they would head for the old Kid Curry Hideaway near Thornhill Butte.

I headed for home in the red afterglow of the sunset. It was near dusk when I unsaddled. I tied Snowflake in his stall and fed him an extra pail of oats, bedded the stall, and forked hay from the loft to fill the manger.

Bob Coburn's horse, Midnight, was in his stall, and his manger was full of hay and the stall bedded down, so I figured that Bob had returned from his overnight stay at the Ruby Gulch Mine. It was long past suppertime when I got to the cook cabin. Al Taylor fried me a thick sirloin steak and said that Bob had left word for me to come over to his house as soon as I finished my late supper.

The Wagner Train Robbery

"What's Bob caught you at this time?" Al asked with a chuckle.

"Danged if I know," I said worriedly. "He told me to put in a full day and I did. I reckon he'll chaw me out regardless, just to keep in practice."

On the way to the ranch that evening I had tried to figure out what had happened. I had taken it for granted that Kid Curry and his outlaw pals had held up a bank somewhere along their back trail. Every outlaw had a saddle slicker tied behind his saddle cantle, and those slickers bulged out as if they might have gunnysacks filled with money wrapped up in them. I recalled that none of the men had called any other by name. Kid Curry was the only one who had come within a hundred yards of me. Even if I wanted to tell anything, which I didn't, I could not really identify the others. They all wore a two-week growth of whiskers. What worried me was if my brother Bob asked me any questions about the horses.

The grub lay heavy as lead in my belly, and I was sweating a little and nervous as heck by the time I climbed the steps to the vine-covered porch at Bob's two-storied log house. The front door stood partly open, and there was a light showing from the big Rochester lamp through the drawn window blinds. Bob called to me to come in and bolt the door. He was reading a newspaper as he sat in a large leather chair near the lamplight. Bob lowered the newspaper and put on one of his left-handed grins.

"How many horses did you spill while you were asleep in the shade of the scrub pines?" he asked. I could tell he was in good humor.

"They were all there when I counted them through the gate," I said. "And I put in a full day's work," I added for a clincher.

"Draw up a chair to the light and read a while," Bob invited, motioning toward the bookshelves.

There was a complete set of Mark Twain's books. I took down a copy of *Huckleberry Finn* and moved an armchair close to the light and sat down. That was the first time in history that Bob had ever asked me to sit down in his parlor, and it had me puzzled.

Bob removed a small cigar from a gun-metal cigar case and lit it.

93

Pioneer Cattleman in Montana

He ordered the cigars by the box from a cigar maker in the East. Then he sat back to read the late copy of the *Great Falls Tribune* that had come by stage in the day's mail. Bob seldom wore Levis, and when he did, he pulled them on over a pair of pants that belonged to an old suit. The pants he had on now were a pair of lightweight gray tweed that had seen better days. The cuffs were rolled up to show the stitching on his black shop-made boots. His unbuttoned vest matched the pants, and from where I sat on his right I could see the black hard-rubber butt of a Colt six-shooter shoved in the waistband of his pants.

I had read *Huck Finn* a dozen or more times, but I pretended I was busy reading. Out of the corner of an eye I could see that Bob wasn't reading the newspaper as he pretended. His head, with the thick black hair, was cocked a little sideways as if he were listening, waiting for something to happen. I couldn't help but wonder if his uneasiness had anything to do with the four outlaws borrowing Circle C horses.

As I began to notice the tense uneasiness that filled the room, I heard the sound of horsebackers. Bob immediately sprang to his feet, dropping the discarded newspaper on the carpeted floor. He stood with his booted feet spread, and his steel-gray eyes narrowed under his heavy black brows.

Then came the stomp of high-heeled boots and the sound of spur rowels on the porch, then a pounding on the front door. Bob turned the lamp on low wick, which threw dark shadows into the hallway.

"See who it is," Bob told me in a low brittle voice, and I stepped into the hallway towards the door. Bob was right behind me, and without having to look around I sensed that he had his six-shooter in his hand.

I slid the inside bolt, and when I opened the door, Bob slipped in behind it. There was enough moonlight to show the vague bulk of a man standing on the porch almost within arm's reach of me. He was a large, heavy-set man with a paunch. A sheriff's star was pinned to his open vest, a wide cartridge belt hung slaunchwise

The Wagner Train Robbery

across his belly, and his hand was on the butt of a six-shooter that was tied down on his thick thigh. I didn't like the way he stood there spread-legged, his hat brim pulled down across his eyes.

"Anybody here besides you, kid?" he asked in a harsh-toned voice.

I gave no answer as I stood blocking the door. My head was level with his law badge, so he would have to shove me aside to get in. Then I felt Bob move in behind me.

"I'm Bob Coburn," Bob said in a gritty voice. "Who the hell are you, mister?"

"I'm the sheriff from Valley County." His voice was pompous and gruff, full of authority. "Kid Curry and his gang held up the Great Northern train at Wagner. Blowed hell out of the mail express car. I'm hot on their trail. I want supper and fresh horses for me and my twenty-five-man-posse. Right now. Our chuck wagon got lost somewhere along the road from Malta."

"Now ain't that too bad about your damned chuck wagon," Bob said, his voice heavy with sarcasm. "You're afoot as far as the Circle C outfit is concerned. You can turn your played-out horses into the pasture below the barn and saddle 'em tomorrow when they get rested. You want a place to sleep, there's plenty of prairie to bed down on."

Bob gripped my shoulder. "Go tell Al Taylor he's not obligated to feed this poolroom posse, but if he does, tell him to charge a dollar a head for their meals, cash in advance. Tell Al he can pocket the money. And you better wake up Pete Olson and tell him to show the sheriff which pasture to turn their horses into. Grab your hat and go out the back door."

As I picked my hat off the hatrack and headed for the back door, I heard Bob say gruffly, "No booze allowed on this ranch, understand? If your posse are usin' whisky for a brave maker, you better bust every goddamned bottle. I'm holding you strictly responsible for the conduct of your men, Sheriff." Then I heard the front door slam in the sheriff's face.

I went out the back door like I'd been hit in the rump by a

bootjack and headed for the cook cabin on a high lope. I knew that when Bob Coburn got his dander up he was a dangerous man and hard to stop once he got started.

I found Al Taylor in the kitchen, his sleeves rolled up above the elbow. He was kneading a big round pan of bread dough with his fists, and his black bread pans were greased and ready for the oven. His blue eyes widened as I brought him up with the latest, and his lips pursed in a soundless whistle when I finished.

"Back East where I come from," Al said, "a lawman with a badge gives the orders, and you take 'em or wind up in jail."

I explained to Al, a tenderfoot pilgrim who had come out West a couple of years earlier, that this was an altogether different situation. This was the Circle C cow ranch, and Bob Coburn gave the only orders right now. I explained that there was a time when Kid Curry and his two brothers, Loney and Johnny, had worked for the outfit, and the sheriff of Valley County had sure come to the wrong place to throw his weight around demanding service.

Al quit his bread making and wiped the flour from his arms on his laundered, white, flour-sack apron. "If I had a bottle of croton oil to put in the coffee, I could delay that man-hunter outfit and give Kid Curry and his gang of train robbers a twenty-four-hour head start."

"What's croton oil, Al?" I asked.

"It's got a dose of castor oil skinned to death," Al explained. "The sheriff and his posse would take to the brush and stay there till Pete Olson's milk cows come home tomorrow evenin'. But the hell of it is I ain't got no croton oil." Al danced a double shuffle as he bustled around the kitchen.

I went to the bunkhouse to wake Pete Olson. The big Swede was in his early twenties and had learned to speak broken English from some farmer in Rosebud Valley he had worked for when he was a kid fresh from the Old Country. Pete called it the "Wosebud" Valley, and "By Cwist" was about his only cuss word. He was strong as a work horse and as good natured as an overgrown Newfoundland pup. Because he spoke with a Swedish accent, he was the butt of practical jokes that at times were crude, but during

The Wagner Train Robbery

the long years I knew Pete, I never once saw him lose his temper. His knowledge of the cattle industry was limited to the range cows he milked and to driving a plow. Pete sure savvied irrigating the hay fields and truck garden, and he was handy around machinery and kept the four windmills in repair. Pete Olson was the only man I ever knew who bedded down for the night with a chew of tobacco bulging his cheek.

I lighted the bunkhouse lantern and shook Pete awake from a peaceful slumber that blesses only men with a clear, untroubled conscience. I told him about the sheriff and his posse and explained that he was to get up and show them where to turn their horses in the pasture below the barn. There wasn't time to explain about the train holdup, but I did tell Pete to inform the sheriff to give his men orders to stay out of the barn on account of fire by cigarettes.

Helping out the cook in a tight like this was a part of my forty-a-month job, and for once I looked forward to the menial chore of dishwashing and fetching in wood and buckets of water and doing any odd jobs that came under the head of bull cook.

Ever since I could remember, I had heard tales and read stories about sheriff's posses, but I had never encountered one before, and I sure aimed to get a close look and keep my ears cocked. I had heard time and again the often-repeated remark by Kid Curry "that you could shoot a whole corral full of posse members and not kill a real man with guts."

According to yarns I had listened to around roundup camps and bunkhouses, a sheriff's posse usually consisted of would-be cowboys who handled a pool cue far better than a gun. Mostly they were saloon bums, tinhorn sports, and bounty-hunter gunslingers. According to most cowpunchers and cattlemen, the outlaws, such as the Wild Bunch, were heroes, whereas a Pinkerton range detective, who wore his law badge pinned to his undershirt, was the lowest specimen of human who ever drew breath. Now I was about to get my first look, although I was prejudiced on the lawless side and would view the posse with a jaundiced eye. Hell's bells, I was practically one of the Kid Curry gang, wasn't I?

Al Taylor stood in the doorway that led into the kitchen. He had a sort of meaningless grin on his sunburned face, and the cowlick on his towhead was sticking straight up. His shirt sleeves were rolled above the elbow, and a flour-sack apron was tied around his waist. Al had been a professional wrestler back East, and he looked like a light heavyweight as he blocked the kitchen doorway. He told the sheriff he had orders to charge him a dollar a head for late supper, cash on the barrelhead. The sheriff said he would make out an order for that amount, and explained it was customary for the sheriff to use the order blanks for all emergency expenses incurred by his posse. Al said to make the order out for twenty-six dollars payable to Alton C. Taylor, cook at the Circle C Ranch. After the sheriff had signed the order, Al told him to keep his men outside until he had supper on the table—nobody was allowed in the mess hall or kitchen. That way nobody got underfoot.

At half-past ten by the alarm clock on the shelf above the stove, Al opened the door to the mess hall and told the men to "come and get 'er." From where I sat peeling spuds in the corner by the kitchen door, I got a ringside view of the posse members as they filed in and took their places on the benches along both sides of the long, oilcloth-covered table. A sorrier-looking motley crowd would have been hard to find in any man's cow country.

They ranged all the way from nineteen- to twenty-year-old poolroom bums to a couple of grizzled sheepherder-looking characters. Mostly they were the type of would-be cowboy found hanging around cow-town saloons bumming drinks. As near as I could figure, there wasn't a genuine cowhand in the bunch. They all packed six-shooters, and some had cartridge belts buckled on. A lot of them came in with Winchester carbines which they stacked against the log wall.

No doubt the sheriff of Valley County had himself a mail-order "Monkey-Ward" lot for a posse. There was the sound of stomping of cheap boots with runover heels, spur jingling, and loud talking as the posse trooped in and sat down to eat, all with their hats on. In no time at all the mess hall smelled of stale booze, and the

The Wagner Train Robbery

whisky talk covered up the nervous tension and dread fear that held every man there as if they expected an outlaw ambush in the night. I thought to myself that if a bunch of Fourth of July firecrackers were to go off outside, it would have resulted in a wild panic.

The sheriff took a seat at the head of the table, with his back to the wall facing the closed door. He wasn't as tall as he had looked when he stood on Bob Coburn's porch. He now had a worried look on his face, and his eyes were restless, as if Bob's cold reception had taken some of the pompous wind out of him. He ate in disgruntled silence, his restless eyes moving down the table, eying each man as if sizing him up for courage in a tight and not liking what he saw. He must have been keenly aware of the danger in tracking down a man like Kid Curry, the most dangerous gunslinger of the Wild Bunch, and his three outlaw companions. But I wasn't about to waste any sympathy on the badge-polishing lawman. I was too busy listening to the chin music, trying to learn the details of the train robbery, separating the grain from the bushwa chaff. There was a lot of wild talk based on a few facts, and when the sheriff corrected a misleading statement, I earmarked it for the truth.

Apparently Kid Curry and one of the outlaws boarded the train at Malta. Kid Curry rode the blind baggage, and his companion (later identified as Harry Longabaugh, alias the Sundance Kid) rode as a passenger. The other two outlaws (later identified as Butch Cassidy and Camilla Hanks) waited at the bridge that crossed Milk River, a few miles east of the small cow town of Wagner. As the train neared the bridge, Kid Curry left the blind baggage, crawled over the tender, and dropped into the engine cab, where he took charge of the engineer and fireman, telling them to halt the train at the bridge.

Harry Longabaugh threw down on the conductor and brakeman, telling them and the passengers that this was a train holdup. He told the passengers to stay in their seats and told the conductor and brakeman to keep them quiet and in their seats and nobody would get hurt. Then he stepped down from the car onto the ground, and when the passengers shoved their heads out the windows, he fired a few shots and warned them to duck back.

Kid Curry told the engineer to uncouple the baggage car and haul it across the bridge. Meanwhile Sheriff Griffiths of Great Falls, who happened to be on the train, opened fire from the rear coach, but when Longabaugh fired a couple of shots, the Great Falls sheriff ducked back and ceased fire.

Kid Curry and Harry Longabaugh rode the engine cab as it hauled the express car, and after they crossed the bridge, Butch Cassidy took over, while Camilla Hanks held the getaway horses. Cassidy ordered the express messenger to open the car door and climb out, which he did. Cassidy had a sack of dynamite which he told Mike O'Neill, the fireman, to hold as he set the charge to blow off the front of the safe. The dynamite explosion blew part of the roof off and shattered one side of the express car. Then Cassidy shot the locked strongbox open with his six-shooter.

A nosy sheepherder, attracted by the sound of the explosion, rode down to get a better look, and his horse was shot out from under him. His bump of curiosity deflated, he hightailed it back to his flock as fast as his legs could carry him. The dead horse was the only casualty in the Wagner train holdup, which netted the robbers eighty thousand dollars.

When the delayed passenger train pulled into the Wagner station, Sheriff Griffiths wired the sketchy details of the holdup to the sheriff of Valley County at Glasgow, the county seat, and the station agent at Malta.

The Valley County sheriff immediately organized a large posse at Glasgow and commandeered a special train to Malta. Getting enough horses at Malta to mount the posse, as well as a wagon and four-horse team to haul grub and bedrolls, caused several delays. At long last the posse got under way and headed for the Little Rockies, the old stomping ground of Kid Curry.

The owner of the livery stable at Malta, who had managed to gather enough saddle horses to mount the posse, had told the sheriff he would do his best to supply the posse with a wagon and a change

The Wagner Train Robbery

of fresh horses which he would send out with a horse wrangler. But the wagon and small remuda of remounts had failed to catch up with the posse that, spread out in groups of four, had followed the stage road from Malta to the Circle C Ranch.

"I can't understand," the sheriff repeated time and again during the meal, "what the hell happened to our chuck wagon and relay of fresh mounts that livery barn man promised to send out. That cowboy driver, Tim Maloney, claimed to know this part of the country."

The mention of Tim Maloney came as sudden as a lightning bolt out of a cloudless sky. I cut a quick look at Al Taylor, who shrugged his shoulders and shook his head, a puzzled look on his face.

"I depended a lot on that man Maloney," the sheriff went on. "When news of the train holdup reached Malta, Tim Maloney and another cowboy named Byron Hurley saddled up and left town to head off the train robbers. In their excitement they forgot to take their guns, and those brave unarmed men were forced to return to Malta."

I covered my mouth with both hands to keep from bustin' out laughing. The notion of Tim Maloney and Byron Hurley starting out without six-shooters and saddle guns to head off Kid Curry and his gang sounded so darned ridiculous. Tim Maloney was well acquainted with Kid Curry, and they were good friends. Tim was working for the Circle C on a hay contract and was in Malta to hire a hay crew at the time of the holdup. It was sure a joke that the sheriff had deputized Tim Maloney to drive the mess wagon. No wonder it was lost, strayed, or stolen—on purpose was my guess.

The sheriff bedded his posse down on the empty bunks in the bunkhouse, and after a talk with Bob Coburn, I bedded down. Bob stayed in the office most of the next morning and told me to keep an eye on the posse. Sometime after breakfast some of the men set up a target and started shooting, but Bob broke up the target practice in short order. Then he took the sheriff to the office for a medicine talk.

Maybe Bob felt a little sorry for the sheriff, who now was following a cold trail, but most likely he had a tongue-in-cheek notion when he advised the worried law officer to take his posse to the Jim Winters-Abe Gill place. Bob knew Winters and Gill would welcome the presence of the law and would probably be more than willing to mount the posse on fresh horses.

About ten o'clock the missing mess wagon pulled in at the ranch. The sheriff, who was fit to be tied, chewed Tim Maloney out. Tim waited until the man had run down, then the big, rawboned, black Irishman told the officious lawman off in no uncertain terms. He said the best four-horse team in the country couldn't make more than five miles an hour hauling that overloaded wagon. He had made the halfway stage station at the Hog Ranch after dark, unhooked the horses, and let them graze in the pasture. He was back on the road with the wheels rolling at daybreak. Maloney also said there was no horse wrangler with fresh mounts on the way, and he didn't expect one, because it had taken every saddle horse in Malta to mount the posse.

Then Maloney said that if the sheriff would take off his tin star and repeat what he had said, he would give him the damnedest working over a man ever got and lived to tell about it. Maloney then handed the four lines to the cook he had brought along, climbed down over the front wheel, and spit on his hands as he took a John L. Sullivan fighting stance. The harassed sheriff mumbled some sort of apology and walked off to gather his posse and the horses.

The cook on the wagon got down and went into the kitchen to tell his troubles to Al Taylor. He said he had plenty of canned goods, a quarter of beef, and two slabs of bacon, but no bread. Al gave him a half-dozen loaves of fresh bread, filled one of his Dutch ovens with navy beans, and gave the cook, who was called Shorty, some advice regarding the value of navy beans for taking the wrinkles out of a man's belly.

George Baker, a tall and lanky wolfer who had ridden in from his cabin in the badlands, volunteered to pilot the wagon, replacing Tim Maloney. The sun was noon high by the time the posse finally got under way with the four-horse wagon in the lead.

George Baker had tied his saddle horse to the nigh wheeler and

The Wagner Train Robbery

sat on the seat beside the cook, who was driving. A long-barreled old Winchester .45.-70 buffalo gun laid across his lap. He had not shaved or cut his long hair for a couple of months, and his battered old hat was slanted down across his eyes. His faded blue-flannel shirt and old Levis were dirt glazed with grease and dried blood from the coyotes and wolves he had caught in his traps and skinned for the bounty on their pelts. Baker had not had a hot soapy bath in a month of Sundays, and he stank of muskrat and skunk, which is the most rank and malodorous combination found anywhere on earth. He always had a fresh chew bulging in his whiskered jaw, and the fact that the grizzled wolfer was lousy as a pet coon added to the personality of the hard-case renegade—that and the fact that he had located a bottle in the jockey box of the wagon and was feeling his oats.

Al Taylor and I watched from the kitchen doorway as the posse and wagon headed out along the stage road. The sheriff, who was leading the posse of man hunters that rode ahead of the wagon, sat erect attempting a saddle swagger.

As the sorry-looking outfit passed Bob Coburn's two-storied log house and strung out along the stage road, a big chicken hawk took wing out of one of the cottonwood trees. As the hawk soared down in a wide and lowering circle above the moving wagon, the whiskered wolfer lifted the old buffalo gun from his lap. Levering a cartridge into the breech without lifting the wooden stock from the wagon seat, Baker squeezed the trigger without aiming and took a give-a-damn shot at the high-flying hawk.

The report of the buffalo gun was cannon loud as the big hunk of cartridge lead, deadly enough to kill a buffalo, struck the hawk dead center. Feathers showered in midair as the lead slug tore the body into fragments. Bits of feathered flesh and bone drifted down on the startled posse members, who thought for a minute they were being ambushed by Kid Curry and his outlaw train robbers. They sat their horses in frozen bewilderment, eying the tall willow thickets along the creek banks that flanked the wagon road.

"S'nabitch!" Baker's harsh rasping voice sawed through the

gun echoes. "Ol' Betsy's seen 'er best days. Aimed fer that hawk's eye to shoot the head off neat and clean, and blowed the bird to hell!" He tossed the Winchester into the sagebrush and reached for the whisky jug. Out of the corner of a bloodshot eye the wolfer marked the high clump of brush where he had thrown the gun to be retrieved at some later date. Thus George Baker discounted the difficult feat of marksmanship, a thousand-to-one wing shot that was well nigh impossible with the heavy, cumbersome, outmoded blunderbuss and that forestalled any challenge of further shooting prowess which might later occur.

The badly upset and frightened posse members, who had sat frozen in their saddles like scared cottontail rabbits, slowly recovered from their bewilderment as they stared slack-jawed and bug-eyed at the bearded wolfer.

"May the howlin' wolves never cease," Baker chanted tipsily as he lowered the jug, then waved it in the air, "till they ketch the sonofabitch that sold Buffalo Bill the tanglefoot. Lead on sheriff! Up and at 'em, you bounty-hunting bastards!"

Once more the scowling, harassed sheriff rode on in the lead of his shirt-tail posse, as the cannon-loud blast of the buffalo gun gave a mocking farewell salute to the man hunters.

Due to the late noon start, the sheriff's posse failed to reach the Winters-Gill ranch. They camped on good feed and water alongside the stage road at the foot of Bear Gulch Hill, a few miles this side of Zortman. There the bad luck that had dogged the sheriff of Valley County once again overtook the already delayed posse with still another slight setback.

During the night a number of the posse members became sick with violent abdominal cramps, diarrhea, and nausea. The sheriff blamed the sudden malady on the large kettle of navy beans that Al Taylor, out of generosity for a fellow cook, had given Shorty. The sheriff claimed the beans had soured, and it was a known fact that a hungry bait of soured navy beans could make a healthy man sick as a coyote that had picked up strychnine bait.

Thus, throughout the Little Rockies spread the maligning rumor that the Circle C outfit had deliberately poisoned the entire law

The Dynamited Express Car after the Curry "Hold Up" between Malta and Wagner, Mont. July 3, 1901. "Kid" Curry's gang got away with $80,000.

Top: The Kid Curry hideaway.

Courtesy of W. J. Nankeman, Malta, Montana

Bottom: Dynamited express car after the Wagner train robbery.

posse to cause them further delay and give Kid Curry and his outlaw pals a long head start leaving the country.

George Baker put in his two-bits' worth and reminded the sheriff that a few members of the posse had sneaked off to Zortman during the night and fetched back a couple of gallon kegs of cheap rotgut whisky. It took a cast-iron stomach and tin-lined guts to withstand that fusel oil without getting sick as a poisoned pup. The posse was a sick and sorry mess when they finally made it to the Winters-Gill ranch.

During their week or two stay the posse had the same bad luck that they had at the Circle C Ranch. Conflicting wild rumors spread like turbulent winds. One of the posse reportedly shot himself in the foot, and another shot a horse. Jim Thornhill had sent word to the sheriff that any members of his posse caught prowling day or night on his ranch could easily be mistaken for prowling coyotes and shot down without warning. Needless to say, they gave the Thornhill ranch a wide go-round.

It was said that the posse members, who rode together in threes and fours, confined their man-hunting activities within hollering distance of one another, never ventured far from their headquarters, and never rode after dark. Their peace of mind was disturbed by the rumors that the Winters-Gill place was haunted by the ghost of the one-armed Johnny Curry and the known fact that Jim Winters expected to be shot down by Kid Curry or his brother Loney.

Another disturbing rumor hovered in the air like a dark cloud. The sheriff had received word, with sufficient proof, that Kid Curry, Butch Cassidy, and two other members of the notorious Wild Bunch, who had held up the train near Wagner, instead of quitting the country, had holed up nearby in the badlands at the unknown Kid Curry Hideaway, said to be somewhere in the vicinity of nearby Thornhill Butte. It was rough badlands country where the outlaws could take a potshot at any venturesome lawmen who were foolhardy enough to get within Winchester range. Small wonder that the posse members, fortified by cheap whisky, stayed closely bunched like frightened sheep scared by a wolf pack.

The Wagner Train Robbery

Finally the sheriff gave up his abortive attempt at man hunting and took his motley crew back to town, but not before he and his blundering men became the objects of ridicule, practical jokes, and humiliating crude horseplay that tended to make the whole man hunt a ridiculous farce.

Bob Coburn's rough treatment of the sheriff and his posse added to the already established rumor that the three Coburn brothers, Will, Bob, and Wallace, were members of the Kid Curry gang. The fact that the Circle C outfit had bought the cattle belonging to Jim Thornhill and Kid Curry after the Kid had killed Pike Landusky and that the money was delivered in cash to Kid Curry at the Hideaway to give him a getaway grubstake was kept a secret at the time. But when the 4T brand belonging to Jim Thornhill and Kid Curry was registered to the Coburn Cattle Company in the next issue of the Montana stockgrowers' brand book, the story revealed itself. Anyway, the news of the cash sale of the Kid Curry cattle shortly after the killing of Pike Landusky had already leaked out during the spring calf roundup when the calves were tallied. It was known that the 4T brand and all cattle in that brand now belonged to Wallace Coburn, and it was rumored that Wallace had delivered the cash at the Kid Curry Hideaway.

It did not take the brains of a Philadelphia lawyer for a twelve-year-old kid like me to know that my half-brother Bob knew in advance about the Wagner train holdup on that third day of July, 1901, when he told me where to hold the remuda that evening. And since the outlaws were riding Thornhill horses, it wasn't hard to figure that Jim Thornhill knew in advance about the train holdup.

It was common gossip that Will, Bob, and Wallace Coburn were members of the Kid Curry gang, but whether or not there was any truth to the rumor I have no way of knowing, for they never confided in me. On the other hand, they made no bones about their friendship with Kid Curry and his brothers, who with Jim Thornhill had worked for the Circle C outfit as cowpunchers.

There was also a time when Jim Winters had worked for the Circle C on the roundups, along with the Curry boys and Thornhill, and they all were friendly enough for a number of years. That was before Jim Winters swore out a warrant against Kid Curry and Loney and Jim Thornhill, falsely accusing them of cattle rustling and brand changing.

When Jim Winters bought the old Dan Tressler place and killed Johnny Curry when he attempted to run him off, the bitter, blood-spattered feud was wide open, and the Curry boys' friends took sides. In those days any friend who was loyal to Kid Curry was automatically branded and earmarked as a member of the Kid Curry gang. Kid Curry's friends included a great many cowpunchers in that vast part of northeastern Montana, not only the Circle C outfit, but the Circle Diamond, the Bear Paw Pool, the Milner Square, the Shonkin Pool at Fort Benton, Spud Stevens' outfit at Lewistown, the Judith Basin Pool, and the DHS outfit. In spite of their tough reputations, Kid Curry and his two brothers had many friends, the sort of cowpuncher and rancher friends who were never backward in declaring their friendship, as well as saloonkeepers and gamblers and a few former cowpunchers who now wore the law badge of sheriff, deputy sheriff, or livestock inspector.

Sift this legion of friends down to a hand-picked few, and you had the Kid Curry gang, whose membership was kept a secret. Few of them had a criminal record. Among the Curry gang was the big, easygoing, soft-spoken Jim Thornhill, the only one marked down, as far as I know, on the Pinkerton files. According to the famous (or infamous, depending on which side of the law you were on) Pinkerton cowboy detective, Charlie Siringo, Jim Thornhill was "Dad" Jackson of the old Sam Bass outlaw gang. But Thornhill later told me that he was only about thirty when he came to Montana—too young to be "Dad" Jackson. Frank Jackson, who was Sam Bass's right-hand man, was the only one of the old gang who had not been killed or imprisoned. Thornhill figured he probably was the original "Dad" Jackson.

The afternoon of the Fourth of July, when the stage from Malta to the Little Rockies stopped at the Circle C Ranch to drop off the mail sacks, there were three strangers aboard. The stage driver told Bob Coburn in confidence that one of his passengers was a

The Wagner Train Robbery

post-office inspector and that he figured the other two strangers were Pinkerton detectives bound for Zortman and Landusky. Whether or not the stage driver was correct in his suspicions of the two strangers was never proven one way or the other. It was natural to assume that Pinkerton operatives, hired by the railroad to investigate the train holdup, prowled the Little Rockies and its environs for a week or two under various disguises. They were range detectives like Charlie Siringo, who had stayed at the Jim Thornhill place and accepted his hospitality while doing his damnedest to pick up the cold trail of Kid Curry.

But if there were Pinkerton operatives on the prowl, they never came within gun range of the Circle C Ranch, and I have no way of knowing what sort of written reports those gents, with their law badges pinned to their undershirts, turned in to the Pinkerton headquarters. All was quiet and peaceful at the ranch that Fourth of July, 1901, when we set off our sky rockets and Roman candles into the star-filled night.

A month or two later, long after Kid Curry and his outlaw partners had quit the country, Charlie Beard, surveyor and justice of peace in the Little Rockies, took me along as rod and chain man on a survey to relocate some section corners in the big pasture near the Coburn Buttes. He showed me where a hidden cave on the east Butte was located.

The sandstone roof of the cave was high enough to allow the six-foot Charlie Beard to stand upright. Unmistakable signs revealed fairly recent occupancy. There were many short, stubbed-out butts of cigarettes on the floor, and in a far corner were half-a-dozen empty tomato cans and a discarded squat brown jug with a couple of drinks of whisky in it.

Charlie Beard said he thought that Kid Curry or one of the Wild Bunch had spent a few days here as lookout until the sheriff called off his posse. When the coast was clear, Kid Curry and his gang pulled out for the Hole-in-the-Wall country. It was typical of Kid Curry, Beard told me, that he had come back to his old stomping ground to try for a South American stake on one final go-to-hell gesture. Eighty thousand dollars was the loot, all of it in incomplete, brand-new, unsigned currency that would require an expert to forge the necessary signatures. It would be many months, even a year or two, before it would be safe for them to pass the money.

I came to know Charlie Beard well during the years. I remember a certain aura of mystery about him as though he kept his real self concealed from all who knew him as a friend. He was a man of strange behavior at times—secretive is as close as I can describe it. He was a man of many parts, inscrutable when he chose to be, with innate honesty and integrity and indomitable courage given to few. I was always proud to be claimed as one of Charlie Beard's friends. It is with fond memory I recall the days and nights I spent with him at the ranch, listening while he told countless stories on a long winter night.

10.

Ambush

For safety's sake Jim Winters and his partner, Abe Gill, welcomed the sheriff's posse that was on the trail of the train robbers. During the posse's brief two-week stay at the Winters-Gill ranch, Jim Winters dwelt in the security of the protective arm of the law. All was well during that brief stay while the posse scoured the surrounding country for traces of the outlaws.

Winters was bound to have been aware of the fact that, despite the boastful assurance of the sheriff that Kid Curry and his three outlaw companions had quit the country, there was a strong probability they had hidden out in the badlands between the Little Rockies and the Missouri River.

Winters became a little fed up with the half-hearted, scared-to-death actions of the posse, and revealed his disgust in his sarcastic reply to the sheriff when he tried to persuade him to join the posse in their man hunt. It was a day or so after one of the posse members shot a saddled horse another member had tied up in the brush because he had mistaken the horse for a train robber.

"Not by a damn sight, mister," Winters is said to have answered the sheriff. "I'm staying right here at the ranch. It ain't Kid Curry I'm scared of. I just don't aim to be bushwhacked by the two-bit posse riders you got prowling the country, using rotgut whisky for a brave maker."

After a couple of weeks of fruitless man hunting, the sheriff took his posse back to Malta, and paid them off, and Jim Winters and Abe Gill went back to their regular business of ranching.

It was the middle of July, and the haying season was coming on. Winters had hired a hay crew. About that time a few college students from the eastern university that Abe Gill had attended showed up at the ranch as Gill's guests during their summer vacation. For those eastern Ivy League students it was a new kind of sport to toil and sweat at the business end of a pitchfork, and their festive college spirit directly contrasted the grim posse of heavily armed men who had recently been at the ranch. The recent train holdup at Wagner was indeed something for the students to write home about.

The safety in numbers of the hay crew and the group of young students with their carefree, fun-loving gaiety could have tended to add to the atmosphere of false security for Jim Winters. It had been three weeks since the train holdup, and neither hide nor hair had been seen of Kid Curry and his outlaw companions. It looked as if the outlaws had gone back to the Hole in the Wall with their loot.

On July 25, 1901, sometime between daylight and sunrise, Jim Winters, who was always the first man up, opened the door of his cabin and stepped outside. He had pulled on his boots and pants and put on his hat, and presumably he was headed for the outhouse a short distance away, which was concealed by the high willows and underbrush along the creek.

Winters had gone no farther than fifty feet from the cabin when the hushed, early-morning silence was shattered by the explosion of a rifle. A .30-.30 slug struck Winters in the belly. He was falling, knees buckling, when a second slug hit him in the abdomen, the bullet passing through his body. The gut-shot Winters, mortally wounded, lay in a widening pool of blood, almost in the same spot where Johnny Curry had died five years earlier.[1]

The gunman who had sent those .30.-30 slugs into Jim Winters was an expert shot. The killer, who must have known that a gut-shot

[1] For a newspaper account in *The Daily River Press*, July 26, 1901, see Appendix A.

Abe Gill

Courtesy of Al Lucke, Havre, Montana

Pioneer Cattleman in Montana

man dies a slow, agonizing death, could easily have shot the dying man through the head as he lay on the ground and put him out of his misery, but that wasn't the way the killer wanted it. He had purposely gut-shot Winters so that he would die slowly and in much pain.

Five years earlier Jim Winters had emptied both barrels of a shotgun into Johnny Curry, and this was the payoff. While there was never any proof that could positively identify the ambusher, Abe Gill and many others never doubted that the killer was Kid Curry.

Before the echoes of the two rifle shots had died out. Abe Gill was aware that Kid Curry, after five long years, had avenged the death of his brother. That fearsome knowledge must have sent a cold chill wiring down his spine and put the fear of death into him.

The rest of that long summer day the ranch was under the threat of death from the outlaws. Abe Gill told one of the hired hands to saddle up and ride to Harlem to notify the law and have them send out a doctor. When the rider started out, a few warning shots sent him back to the barn. Much later in the day another horsebacker was permitted to leave the ranch unmolested by warning shots.

Only after the arrival of the sheriff and his posse was there any attempt to hunt for signs. The signs showed that at least two or three men had waited in ambush behind the high willows and brush along the creek. Stubs of hand-rolled cigarettes and empty brass-shell casings of .30-.30-caliber Winchesters were on the ground, as well as piles of manure and the shod tracks of horses.

Once more the sheriff's posse made their headquarters at the Winters-Gill place while they rode in pairs or groups of three or four in a vain hunt for the man or men who had shot Jim Winters from ambush.

Because Abe Gill was concerned about the safety of the college students and felt responsible for their lives, he sent them back home. Needless to say, they needed no persuasion. They had witnessed sudden violent death followed by a day of terror. The romance of the Wild West which had brought them to the ranch in Montana had been shattered by the gun blasts on that early morn-

Ambush

ing, and their dreams of the wild, carefree life of a cowhand were forgotten. The sooner they left this ranch in the Little Rockies, the better.

The sudden death of Jim Winters left Abe Gill the sole owner of the ranch, the disputed land where two men had met violent death. During the brief years of their partnership, Jim Winters and Abe Gill had become close friends. Winters had told his partner that it was only a matter of time until Kid Curry would kill him to avenge his brother Johnny's death, and they had discussed the problem from all angles many times.

But it was not until Winters' prophecy came to pass that the full impact hit Gill. The manner of his partner's death, shot down in cold blood from ambush, came as a sudden shock. For the first time the pilgrim from back East fully realized his helpless position of being left alone to face the unknown. On that long summer day of July 25, Abe Gill had stood in the shadow of death. The man who had shot down his friend and partner could be none other than Kid Curry, and Gill never doubted that if he stepped outside the cabin door he, too, would be shot down.

One of the hay hands said that most likely Kid Curry had pulled out and left two of his friends hidden behind the brush to keep any mounted messenger from informing the law of the killing. That would give Kid Curry a few hours' head start. This was a logical conclusion since later on in the day a hired hand was allowed to ride away from the ranch without being sent back by warning shots.

Not until the sheriff and his posse arrived did Abe Gill feel it was fairly safe to saddle a horse and lend assistance to the law. Several days later, after the sheriff took his posse back to town, Abe Gill had to summon all his courage to face the responsibility and danger of owning the controversial, blood-spattered ranch that had been claimed by Johnny Curry.

Abe Gill was a novice in the cattle business, but his courage to stay and continue ranching gained him respect and admiration in that section of the Montana cow country. Gill was a peaceful man, quiet mannered and soft spoken, a gentleman by breeding and by nature. His only wish was to be left alone. He had no personal enemies and wanted no part in the violent feud between Jim Winters and the Curry brothers. Jim Winters had been killed, presumably by Kid Curry, a notorious outlaw. It was up to the law to hunt down the killer. Abe Gill was content to let the law take its course, and more than once he quietly voiced that opinion in his soft eastern accent.

Gill had enough experience handling cattle to make it pay. According to those who knew the ropes, he was sitting pretty as long as he had sense enough not to pick up his dead partner's hand or play stool pigeon for the Pinkerton Detective Agency.

Gill had been an eyewitness to the murder of Jim Winters. If he had caught a glimpse of the killer, he knew enough to keep his mouth shut. The old Kid Curry Hideaway near Thornhill Butte was still used by men who rode the outlaw trail. Kid Curry had friends in the Little Rockies country. If Abe Gill had talked out of turn, the rustling leaves along the outlaw trail, which extended to Robbers' Roost and the upper Animas Valley in New Mexico, would have carried word to Kid Curry, no matter where the outlaw was.

11.

The Disappearance of Abe Gill

AFTER THE KILLING OF JIM WINTERS, Kid Curry went to Knoxville, Tennessee, where he had relatives. He attempted to pass off some of the incomplete currency from the train robbery in a clothing store. He gave a fifty-dollar bank note to the clerk, who went to a nearby bank to get change for the bill. The bank cashier recognized it as part of the Wagner holdup money and notified the police. Two officers entered the store with drawn guns, and Kid Curry pulled his gun and shot at the policemen. He wounded both of them, one seriously. Then he ran out into the street, jumped into a passing ice wagon and made a spectacular getaway. He was captured later at Jefferson City.

Kid Curry was duly tried in Tennessee for his part in the Wagner train holdup. Mike O'Neill, the fireman on the passenger train at the time, was summoned to identify the prisoner, and Kid Curry was sentenced to serve from thirty to ninety years in prison.

Meanwhile Jim Thornhill, with a bank roll in his pocket, quietly left his ranch in Montana and boarded a train for Tennessee. Whether or not he ever visited Kid Curry while he was in jail has never been verified, but most likely he did visit the Kid to give him the bank roll.

On June 29, 1903, while Kid Curry was in jail at Knoxville awaiting his transfer to the penitentiary, he reached through the cell bars and snared the jailer around the neck with a noose he had made from wire he unraveled off the broom he used to sweep out his cell. He took away the jailer's keys and left him hogtied and gagged in the locked cell. The Kid got a six-shooter and saddle gun from the jail office and made a fast getaway on the sheriff's grain-fed horse, headed for the Hole-in-the-Wall country.[1]

There are a number of conflicting accounts of the death of Kid Curry. Charles Kelly, in his book *Outlaw Trail*, wrote:

> At the old hideout Logan stayed with Walt Putney, one of the men who had helped him rob the Belle Fourche bank in 1897. The two outlaws stole some horses from the Tisdale ranch belonging to Mc-Donald and John May. Word was sent to Buffalo and Sheriff Beard and Alva Young went to the Putney ranch to arrest the thieves. Logan and Putney saw the officers coming and rode away. The sheriff fired, wounding Logan. Putney helped him back on his horse and they both disappeared.
>
> Two nights later Dr. Julis A. Schulke was held up in his office in Thermopolis and forced to drive several miles into the country to attend a wounded man. A few nights later he was forced to make a second call, when he found the patient's wound badly infected and recovery doubtful. He received no more calls, and believes Harvey Logan, the mysterious patient, died.[2]

There was a train holdup near Parachute, Colorado, on July 7, 1904, and when the law posse overtook the outlaws a few days later, there was a running gun fight. A cowpuncher known as Tap Duncan was wounded, and he shot himself in the head rather than be taken alive. He was later identified as Harvey Logan, alias Kid Curry. Although I can't be sure, I think the body was identified by Jim Thornhill and John Troop of Landusky, Montana.

Sometime later a bank was robbed at Cody, Wyoming, and one of the bank robbers was thought to be Kid Curry. Therefore the body of Tap Duncan was exhumed, photographed, and again identified as Kid Curry. In 1904 a Pinkerton operative took the photograph to Knoxville, Tennessee, where the Kid had broken

---

[1] For a newspaper account of Kid Curry's escape, see Appendix A.
[2] *Outlaw Trail* (Salt Lake City, 1938), 280.

The Disappearance of Abe Gill

out of jail. The law officers there also positively identified the picture of the dead man as Kid Curry.

Of course, the reports of Kid Curry's death reached the Little Rockies. Jim Thornhill, whenever he was questioned, said he was sure Kid Curry was dead. While the friends of Kid Curry mourned the passing of the notorious outlaw and gathered in the saloons of Landusky to salute his memory by passing the bottle, Abe Gill must have breathed easier when he learned that the Kid was dead. He no longer had to fear that someday Kid Curry would return to kill him for being Jim Winters' partner.

No one doubted that Kid Curry was dead until Abe Gill accompanied Will Coburn and John Survant to South America. While they were down there, they heard rumors that Kid Curry, under an assumed name, and Butch Cassidy and Harry Longabaugh (the Sundance Kid) were ranching somewhere in South America. Abe Gill wanted to notify the South American authorities and the Pinkerton Detective Agency, and I think he eventually did before they departed for home. The South American authorities at Buenos Aires seemed to ignore the rumor and did little or nothing about apprehending the North American outlaws. But the Pinkertons later sent one or two operatives to South America to make an investigation.

Abe Gill returned to his Montana ranch a troubled, worried man. The knowledge that Kid Curry might still be alive stuck like a bothersome sandbur in the back of his mind. Although the name of Harvey Logan, alias Kid Curry, was probably marked deceased on the Pinkerton files, throughout the Little Rockies there was a spiderweb of conflicting rumors about whether or not Kid Curry really was dead or alive, whether Abe Gill corresponded with the Pinkertons, and whether a Pinkerton range detective was snooping around Landusky and Zortman.

If a strange cowpuncher showed up in that part of the cow country, riding the grub line or asking for a job, he was suspected of being a Pinkerton man. And if that strange cowpuncher began asking careless questions at the cow camps or in town, he was apt to get any number of conflicting answers. It would have taken a Philadelphia lawyer to sort out the truth from the big windies, for in spite of the ambush killing of Jim Winters, supposedly by Kid Curry, the Kid had plenty of friends among the cowpunchers, ranchers, and saloonkeepers.

Around the Little Rockies country the general opinion on the the killing of Jim Winters was that Winters had signed his own death warrant when he killed Johnny Curry and should have quit the country then instead of hanging around. Winters knew that sooner or later Kid Curry was bound to come back and play out his brother's hand.

The local sheriffs and deputies still rode wide around the old Kid Curry Hideaway. If any Pinkerton range detective knew its hidden location, he never rode within rifle shot of the one steep trail leading down to the hidden log cabin, the only entrance to the Hideaway. A stranger could ride within a hundred yards of the Hideaway and never know it was there, blissfully unaware that every movement was being watched by wanted men who still used it now and then.

For five years after the killing of Jim Winters, Abe Gill lived at his ranch in the Little Rockies. Old-timers still called the ranch the Dan Tressler place, and to others it was known as the Jim Winters ranch. Few called it the Gill ranch, for in spite of Abe Gill's five-year tenure, he was still considered a dude from back East and a tenderfoot. He never lost his eastern accent in spite of his attempts to acquire cowpuncher lingo and the cow country vernacular. His eastern background and college education remained noticeable although he made every effort to adjust his ways and mannerisms to the cow country. In spite of his painstaking attempts, Abe Gill had never been able to sit a horse with the natural ease of a cowhand. Rather, he sat a western saddle like a cavalry trooper, and he never was able to handle a ketch rope or sit with a natural easy balance in the saddle while riding a dodging cutting horse.

Despite Abe Gill's cordial manners and his eagerness to be ac-

The Disappearance of Abe Gill

cepted among the cowpunchers on the roundup, the easterner never quite made the grade. Perhaps this was because the old-time cowhand was a strange breed of mankind, clannish and stand-offish, accepting no stranger not of their own special breed. After a five-minute talk with a stranger, those old-timer cowhands knew if he was one of them or a phony trying to pass himself off as one of their breed. The cowhands sized up Abe Gill and accepted him at face value as a pilgrim rancher, but he was always considered an outsider, never one of them. He was not a man with whom a cowpuncher could talk confidentially or share a bottle down to the last drink. Even the cowhands who worked for Gill never confided in him, although they claimed he was a good employer.

While Abe Gill was always considered a good neighbor, easy to get along with and friendly enough, his eastern background kept him from ever really belonging. His cultural background and college education, along with his loyalty to Jim Winters and his desire for the apprehension and punishment of Winters' murderer, although laudable characteristics, tended to make certain types of men in that tough vicinity suspicious of Abe Gill.

The cold-blooded murder of his partner left a mark on Gill as plain and permanent as a brand on an animal's hide. The murder had forever destroyed the pilgrim's romantic dreams of the West. Gone was the glory of having a partner who had shot and killed one of the Curry outlaws.

Abe Gill was now on his own. This posed no difficult problem, for he could hire a good, trustworthy cowhand, and during the years Gill prospered as a stockman. But he must have always feared that Kid Curry was alive and ranching in South America and might someday return to the Little Rockies. Perhaps that was why Abe Gill finally decided to sell out and go back East where he belonged. He sold his ranch and all the cattle in his brand to the Coburn Cattle Company in the fall of 1906.

I now recall a certain incident in late August of that year. I was seventeen and was due back in school at Great Falls after Labor Day. I had come in late for noon dinner and was sitting alone

Pioneer Cattleman in Montana

at the long mess table when Abe Gill and George Hall, the stock inspector, came in for coffee. Gill began talking about why he was selling out his ranch and going back East.

That day George Hall was at the Circle C Ranch in his official capacity as livestock and brand inspector to tally the cattle Abe Gill was selling to the Coburn Cattle Company. Hall had been a passenger on the train in the Wagner holdup, and he remarked that when Sheriff Griffiths from Great Falls, who was also on the train, claimed he had swapped shots with the train robbers, "he must have shot down his bootleg."

I was at the age when I took special notice of the way different cowpunchers dressed in order to imitate anything special. George Hall wore the garb of the typical Montana cowpuncher Charles M. Russell depicted in his paintings. Abe Gill favored the Frederic Remington type of dress, with the wide-brimmed hat that was creased down the middle and turned up in front and spurs with big rowels that dragged the floor of the mess hall.

When the stock inspector dropped the name of Kid Curry, I had both ears cocked. It was George Hall's opinion that Kid Curry had left South America, if he had ever gone there, and was back in the Hole-in-the-Wall country and that one of these days he would show up in the Little Rockies at his Hideaway or at Jim Thornhill's ranch.

Abe Gill was dead serious when he admitted that was one reason he was selling his ranch holdings and going back East. He said he knew if he stayed on, it would only be a matter of time until Kid Curry or one of his gang shot him down in the same manner in which Jim Winters had been murdered.

"If and when that time ever comes before I go East," Abe Gill said with quiet conviction in his eastern accent, "I will die the death of a martyr." Those were his exact words spoken in the mess hall at the Circle C Ranch on that late August day in 1906. I remember because he pronounced the word martyr "mahtah."

Just after Abe Gill sold his ranch to the Coburn Cattle Company, he mysteriously disappeared. He supposedly rode away from his ranch on his favorite horse, White Cloud, and neither he nor

The Disappearance of Abe Gill

his horse were ever seen again. The *Fort Benton River Press* reported his absence on December 10, 1906:

> The eastern friends of A. D. Gill, the well known Landusky stockman and farmer, are making enquiries of the Chouteau County authorities as to his present location, nothing having been heard of him for nearly two months. Mr. Gill, it will be remembered, sold his ranch to the Coburn Cattle Company last fall, and it was understood he would immediately go east. His grip was sent from Landusky to Harlem about six weeks ago, but Mr. Gill has not been seen by his neighbors since that time, and his present whereabouts are unknown.

Sixty years have now passed, and to the best of my knowledge, the mystery of Abe Gill's disappearance has never been solved. It was rumored that relatives and friends back East hired a Pinkerton operative to make a thorough and extensive search for the missing man, but that no trace was ever found of him or his horse.

The Little Rockies and the badlands country north of the Missouri River was extremely rough and broken terrain. From the mouth of the Musselshell and Rocky Point to the Cow Island Crossing on the Missouri was outlaw country where men with a bounty on their hides could hole up for weeks and months in comparative safety from the long reach of the law. The swift-moving, wide Missouri River was iced over during the winter, and its treacherous open air holes offered a watery grave for a man and horse. After the spring thaw, the floods would obliterate any trace of a murderer's foul deed. The stretch of rough badlands along the Missouri offered countless deep canyons and cut coulees where Abe Gill's body and the carcass of his horse could have been concealed. In the badlands the coyotes and wolves ran in packs and the mountain lions lurked in their caves.

It was a foregone conclusion that Abe Gill had met with foul play. Any man who was or had been a friend of Kid Curry and his two brothers was under suspicion. Jim Thornhill, the former partner of Kid Curry, was the prime suspect. And because it was a well-known fact that men on the dodge were welcome at the Thornhill ranch, any man who worked for Thornhill was also a suspect, whether or not he was just an honest cowpuncher riding the grub line. The Circle C outfit lived under a cloud of suspicion for a long time. Will, Bob, and Wallace Coburn were questioned, along with Jake Myers, who had replaced Horace Brewster as ranch foreman and wagon boss.

Although Charlie Siringo did not mention Abe Gill's disappearance in his book *A Cowboy Detective,* written in later years when he was no longer in the employ of the Pinkertons, the prevailing rumor remained that Siringo was one of the Pinkerton range detectives sent out to the Little Rockies country to investigate the mysterious disappearance of Abe Gill.

Those given to superstition claimed that the old Dan Tressler (Winters-Gill) ranch was ghost haunted. On a bright sunny day in summertime, it was a peaceful place, with its green hay meadows and the air sweet-scented by the wild roses in bloom. Meadowlarks warbled their early morning and sunset song, and you could hear the sound of the gently flowing waters of the creek, which had tall leafy willows along the banks. The ragged outline of the Little Rockies formed a background to the sod-roofed log cabin and barn and pole corrals. It was a peaceful, quiet setting that gave no hint of tragedy or violence. Even on a cold winter day when the ground was covered with snow, the ranch formed a yuletide setting.

It was only at night that the ranch seemed haunted. Ghostly tales were told by cowpunchers who spread their bedrolls in the cabin. The creaking sound of the pine-board floor became the cautious tread of Jim Winters as he crouched there with his double-barreled shotgun. The pounding hoofs of the bucking bronc Johnny Curry rode that bleak February morning when Winters blasted him from the saddle could be heard in the night. The dying groans of the gut-shot Winters came from the willows, and the scratching sound outside the cabin was Abe Gill trying the door latch to gain entrance.

Perhaps the ghost stories, told in good faith around bunkhouses and roundup camps, resulted from the strong superstition among the old-time cowhands that the ghost of any cowpuncher who died

The Disappearance of Abe Gill

a violent death by gunshot or night stampede or was dragged to death by a bronc came back from the grave to roam the night, earthbound forevermore.

Later, when the Gill ranch became a Circle C line camp, I lived in the cabin for weeks at a time, summer and winter, spring and fall. It was easy to imagine I heard ghostly night sounds that in the light of day could easily be explained as pack rats gnawing or scampering across the floor, the night prowl of a skunk, or the night wind at the door or window. But there was a time in my cowpuncher youth when I shared the belief of the other superstitious cowhands that the ranch was haunted.

Because of his mysterious disappearance, Abe Gill played a minor role in the saga of violence and bloodshed in the feud between Jim Winters and the Curry boys.

The town of Landusky in the heart of the Little Rockies is now a ghost town in every sense. But in the early days outlaws from Robbers' Roost, Brown's Hole and the Hole-in-the-Wall country were frequent visitors. Gunslingers from both sides of the bloody Johnson County war in Wyoming rode the wide streets, shooting up the town. For years Kid Curry and his two brothers and the notorious unknown members of the Curry gang made Landusky their headquarters. Butch Cassidy and his Wild Bunch, sometimes called the "Train Robbers' Syndicate" left their sign there. Millions of dollars in rich gold-bearing ore was taken from the mines of the Little Rockies that were surrounded on all sides by big and little cow outfits. In recent years a raging forest fire burned down many of the old historic landmarks, including Jew Jake's saloon and store at Landusky.

12.

The Circle C Cowhands

THE NORTHERN MONTANA ROUNDUP ASSOCIATION, well established in 1896, created better understanding and closer unity among the big outfits and the smaller ranchers in that section of the cow country. Boundary lines between the big outfits were drawn along nature's barriers that had been there since time began. There was the Missouri River to the south, the Milk River to the north, the Bear Paw Mountains and the Little Rockies to the west, and the Larb Hills and the Dakota boundary to the east. North of Milk River was the Canadian border.

The association set dates for the calf roundups in the spring and the beef roundups in the fall. Reps were sent out from all the big outfits to work with each wagon. The reps were top cowhands, and each one traveled with his own string of ten horses. For example, there were ten or twelve reps working with the Circle C wagon. They came from all directions—from south of the Missouri, from the Shonkin at Fort Benton, from the Bear Paw Pool, from the Milner Square and the Circle Diamond, from the Bar N Bar, from Sun River near Great Falls, from Flowerree's F outfit on Sun River. They came from the DHS in Judith Basin and from Big Sandy and the Marias Pool, and at least one rep came from the Canadian border. They represented the territory of more than a hundred-mile radius of the ranch.

Jim Adams on Sun River left his string of cow horses in the Staple

The Circle C Cowhands

brand at the Circle C Ranch the year around, and John Green from Fort Benton left his string of JHG horses. In return the Circle C left rep strings at their ranches. Since Jim Adams and John Green of the Green Cattle Company were both related by marriage to Robert Coburn, it was a sort of family deal.

When the outfit left the home ranch on both the spring and fall roundups, the reps almost equalled the number of Circle C cowhands. On each roundup of the Circle C range, as the wagon moved on its rounds, seldom a day passed without one of the small ranch owners showing up at camp with his bedroll and a couple of horses in his short string. He would work a day or two with the wagon or as long as the roundup was working in the vicinity of his ranch.

Horace Brewster was the Circle C foreman and wagon boss, and no better an all-round cowhand and wagon boss ever forked a cow horse or led his men on early morning circle. The following lists some of the regular Circle C cowhands:

Frank Howe	Tom Ball
Wash Lampkin	Jim Brown
Scott Miller	Rufus Warrior
Harry Green	Art Mayberry
Joe Contway	Tom Mayberry
Tex Alford	Charlie Green
Fred and Lew Roberts	Walter Green
Pete and Beulah Davenport	Harry Asher
Charlie Summers	George Rock
Ike Neibauer	George Chase
Pryor Smith	Joe Holt
Bill Jacobs	Clay Hill
Pete Walters	Slim Fletcher
Charlie Stuart	George McNeill
Con Price	Bob Atkinson
Walt Sizer	Jim Loughlin
Charlie Brewster	Danny Thompson
Jack Davis	Kid Curry
Charlie Leep	Loney Curry
Coonie Granath	Johnny Curry
George Hall	Jim Thornhill

Ott Cassidy	Bob Smith
Al Shaw	Johnny Stevens
Puck Powell	Frank Stevens
Ed Powell	Tim Maloney
Tom McDonald	Aleck Black
Letch Lemmon	Harry Isom
Doc Corrigan	Tom Gordon
Ringbone Sam Frazier	Jake Myers
Charlie (Dude) Parks	Joe Myers
Riley Brooks	Joe Legg
Everett (Cotton) Thompson	Rawhide Dan
Pete Ferguson	Frank Hutchins
Roy Long Knife	Jeb Prouty

All of them were top-hand, all-round cowpunchers, capable of running a roundup outfit or even a big spread. But for the most part they didn't want the responsibility or lacked the leadership it takes to handle men. There was a hungry tune that expressed their feelings:

I punched cows for a long, long time,
And I ain't run a wagon yet!

And the ribald verses gave several reasons why.

For the most part the cowhands were honest, hard-working men who managed to keep out of serious trouble—the sort of men who could be depended upon to stay in an isolated winter line camp. They were level-headed cowhands who knew how to get along when they were repping with some outfit—easy to work with but at the same time able to take their own part and stand up for the outfit they worked for if there was an argument over a mistaken brand.

Usually the man who was ramrodding the roundup or one of his top hands did all the cutting and roping. If some rep was an expert heeler, he got the job. The one-eyed Charlie Stuart, who wore a black patch over his blind eye, was one of the best heelers I ever saw, and he rode top rope horses. He and his horse knew how to slip into the herd like a carving knife into butter and ease the cow and calf to the edge of the herd. Then dipping his loop with a twist

Top: Cowhands at the Circle C corrals

Bottom: Letch Lemon, Circle C cowhand, wearing angora chaps and typical cowpuncher garb.

Courtesy of Mrs. Ethel Seaford, Zortman, Montana

of the wrist, without a swing of the noose, he jerked the slack and took his dallies without a lost motion. He seldom missed.

Any old-time cowpuncher worthy of the name knew every brand and earmark listed in the Montana brand book, as well as many out-of-state brands from Wyoming, Colorado, and Texas.

In those days a man could tell which part of the cow country a cowpuncher came from by his clothing—his hat, boots, and spurs—and his outfit—his saddle, bridle, bit, and ketch rope.

The Montana and Northwest cowpuncher wore a narrow-brimmed, low-crowned Stetson hat creased in four separate dents, *never* with a leather or braided horsehair hatband like you see today. His small tally book and stub pencil were kept in his upper vest pocket. He carried his sack of Bull Durham and white rice cigarette papers in his lower vest pocket, because more often than not the shirts he wore had no pockets. In the winter he wore what were called California pants, which were made of heavy wool in a large, subdued plaid pattern and had a buckskin foxing in the seat and down the inside of the legs which was Indian tanned and sewed into the pants by some Indian woman. The buckskin and sewing cost four bits at the nearest Indian camp.

The old-time cowpuncher wore a large silk handkerchief loosely knotted around his neck. It was usually black which would not show dirt. This silk neckerchief was mainly ornamental, but it became useful for the boys who brought up the drags of the strung-out trail herds on the long drives to the north. They could pull it up across their noses and mouths to keep from breathing dust. It was also handy for road agents who held up the stages. But, as I said, the neckerchiefs were worn mostly for style, like the fresh rattlesnake skins that were used to decorate the saddle cantles and the long tapaderos that went out of style during my generation. As Frank Howe once said, "Them long taps was hell for looks but a damned awkward drag when you bucked four-foot snowdrifts."

The Montana cowpuncher wore angora wool chaps that on a cold winter day kept a man's legs warm. The chaps came in snow white, black, burnt orange, and red. They were cumbersome and worse than useless in Arizona where the sharp barbs of cat's-claw

The Circle C Cowhands

and mesquite and cholla cactus snagged the long wool. The angora chaps belonged to Montana and the Northwest plains country, the leather chaps to the Southwest.

The old-time cowhand wore suspenders called galluses to hold up pants and Levis, instead of the belts with fancy silver buckles like the present-day cowboy wears. The galluses ranged from heavy-duty, wide-elastic, red suspenders worn by firemen to the fancy silk-embroidered galluses the gamblers and bartenders wore with ladies' red garters for sleeve bands. Some of the cowhands wore leather galluses or shoulder braces.

For quite a number of years some of the early-day cowpunchers wore leather cuffs made from saddle leather with a glove snap at the wrist. The average length of the cuff was about four inches. Some were made of plain leather, some carved. They were mainly ornamental although they protected the shirt cuffs and a man's wrists from winter cold. Winter and summer the cowpunchers wore buckskin gloves. In winter they were usually the fur-lined gauntlet style. Also in winter the cowpunchers wore fleece-lined overshoes made to fit over their high-heeled boots.

The early-day cowpuncher wore a filled cartridge belt that carried his holstered Colt .45 six-shooter. The cartridge belt was slanted and the holster tied down by a whang leather string around the thigh. But in my time, which was the generation of the pioneer sons, the wearing of cartridge belts and holstered guns ceased. The cowhand usually owned a single-action Colt six-shooter, but he wore it tucked inside the waistband of his pants, the flange of the cylinder swung out to keep the gun from sliding down the pants' leg. The heavy six-shooter carried in this manner put a callous on the hipbone of the gun toter.

The popular boot among the Montana cowhands was made to order at Olathe, Kansas, by the J. C. Hyer Boot Company, now known as Hyer and Sons. The work boot was made of cowhide, and the dress boot had an alligator leather foot and a calfskin, stitched, stovepipe top. The pants were worn outside the boot tops. Every ranch bunkhouse and saddle shop in town had a Hyer boot catalog with a stack of order blanks. The cowhand put his sock foot on a piece of brown wrapping paper while somebody penciled the outline and measured the instep with a tape that was kept handy. The alligator boots were not guaranteed for wear and tear, but the work boot was custom-made to take plenty of abuse.

There was also a spur-and-bit catalog and a saddle catalog in every bunkhouse and saddle shop in town. Saddles were ordered from the Garcia Saddle Company at Elko, Nevada, and the Visalia Saddle Company at Visalia, California. Spurs and bits could be purchased from Al Fustano at Miles City, who carried a good supply, or ordered from Garcia and Visalia. Most of the spurs listed in the catalogs had curved shanks, and made-to-order spurs would have a silver quarter attached to the inside of each spur rowel next to the shank. The dip of the curved shank varied according to the purchaser's liking.

The style of bridle bits varied from the short-shanked grazing bit to the more ornate spade bit. A popular style of bit was the U.S. Cavalry, long-shanked, curved bit with silver-mounted conchos. The lighter weight bit used by the Northwest Mounted Police was also popular. It had a smaller silver concho which could be engraved with a brand or initials.

As a rule, the Montana cowpuncher rode a single-cinch, three-quarter-rigged saddle, a compromise between the center-fire and the front-ring, double-rigged saddle that had a flank cinch. Forty or fifty dollars would buy the best full-stamped saddle, and five or ten dollars more would pay for a pair of long-pointed tapaderos that varied anywhere from twelve to twenty-four inches in length and had sheepskin lining over the stirrups for winter use. The long taps were worn for style in those days. When a cowpuncher wanted to show off in town and buck his horse down the street, he would let out a big holler, and instead of spurring his horse in both shoulders, he would swing the long taps forward and back along the horse's shoulders and neck, and the bucking show would be on.

Early-day saddles had a high narrow fork (called a slick-fork) that sloped back at an easy low angle to the high cantle. For the most part, that was the only form of saddletree. Handmade and rawhide-covered, they were built to last. The hardwood saddle

Roping a Cow,
For the history of thi

Charles M. Russell
painting, see Appendix D.

horns were leather covered, and when a cowhand head-roped a big steer and took his dally wraps around the horn, he played the big ox like a trout on a fishline, wearing the wooden horn down to a nubbin the size of a hickory walking cane. It required a good roper and a trained rope horse to get the job done.

The old-time cowhand was considered well dressed when he wore the best grade of hat John B. Stetson manufactured and a pair of custom-made boots, regardless of the rest of his apparel. There were a few range dudes who took pride in wearing red flannel shirts and California pants. Those so-called range dudes, who set the fashion for the cowpuncher, were apt to be the top hands in any man's cow country. In those days "dude" did not have the connotation it has today.

The average cowpuncher owned two good horses, one to ride and one to pack his roundup bed. His forty-years gatherings were kept in a canvas bean sack (called a war sack) which he used for a pillow when he bedded down at night. His bedroll consisted of a pair of Hudson's Bay blankets or quilted sugans and a heavy canvas bed tarp.

The old-time cowpuncher was a drifter by nature, and was free to roam where he chose, riding the grub line in the summer between the spring and fall roundups, hiring out during roundups, and after the beef roundup in the fall finding a winter job at some line camp. If he was lucky, he hired out as a bartender and lived the life of Riley in some cow town.

It was the dream of the run-of-the-mill cowpuncher to own a saloon someday and retire for life, but the ones who made that dream come true were few and far between. Puck Powell and Ed Powell (not related as far as I know of), and Long Henry Plott all owned saloons at Malta. Loney Curry and his cousin, Bob Lee, who went by the name of Bob Curry, ran a saloon at Harlem.

When Frank Howe fell heir to a saloon at the cow town of Dodson, Montana, it was one for the book. Just exactly how, why, and when the big, good-natured cowpuncher, who had been a straw boss for Horace Brewster for a good many years at the Circle C, fell heir to the Bucket of Blood Saloon is a mystery. Howe, who was a natural teller of tall tales, with a flair for practical jokes, was known as the most entertaining liar in those parts, so any story he told about how he became the owner of the saloon could hardly be believed. He was a ladies' man, and his popularity with the honky-tonk girls was indicated by the many fancy, embroidered sofa pillows, fragrant with sachet bags that saturated the blankets of his roundup bed. Howe's perfumed roundup bed could be smelled a mile away, and, according to Charlie Stuart, it guided many a man back to camp on a stormy night.

There were conflicting rumors concerning Frank Howe's heritage of the Bucket of Blood Saloon. One version was that a madam known as Big Casino bought the saloon and gave it to Howe for sentimental reasons. Another story was that Howe was tending bar at the saloon when the owner died of delirium tremens. He willed the saloon to Howe who had nursed him through former bouts of the d.t.'s. Still another yarn was that Frank Howe had won the saloon in an all-night poker game. The most appealing story was that an outlaw had owned the saloon and Howe had tipped him off that a Pinkerton detective, posing as an outlaw, was about to arrest him and claim the bounty money on his hide. Howe, who was tending bar that night, had put knockout drops in the bounty hunter's whisky. While the detective was knocked out by the Micky Finn, Howe gave the outlaw his private horse to make his getaway in exchange for a bill of sale to the saloon. There were other more or less plausible yarns concerning the saloon heritage, all of them circulated by the new owner as he played genial host as bartender and bought drinks for the house.

The big cowpuncher was in his glory. At long last his dream of owning a saloon had come to pass. In no time at all, the Bucket of Blood was the most popular saloon in town. Every cowpuncher Howe had ever known (and that took in a vast territory) had unlimited credit. When a customer bought a round of drinks, Howe set them up in return.

There had been a large supply of barreled whisky and draught beer on hand when Howe took over. In less than a month the

The Circle C Cowhands

Bucket of Blood had gone dry as the Sahara Desert and the cash register was empty. The I.O.U. ledger was filled with the names of every cowpuncher Howe had ever known, along with the names of strangers. But Howe, in a gesture typical of him, tossed the ledger into the potbellied stove and set fire to it.

When the fall beef roundup was due to start, Howe showed up at the Circle C Ranch, a satisfied grin on his homely, battered face. It had been fun while it lasted, he said. He'd had the time of his life and had no regrets, but now it felt good to get the town stink out of his system.

There was another incident that gained Frank Howe a certain measure of immortality. In 1916, Charles M. Russell painted a picture of three cowpunchers roping a bear in the Larb Hills of Montana. The painting was titled *Loops and Swift Horses are Surer than Lead*. The cowpuncher in the foreground on the bald-faced roan horse, head-roping the bear, was none other than Frank Howe. The cowpuncher on the white horse, who had roped the bear by the hind legs, was Joe Reynolds, part owner of the Long X outfit. The third rider on the spooked horse was the Shufeldt Kid who rode the rough string for the Bear Paw Pool. The bear roping had taken place during the fall roundup a year before the painting was done.

Wallace Coburn had told the bear-roping story to Charlie Russell, and the artist, who was a stickler for correct detail, took a pack trip with Wallace into the Larb Hills. He took Frank Howe along to get the factual background for the painting. The scene of the bear roping was near the place where a few years earlier Wallace Coburn had killed a silvertip grizzly she-bear and her three nearly grown cubs without moving from where he was crouched behind a dead tree. That was some sort of record for bear hunting.

Through Russell's painting, Frank Howe attained his place in the sun. Even in Arizona, where he later went to ramrod the outfit Will and Bob Coburn owned near Globe, Howe was known as the cowhand who roped the bear. The glass showcase that held an old gun collection at Charlie Collins' Saddle Shop at Globe, Arizona, displayed a somewhat pocket-worn, fly-specked card with the inscription:

BUCKET OF BLOOD SALOON, DODSON, MONTANA. FRANK HOWE—THE MAN WHO ROPED THE BEAR, OWNER AND PROPRIETOR. HAVE ONE ON THE HOUSE!

Never a man inclined to hide his candlelight under his bed tarp, this raconteur of the Montana cow country sang his own saga and fashioned his own legend from the warp and weave of the tall tales told at roundup campfires and in ranch bunkhouses on a long winter evening.

Some big Texas outfits had trailed herds of cattle into Montana and located there. Among them were the Matadors, the Long S belonging to the Slaughter outfit, the Reynolds Long X located in the Larb Hills and the badlands north of the Missouri. The XIT, the biggest of the Texas spreads, claimed a lot of territory around Fallon and Custer counties on the Yellowstone. The 777 outfit belonging to Gudgell and Boice was located on the Little Missouri. There were other Texas outfits, such as the IXL and the Turkey Track.

The Texans were born and raised in the cattle industry, and the owners, trail bosses, and cowhands who trailed the cattle from the Lone Star State had the cow savvy it took to make a hand in any man's cow country. Some of the cowhands who came up the long trail from No Man's Land, the Panhandle, the Red and Canadian rivers, and the town of Tascosa were tough gun hands and well able to take their own part. They were a different breed of cowhand for the most part, and most of them spoke border Mexican like natives.

They wore a higher-crowned, wider-brimmed hat, the ten gallon style with no dents in the high crown except perhaps a crease down the middle. Some of them tucked their pants legs into their boot tops and wore either long-shanked spurs or Mexican spurs with large rowels that chimed like tinkling bells. Those spurs were called

The Circle C Cowhands

Cross L spurs for some reason. Perhaps they had been named by a cowpuncher who worked for the Cross L outfit.

The Texas cowhands rode a double-rigged saddle, and those who came from rough brush country tied their ropes by a slipknot in the end of their ketch ropes, which were shorter than the ropes used by Montana cowhands. The Texans wore leather chaps—shotgun, pull-on chaps with leather fringe or batwing chaps made of stiff steer hide—and a larger-sized silk handkerchief around their throats.

The big Texas trail outfits had their own remudas of cow horses. As a rule, the horses were a smaller breed that traced back to the Spanish horses imported from Spain into Mexico. The Texas horse was apt to be stout, deep chested, close coupled, and broad rumped with heavy, muscled hindquarters. This quarter-horse type was bred for short bursts of speed and the endurance necessary for long distances.

On the other hand, the Montana and Northwest cowpunchers rode a larger-boned, longer-legged horse, stout enough to buck the winter snowdrifts. The horse breeders who experimented with this type of cow horse favored the Morgan breed or a cross between a Percheron stallion and a Hambletonian mare of the trotting type. Or they bred a Morgan stud to a Morgan mare or a Hambletonian mare or even an Indian mare of the Nez Percé Appaloosa type.

A remuda of two or three hundred good cow horses would have almost any type saddle horse with a strain of Thoroughbred or a trace of Steel Dust. The crossbreeding tended to produce good "circle" horses to carry a man twenty-five or thirty miles and come in fresh and stout after driving cattle to the holdup ground.

Some of the big outfits raised their own horses, while other outfits bought their two-year-old colts from various horse breeders.

Every outfit had its own bronc riders to halter break, saddle break, and train the horses for all-round cow work. The schooling required days and weeks to turn out a good rope horse—to hobble break the horse and graze it on a picket rope and the horse to stand ground-tied when a rider got off and dropped the bridle reins.

The bronc riders rode their string of broncs, called the "rough string," on the roundup to complete the horses' training in actual cow work. When a rider turned his string of broncs over to the outfit, they were usually "green broke," and it was up to the cowpunchers to complete the training until they were all-round cow horses. As a result, each cowhand had one or two "green broke" horses in his string of ten mounts. Most of the broncs would have a hump in their backs on a frosty morning, and it was a case of ride or get thrown.

When some hot-headed cowpuncher fought a horse, quirted it over the head, or abused it in any way, that man got fired, regardless. Some outfits barred the use of a spade bit or a bit that had a ring for a curb strap. Unless a man knew how to use a spade bit, which could tear a horse's mouth, he had better sell his saddle and travel on foot.

The old-time bronc rider working for a big outfit started with a hackamore, then used a snaffle bit, and then a grazing bit with curb enough to control the horse. Some favored a "cricket" bit, a hollow copper cylinder inside the curb, which made a metallic sound when the horse tongued the bit. Some horse handlers argued that the sound of the cricket tended to take the bronc's mind off his troubles.

The term "bronc riding" was used in a broad sense that included everything from halter breaking through turning the horse over to the cowpuncher. While the qualifications of a bronc rider were few, they were vitally important. First, the bronc rider could have absolutely no fear of the unbroken horse he was handling. Second, he had to have unlimited patience and an even temper. Third, he had to have the necessary love for horseflesh and a thorough understanding of horses—knowledge based on kindness. Gentle handling was needed for a scared two-year-old range colt that had never known the touch of a man's hand except the rough manhandling when it was branded and gelded. That rough treatment frightened the colt, and it was up to the handler to overcome the colt's fear of man. The job required all the patience a man ever had and tested his temper at times.

The man who was afraid of his horses was the man most likely to mistreat his mount. That type of bronc rider would tie a green colt he was halter breaking to a corral post or snubbing post, and when the scared bronc reared back and fought the halter rope, which was natural, the man would stand just far enough away to keep from getting kicked. With a bullwhip or a length of stay chain, he would work the bronc over until it was exhausted and stood dripping sweat, its hindquarters ridged with whip and chain welts. When the colt was too weak to fight against total odds, its spirit broken, the brave hombre would ease into the saddle and quirt and spur the horse around. That type of bronc rider, whose fear was poisoned with hatred, was in the slim minority and never held a job for any length of time.

There was another type of horse breaking called "whip breaking," in which a long lead rope and buggy whip was used. Since I have never seen this method used, I can't judge it one way or the other. I have never heard of whip breaking being used by any big cow outfit or by any old-time bronc handler.

Good bronc handlers were a breed of men set apart from the average cowpuncher. Since they were few and far between, they were sought after by the big outfits. As a rule, the bronc rider was paid ten dollars a head, and he usually handled six or eight head at a time. Sometimes he worked alone, but usually he had a cowpuncher to help him around the corrals. When he rode a bronc outside the corral, the helper "hazed" for him. If the bronc cold-jawed and stampeded or bucked towards a cut bank or barbwire fence, the hazer spurred alongside and acted as pickup man.

There was the constant danger of a bronc rider getting bucked off or hanging a foot in a stirrup and being dragged to death. A good hazer or pickup man had to know his job, or he was apt to be underfoot or left behind when most needed. He had to be mounted on a fast horse that had plenty of savvy.

Charlie Brewster (brother of Horace Brewster) who rode the rough string for the Circle C was as good a rider and all-round handler of green broncs as any other in Montana. Despite the fact that Charlie had picked up a few busted bones during his bronc-riding career and had been thrown many times and kicked and tromped on, he had absolutely no fear of any rank-spoiled bucking horse that ever wore hair.

Charlie Brewster was a natural, as the cow country saying went. He had a way with horses and liked to handle green broncs. It was a pleasure to watch him, and he usually had an audience of rail birds when he was working. Charlie rode with a hackamore, a ten- or twelve-foot length of braided rawhide bozal. He would spend a long time gentling a colt before he saddled it. He would rub behind the nervous ears and jaws, along the neck and withers, down the back and along the ribs and under the belly, working his way slowly towards the rump and hindquarters. He would talk to the colt in a quiet voice and chuckle to himself as the bronc lashed out in a cow kick. Holding the horsehair rope in his left hand, he would cuss good-naturedly at the near miss of the unshod flinty hoof, calling the colt a wall-eyed son of a stud and telling it that its mammy was gentle and other nonsense. He would rub the colt down with a piece of gunnysack, and then, holding onto the saddle horn, he would ease the saddle onto the colt's quivering, sweat-wet back. Sometimes the bronc pitched the uncinched saddle off into the corral dust half-a-dozen times before the cinch was slowly tightened. By that time both bronc and man were sweaty and dust powdered. Charlie would let go of the rope and hunker down with his back to a corral post and roll and smoke a cigarette, while he passed a few words of comment about the colt to any rail birds on the fence.

"That 'un," Charlie Brewster would pass judgment, "shore gave up easy. Even if he bogged his head, he couldn't pitch a lick. A child could set 'im."

Or, if the bronc stood with his back humped and had to be sacked from his balky tracks, Charlie would say, "That 'un will bear watchin'. Been savin' his strength like he knew what was comin'. Like as not he'll sull when I ease into the saddle. He's the kind that's apt to rear up and fall over backwards. When he shows too much white when he walls his eye, that's the danger signal."

Another bronc might sink his head and pitch, then stop stiff-legged and whistle through flared nostrils. "That young feller thinks he's a plumb warthog," Charlie would comment. "He's fixin' to give a man a hard time. The way he sunfishes, he's showed me his hole card. I aim to call his bluff while he's still in the notion." Charlie would stub out his short cigarette butt and pull on his chaps.

> *Never was a bronc never got rode,*
> *Never was a rider never got throwed.*

Charlie would quote the time-worn axiom of the bronc rider and say, "Time me 'n you got this here argument settled, young feller, once and for all."

If there happened to be cowpunchers sitting on the corral fence, Charlie would try to get a bet—anything from a bottle of beer to a month's wages—that he could ride the bronc straight up and blow smoke from his cigarette on every jump.

Charlie Brewster claimed that every green bronc had some buck in him, and his idea was to get the buck out of the bronc's system at the start. He never tightened the slack in the horsehair rope, and although he used a quirt that he held by a wrist loop, he quirted over and under and always behind, where the tails of the quirt would hit the flanks or hind legs, never across the withers, neck, or head. The rowels of his spurs were blunt and left no raking spur marks that would draw blood on shoulders, ribs, and flanks.

Only on rare occasions was there some ornery outlaw bronc that Charley declared could never be "gentle broke." Those were broncs that, instead of pitching, reared up and fell over backwards or pitched limber-legged and turned somersaults. They were classed as spoiled outlaws, likely to kill or cripple a rider.

The Circle C had twenty or thirty outlaw broncs, called the Wild Bunch, turned loose on the range. All of them were big, stout, good-looking geldings by a horseman's standards. But those potential man killers were worse than useless, and now and then there were arguments regarding their disposal.

Some of the cowpunchers who had no love for soldiers in general and the cavalry in particular, because of several free-for-all fights with the troopers, suggested selling the spoiled man-killer horses to the remount station for fifty dollars a round. Frank Howe and Joe Contway volunteered to deliver the bunch at Fort Assiniboine, and it seemed like a good notion at the time.

At the beginning of the general argument, the wagon boss, Horace Brewster, had argued that every spoiled outlaw horse should be shot. But when he called for volunteers for a firing squad and even offered to pay five bucks a head for each horse killed, there were no takers. Old Tex Alford, who was repping for his own little spread at Rocky Point, declared he would rather shoot a man that needed killing than shoot a sound horse. The white-whiskered old cowhand voiced the thoughts of all the hands, and no more was said.

Walter Hill, son of the Empire Builder, settled all the arguments and saved the day by buying the whole bunch of renegade horses for the Wild West Show he was putting on at St. Paul. The cowhands sensed an odd mixture of sheer relief and nostalgia as the bunch of broncs were driven to the Malta stockyards, loaded into stockcars, and taken East by a special train. There was no sound more mournful than a locomotive whistle at sundown on a Montana prairie, and it was said there were moist eyes when Frank Howe, Charlie Brewster, and Joe Contway stood on the loading platform at the Malta stockyards and watched the horse train until it was out of sight.

Frank Howe said later that the three of them rode every bronc in the Wild Bunch into every saloon in Malta that night as they made the rounds on both sides of the tracks. As the three cowhands lined up at each bar, Joe Contway would say, "Well, hombres, let's have another horn." And once again they would ride Bogus Brown, the mouse-colored Lizard, the big black-and-white War Paint, Zebra Dun, Bald Hornet, the buckskin Yellow Jacket, Sidewinder, Scorpion, Black Maria, Bear Trap, Black Coffin, the flax-maned sorrel Gold Heels, Sittin' Bull, the strawberry roan Pitchfork, Pinwheel, Cyclone, Hurricane, Hell to Set, and Sundance. In the saloons, the three men toasted each bronc in turn.

"Well, hombres," Joe Contway would repeat, "time for another

The Circle C Cowhands

horn." They speculated with mournful misgivings what would be the fate of the professional bronc riders in Walter Hill's Wild West Show when they tackled the man-killer, renegade, outlaw broncs.

The three cronies traveled the rounds of the saloons in what Frank Howe called a "three-man bronc wake," and before they departed from each saloon, their tipsy, somewhat off-key voices joined in the mournful dirge:

Never was a bronc never got rode,
Never was a rider never got throwed.

Their spur straps let out to the "town hole," their spur rowels dragging on the plank sidewalks, they wended their way from Puck Powell's to Long Henry's, Ed Powell's, and Cavanaugh's, and wound up at Big Casino's dance hall in the red-light district on the north side of the tracks, where Piano Jim, the professor, tickled the ivories to the accompaniment of the mournful bronc-rider's dirge.

Some weeks later Frank Howe, who had gone to Chicago with a trainload of Circle C beef steers, returned with the latest news of the big city. The way Howe told it, the train trip East must have broken the spirit of every renegade bronc in the Circle C Wild Bunch. Either they got train sick or homesick or were frightened by the big crowds and the noise of the brass band in the circus tent. Or perhaps the oats they were fed to make them rollicky were too rich for their range blood. Anyway, the renegade broncs failed to live up to their billing as bucking horses, and they acted for all the world like gentle-broke ladies' horses. All of them refused to buck, and all they did was sull and balk or dog-trot or lope. A few of those man-killer outlaws even laid down. The arena boss had to substitute trained bucking horses from Buffalo Bill's Wild West Show, and the windup was that the disgusted arena boss had the broncs auctioned off to a bunch of hayseed farmers who had come to St. Paul to take in Hill's Wild West Show—one hell of a comedown for the rankest broncs in Montana to wind up pulling some sodbuster's plow.

"It was a horse on Walter Hill," Howe chuckled, "payin' a hundred bucks a round for them broncs that the Circle C outfit had a mind to crowbait. Anyhow, I reckon Jim Hill's Great Northern Railroad can stand the financial loss. By now them renegade outlaws will be collar marked. A hell of a note when you come to think it over, kinda sad to ponder about."

Frank Howe shook his head and put on a sad face as he said to Charlie Brewster and Joe Contway, "Us fellers got another cryin' jag comin' next time we get to Malta."

13.

The Pioneer Jerk-Line Freighters

DURING THE PIONEER DAYS of Montana Territory, the Pony Express rider carried the mail. By the same token, the bullwhacker, the mule skinner, and the jerk-line freighter carried supplies to the remote mining camps, cow towns, and scattered ranches of the early settlers and their families.

The Pony Express rider was a colorful, romantic, and legendary figure, clad in buckskins, armed with pistol and saddle gun, mounted on the fastest horse obtainable, his saddle bags bulging with precious letters from home. He spurred his horse to a run between frequent relay stations where a stock tender was ready with a fresh mount and rode full tilt through hostile Indian country, risking his life to carry the mail in record time to the pioneer women who eagerly awaited the precious letters from home. The Pony Express rider was their sole contact with loved ones back home. Therefore he gained heroic stature and became a part of the legend of the old West.

During that same era, when the soil of the wilderness of Montana Territory was blood spattered by the Indian wars, the jerk-line freighter, with his slow-moving, heavy-laden wagons of life-giving supplies, was enduring the same dangers, along with more gruelling hardships. Every inch of the way was fraught with the constant danger of attack by some marauding war party of hostile

Indians. Those laden freight wagons were the lifeline of the pioneer settlers who lived in remote places.

The bullwhacker, mule skinner, and jerk-line freighter were not dashing romantic figures with their bearded faces, mud-spattered clothes and clodhopper shoes, and grimy, calloused hands. But the freighter's unsung brand of downright courage and fortitude, in the opinion of many old-time pioneers, far surpassed that of the hard-riding, heroic Pony Express rider. Often somewhere along the trail of the freighter would be found the charred remnants of looted wagons (the oxen, mules, or horses stolen) and the mutilated and scalped body of a freighter who had fought an Indian attack against overwhelming odds.

The pioneer jerk-line freighter was a unique breed of mankind, tough as rawhide. He endured untold hardships, such as the winter blizzards, the merciless summer sun and winds that dried up water holes, and the rainy season that bogged down the laden wagons to the hubs. But to the freighter, who had unlimited patience, these hardships were all taken as part of a day's work. The sacrifice of life by these men during the Indian raids was a trait that became legendary.

The old Circle C Ranch was about forty miles by wagon road from the cow town of Malta on the Great Northern Railroad. Most of the road crossed rolling prairie country that was usually easy to travel by buggy, buckboard, stagecoach, and wagon. But there were times when the winter blizzards drifted the snow high in the coulees and slowed down travel between the ranch and Malta, Zortman, and Landusky.

The high piled snowdrifts, combined with temperatures of twenty to forty degrees below zero, were extremely hard on the jerk-line freighter and his outfit. He had to provide hay for the teams, chop ice from the frozen creeks for water, or shovel snow to uncover a harness on an early morning. Harnessing eighteen to twenty head of stock in forty-below weather was not easy when the freighter's hands, in spite of fleece-lined gloves, were numb with cold. In spite of high, four-buckle overshoes and wool socks, a man's feet

The Pioneer Jerk-Line Freighters

got cold. He had to suffer frozen fingers and toes and frostbitten cheeks and nose.

There were hame-strap buckles to fasten (the leather straps stiff from cold), bridles to put on, tugs to fasten to singletrees, and collars to adjust to felt pads to prevent collar sores on necks and shoulders. Wet snow balled up between an animal's cleated shoes and had to be pried out with a pocket-knife. Packed snow between wagon spokes had to be knocked out with an ax or short crowbar. Nose bags had to be filled with oats and the teams harnessed as they stood in their proper places, munching their grain.

During the rainy season the wide, hard-clay lane between the Phillips' sheep ranch and the Hog Ranch stage station at the south end of the road from Malta became one long stretch of sticky gumbo mud. The freight wagons would sink hub deep to the big wheels and hock deep to the stock. The best of the jerk-line freighters had to drop trail, uncouple the wagons, and haul one wagon out at a time through the gumbo lane onto the high ground at the Hog Ranch. There were times when part of the load had to be left behind for a second trip.

Even when hauling one wagon at a time, there were frequent stops. While the horses on slacked tugs got their wind, the freighters had to chop out the gumbo mud balls from the wagon spokes and clean mud from the hoofs of each animal. Such times taxed the patience of the freighter to the breaking point. It was hard, gruelling work, and the tedious delay in the freighter's schedule cost him money.

The cowpuncher riding the range welcomed the sight of a freight outfit, and he would ride five miles out of his way on a hot summer day for a quart bottle of beer. It was almost a sure bet that any freight outfit headed for the Little Rockies would have one wagon loaded with beer, and without exception, it would be free beer for the cowpuncher. To offer to pay would have been an insult.

On a cold winter day there would be a jug of whisky in the canvas-covered caboose that was the freighter's home on wheels. It was well known how he got his jug of good barrel whisky. Freighters were experts at tapping down one of the barrel hoops and boring a small gimlet hole in the hardwood. The whisky was drained off into a gallon jug through the stem of a corncob pipe or a hollow macaroni straw or a short length of rubber hose. Then a whittled boxwood plug was tamped into the gimlet hole and the iron hoop tapped back in place. If necessary, a small hole was bored in the top of the barrel to let the whisky flow faster. This hole was plugged and seared over by a hot iron.

Barrel tapping was indeed an art. The saloon keepers called it "freighter's shrinkage" and grinned it off as a joke on themselves, knowing full well that they would be more than repaid, because the freighter was a free spender when he got to town.

Some jerk-line freighters went in for fancy trimmings on their harnesses. Sleigh bells were attached to the polished, brass, hame knobs, and red, white, and blue ivory rings were fastened on the harness of the lead team.

Zortman, Montana

Courtesy of Dave Nichols, Malta, Montana

Top: Twelve-horse freight team, believed to belong to Frank Whitmore, leaving Malta about 1900–1906. Hank Sanford, teamster.

Courtesy of 50th Year Magazine, *Malta, Montana*

Bottom: Big Foot Sturman's jerk-line freight outfit at Zortman.

Courtesy of Dave Nichols, Malta, Montana

Pioneer Cattleman in Montana

Among the jerk-line freighters I knew were Joe Hartmann and his brother Tim.[1] Others were Jim Murray and his son-in-law Joe Malette (who inherited the freight outfit when Jim Murray died), Frank Whitmore, and Big Foot Sturman and his sons. Another was Big Bozark, the heavyweight prize fighter who worked as a swamper for Joe Malette and did his road work along the route from the Little Rockies to Malta. He would jogtrot and shadow-box ahead of the slow-moving freight wagons. There was also Hard Luck Smith with his unkempt, long, dirty yellow hair and graying, straw-colored beard and scabbed, dirt-crusted hands. He bragged he couldn't remember the last time he had taken a bath.

Hard Luck Smith, a teller of tall tales, often recalled the time a good-looking schoolmarm came to Landusky. He claimed that he decided to gussie up some and wore out two hoof rasps at the blacksmith shop trying to get the crusted grime off his big hands. Finally he gave up the job as hopeless.

Another of Hard Luck's windies concerned the time some freighter hauling freight from Malta to the store and saloon at Rocky Point lost his fourteen-horse team. The freighter was traveling along the old freight road that crossed Sun Prairie when a three-day rain caught him. He unhooked his teams, slipped off the harnesses, and turned the horses loose to graze. When the rain let up, the freighter started out to wrangle in his horses, but when he found them, they were dead. The sticky gumbo mud had caked onto their long tails until it reached the size of beer kegs, and when it dried, the mud was heavy as lead. The weight of the horses' tails stretched their hides tight as drumheads, so they couldn't close their eyelids, and, so Hard Luck claimed, the fourteen horses died from lack of sleep.

Jake Myers, the foreman at the Circle C Ranch, liked to tell about the time he rode into the camp of Hard Luck Smith and his swamper, Two Dog Moore, one early morning. The only water available was in a keg in the caboose. Hard Luck was preparing breakfast and invited Jake to eat.

[1] For an original account of jerk-line freighting by Joseph M. Hartmann, see Appendix B.

The Pioneer Jerk-Line Freighters

"Reckon we got enough water, Two Dog, to mix up a batch of flapjacks?" Hard Luck called out to his swamper.

"Reckon so," Two Dog Moore replied, "providin' you don't spill none."

While Hard Luck was in the caboose cooking breakfast on the little sheet-iron stove, Jake helped fit oat-filled nose bags on the horses while little Two Dog did the harnessing.

When Hard Luck hollered "come and git 'er," Jake filled his plate with a stack of brown flapjacks and covered the stack with corn syrup from the can. There was crisp bacon and strong black coffee, and Jake wolfed his grub like a hungry man.

"Them's shore good buckwheat flapjacks, Hard Luck," Jake complimented the freighter as he ate hungrily.

"Hell, them's not buckwheat cakes, Jake. We're dry camped. I used last night's dishwater to stir up the batter."

Jake said later that a man sure had to have a tin-lined stomach to eat a bait of grub at Hard Luck's freight camp.

There was a tale about Hard Luck Smith and his swamper, Two Dog Moore. Hard Luck was hauling dynamite when his wagons bogged down on Rolling M Flat on the Circle C range. He got up on top of the load and heaved case after case of dynamite and black cans of blasting powder off the wagons to lighten the load. One wheel had to be jacked up, and Hard Luck shoved a case of dynamite sticks under the jack and told Two Dog to "jack 'er up." Two Dog, scared to death of dynamite, quit the flats, leaving Hard Luck to do the job. When the freight outfit moved on, the swamper came back.

The first time I ever met Hard Luck Smith and his swamper was early one morning when I was headed for a winter line camp. I had hit the Landusky road a ways back for easy traveling through the snowdrifts. A beer bottle filled with kerosene for the lantern at the line camp was shoved in the pocket of my angora wool chaps.

Hard Luck was hauling cordwood to the powder plant below the Little Rockies where the Alder Gulch and Ruby Gulch gold mines were located. It was about twenty below, and he had the wagon gears on bobsled runners. The cordwood was piled high and Hard Luck was riding the bull board that stuck out on one side about six feet. His blacksnake whip was coiled around the neck of his mangy old coonskin coat.

As I rode alongside, Hard Luck spotted the neck of the bottle of colorless kerosene sticking partly out of my pocket. He grinned and spat out the chew of tobacco in his mouth.

"Alky!" his eyes lit up like blue flames. "Alky!" He reached out a long arm quickly and yanked the bottle from my chaps. Before I could open my mouth to warn him, he had pulled out the cork with his teeth and had the bottle tipped up. I watched the first gurgle as the stuff went down and saw his Adam's apple bob a a couple of times before I rode away at a high lope.

Hard Luck had one of the farthest-reaching voices I ever heard, and I could hear him a mile away as his voice echoed through the frosty air in the scrub pines. I dreaded the next meeting with the big, yellow-whiskered giant. I later heard the story he told around the saloons. He had drunk the quart before he took time to get the taste of the kerosene. For a week, he claimed, he didn't dare light a cigarette or stand near an open flame. He backed away from the stove till he nearly froze to death. He also said what he would do to the short-complected Circle C kid if he ever caught up with him.

I met him in Dutch John's saloon at Landusky, and before I could back out the door, he reached out and collared me. He poured enough drinks to last a lifetime into me and into himself and everybody who came into the saloon. It took half a month's pay to foot the bill. And it wasn't coal oil we drank.

In contrast to Hard Luck, the Hartmann boys, who also were freighters, were finicky as old maids about their caboose. They kept it neat and clean as an advertisement for soap. The Hartmanns were sober by habit, both on the road and in town, and they were hard workers who took excellent care of their horses and wagons. Because of their dependability, they were successful in their jerkline freight business. The same was true of Frank Whitmore who made the Jim Thornhill place his headquarters.

The Pioneer Jerk-Line Freighters

The last time I saw Hard Luck Smith's freight outfit was on the road to Malta at the crossing of the dam at Rolling M Flat. I was sitting my horse looking down on the green hay meadows and the old log buildings and pole corrals of the Circle C home ranch just before the outfit was sold. I twisted around in my saddle to watch the twenty-horse freight outfit coming around the bend in the road. I listened to the jingle of sleigh bells and the creak of the wagon wheels and watched until they were out of sight. It was the last jerk-line freight outfit I ever saw.

14.

The Hungry Plight of the Indians

SINCE ROBERT COBURN HAD BEEN ORPHANED at an early age, he was made a carpenter's apprentice, as was the custom in Canada at that time. Schooling became secondary; he had learned the three R's, which was the extent of his education. At the age of sixteen he ran away from his apprenticeship in Smith Falls, Ontario, and entered the United States in 1853. Somehow he made his way to Montana Territory in 1863. Coburn's limited knowledge of the carpenter trade, which he heartily disliked, was his only asset. A green young man in a strange land, he was forced to earn his own living by making rockers and sluice boxes for the placer miners, which left no time for further education.

As the years passed, Coburn saved the money he earned with pick, shovel, and gold pan. He had the foresight to invest it in land and cattle. Starting from scratch, he gradually built up a sizable cow outfit. Perhaps his love for horseflesh and his natural understanding of horses came from his Irish ancestry, but his knowledge of cattle was acquired the hard way, by experience, and from listening to cowmen who knew the cattle industry. Instead of raising a Texas longhorn breed of cattle that he described as "all horns and bushy tails," he experimented with a cross between the shorthorn and Hereford, to produce a hardier breed of beef cattle.

Robert Coburn was a long-time member of the Montana Stock-

The Hungry Plight of the Indians

growers Association and attended most of their meetings. At meetings of the association, when Granville Stuart and other cattlemen of higher education were appointed to represent the stockmen of Montana, he deeply felt the handicap of his lack of learning. He admired and envied men like Granville Stuart who had the ability to express themselves in forceful, correct language, verbal or written.

Coburn was a proud man, keenly aware of his lack of education, and he forced himself to be content to listen to the speeches of more learned men who championed the cause of the cowman whenever some bill favoring the stockgrowers association needed passing in the territorial legislature. Coburn's knowledge of the cattle industry and its many problems was equal and sometimes better than the spokesman for the association, and there must have been many times when his inability to express himself in spoken or written words was bitter medicine to swallow. Because of this, Coburn decided he would give his children the best education that his hard-earned money could provide. It must have been a bitter disappointment when none of his five sons took advantage of the college education offered them.

By the time the Coburn Cattle Company was formed in 1901, the outfit had grown in spite of occasional dry summers and severe winters, the high rates for shipping beef steers to the Chicago markets, and the low price of beef. Robert Coburn had bought out many small ranches that were used by the Circle C for winter line camps. With a permit to run a certain number of cattle on the Fort Belknap Reservation and with the free range all around from the Missouri River to the Milk River and the Larb Hills, there was good feed and plenty of water to graze the increased herds.

My father and half-brother Bob attended the meetings of the Montana Stockgrowers Association, while Will Coburn met with the Northern Montana Roundup Association. My other half-brother, Wallace, usually went along with our father to take notes at the meetings on discussions about the diseases of cattle and subsequent quarantine, the eternal strife with the railroads regarding the high price of shipping beef, the constant effort on the part of the cattlemen to boost the price of beef, and the war against cattle rustling.

The differences of opinion on some subjects brought up at the meetings caused a lot of jangling among the stockmen from different sections of Montana. There was a jealous sort of rivalry among the southern Montana outfits, the northern spreads, and the big Texas outfits that trailed in the longhorns carrying ticks. When it was discovered that the Texas tick fever not only destroyed cattle but also human beings, a quarantine barring the longhorns was established, and all cattle of all brands had to be dipped at the dipping vats.

There also were discussions over the problem of overstocking the range. In a few instances, trainloads of cattle were shipped in and turned loose to rustle on ranges that were already stocked to capacity. There was the problem of Indians of all tribes throughout Montana killing the cowman's beef steers. Even after the Indians had been rounded up by the soldiers and confined on reservations, the beef butchering continued.

The Indians had become wards of the United States government, and it was the Bureau of Indian Affairs' duty to feed and clothe the reservation Indians. That they did not live up to treaty terms is the understatement of the century. The Bureau at Washington was sadly and criminally out of touch with the grim facts of the starvation and lack of warm winter clothing, warm blankets, and other necessities of life on the reservations throughout Montana.

There were instances of skulduggery and larceny by some of the Indian agents and subagents. Their criminal negligence meant that beef, flour, and other food supplies were not issued to the starving Indians on ration issue day. The Indians, who had traveled miles through winter storms and high snowdrifts to the agency or subagency, were kept waiting, empty bellied and freezing, for hours and days, only to be sent back to their lodges empty handed. Little wonder they were bitter and hated the Great White Father who had failed miserably to keep the terms of the treaty signed by the generals who had conquered the Indians.

The Hungry Plight of the Indians

In a few instances the Indian agent pocketed the money allotted him by the Bureau of Indian Affairs at Washington for the purchase of beef steers and food supplies and blankets. Stockmen like Granville Stuart (who was married to an Indian woman), other spokesmen for the Montana Stockgrowers Association at the Helena legislature, and United States senators and representatives from Montana pleaded in vain for the Bureau of Indian Affairs to feed the reservation Indians and quoted facts and figures to back up their arguments.

The government buffalo hunters had slaughtered the buffalos, and the young Indians were fenced off from their hunting grounds. So the starving Indians who killed the white man's beef were not to blame. The burden of guilt lay with the Bureau of Indian Affairs and the Indian agents. The stockmen argued that it was time the Great White Father took the blindfold off, cleaned the wax out of his ears, and woke up to the grave situation that existed on the Indian reservations.

The disgraceful condition that prevailed on the Fort Belknap Reservation especially concerned the Circle C outfit and other outfits that grazed cattle in the vicinity of the reservation or had permits to run cattle on government land. Those cattlemen all suffered a loss of beef steers from Indians butchering their cattle. Scarcely a day passed without some old Indian coming to the ranch to beg for meat, and no Indian left without a chunk of beef for his hungry family.

Wallace Coburn, who championed the cause of the Assiniboins and Gros Ventres, had learned the Indian sign language and sign talk. He visited the old men in their lodges where he smoked and talked and listened, and more than a few times he rode to the subagency at Lodge Pole on ration issue day. He had seen the subagent turn the hungry Indians away empty handed. When Wallace had compiled sufficient evidence, the Circle C and other cow outfits with cattle on the reservation preferred charges against the agent and subagent. In behalf of the Indians, Wallace Coburn sent a personal letter to President Theodore Roosevelt, whom he had met at a meeting of the Montana stockgrowers where they had discussed big game hunting.

Top: Robert Coburn's house at the Circle C Ranch. Wallace's house at rear left.

Bottom: Bob Coburn with old Assiniboin chief Dog Rump and Dog Rump's wife, about 1900.

The Hungry Plight of the Indians

The letter got the desired results, more or less. The Indian agent at Fort Belknap dodged the issue by shifting the blame to the subagent, with the result that the luckless subagent served time in the federal penitentiary. As a result, the Bureau of Indian Affairs purchased a somewhat inadequate number of beef steers to be divided among the Indians and issued them a certain number of cows. Each Indian was given his individual number for a brand, and bulls to service the cows were scattered on the reservation land.

But there was a catch to the deal. No Indian was allowed to kill his own beef. When the steers were four years old, they were rounded up and shipped to the Chicago market. Every Indian on the Fort Belknap Reservation was supposed to receive the cash value for his steers sold at the Union Stockyards at prevailing prices, the cost of shipment deducted from the sale. There were a few years when the price of beef sold in Chicago barely covered the cost of shipment.

The hell of it was that the low market price did nothing in the

Ration day at Ft. Belknap Reservation.

Montana Historical Society

way of filling the empty bellies of the starving Indians. By that same token, it failed to solve the problem of the cattlemen whose cattle continued to be butchered by the Indians.

The hungry Indian tried to solve his own problem. During the summer months and rainy season, if a black cloud appeared in the sky and there was distant thunder and chain or even sheet lightning, in perhaps half-a-dozen scattered places within a radius of ten miles there would be a dead beef steer on the ground. The Indians would draw a wagon or two up to the carcass, and half-a-dozen women with skinning knives and an ax to quarter the beef would swarm around the dead steer. In less than thirty minutes the wagons and squaws would be gone and only a pile of sodden paunch grass and drying blood would remain on the ground. The Indians used everything but the paunch grass when butchering a beef—hoofs, horns, hide, and meat—everything but the beller, as the cowboys used to say.

As a result of the issue of cows and bulls to the Indians on the reservation, the killing of the Circle C steers slacked off considerably. The Indians were eating their own beef regardless of the unfair government ruling that forbade a hungry Indian and his starving family the right to butcher their own beef. The ruling that Indian-owned beef steers had to be shipped to the Chicago market offered the chance for larceny by the Indian agent and his political cronies who had him appointed. The money for the beef steers came to the Indian agent in the form of checks to hand over to the Indians. The Indians, who spoke or understood no white man's talk, signed their names with an X or thumb print on the back of the check. The Indian agent found that cheating them was easier than taking coins from the tin cup of a blind beggar.

The interference in Indian affairs by the Circle C and a few other cow outfits that ran cattle on the reservation incurred the wrath of a few squaw men who by marrying Indian women had obtained land on the Fort Belknap Reservation. William James Allen, the subagent at Lodge Pole, was a squaw man and a constant troublemaker who had the backing of a few other squaw men. At the drop of the hat he would write letters of complaint to the Bu-

The Hungry Plight of the Indians

reau of Indian Affairs at Washington and demand that all cattle belonging to the outside cattlemen be removed from the reservation and their permits to run cattle on government land be revoked.

But there were other squaw men who wanted no part of Allen's activities and refused to join his abortive campaign against the cattlemen, the Circle C outfit in particular. Those men could foresee trouble and preferred to remain neutral.

When the Indian Department refused to cancel the cattle permits of the cowmen, Allen and his followers attacked from another angle. They contested the Circle C's water rights to Beaver Creek, Little Warm and Big Warm creeks, and Rock Creek, whose headwater springs lay within the boundary of the Fort Belknap Reservation. Under the guise of protecting Indian rights to the creeks, the subagent filed lawsuits in the federal court at Helena and held secret meetings with the clique of squaw men at the Lodge Pole subagency.

Allen's request that the full-blood tribal chiefs meet with the squaw-man clan for a council was more like a command. The wily subagent had drawn up a petition for the tribal chiefs and medicine men to sign with their mark and thumb print. The petition was a formal protest against the Circle C for the water rights to the above-mentioned creeks.

Under the duress of thinly disguised threats and false promises, the old men put their marks on the petition that was to be used in court. It was significant that no white squaw-man's name was signed to the petition. The subagent assumed the role of representing the Indian Department in the protection of the water rights of the full-blood Indians.

The lawsuits against the Circle C outfit were long, drawn-out affairs. In the end it was proven in court that the DHS Cattle Company had located the land they sold to Robert Coburn prior to the government survey of the Fort Belknap Reservation and that the land included the first water rights to Beaver Creek and Little Warm and Big Warm creeks. The court agreed and granted the Circle C the first water rights.

Thus defeated in court, Allen went back to the Lodge Pole subagency to lick his wounds, and subsequently to call a secret meeting of his squaw-men cronies to hold a medicine talk. What transpired at that secret meeting was not known to any outsider. But disturbing and somewhat alarming rumors spread throughout the Fort Belknap Reservation, and were talked about in lowered voices in the Indian lodges. The subagent, seeking revenge against the Circle C, was stirring up trouble.

15.

The Allen Killing

DURING THE EARLY DAYS of the reservations, the Indians, who since the beginning of time had governed their own affairs through able chiefs and medicine men in tribal councils, had no voice in their own governing. The Bureau of Indian Affairs established a head agency and one or two subagencies for every reservation and appointed white men as agents. All rules and regulations governing the Indian wards of the United States government were sent from Washington to be carried out by the Indian agent and his staff of subagents, clerks, Indian police, and laborers.

The Fort Belknap Reservation was originally intended to hold only the Gros Ventres, a tribe of the Blackfoot Nation. For some reason never satisfactorily explained by the Indian Bureau, the Gros Ventres were forced to share the land with their lifelong bitter enemies, the Assiniboins, a Siouan tribe.

The agents and subagents had almost dictatorial power over the Indians. On days when government rations were issued, Indians of both tribes traveled from miles around to the subagency store at Lodge Pole, where the subagent and his clerks were on hand. Several beef steers in the ID brand would be butchered, and the meat and the rations of salt pork, flour, sugar, coffee, and tobacco were divided among the Indians. Therefore it behooved all Indians to "stand in good" (to use an Indian phrase) with the subagent. The same held true for the so-called squaw men (white men married to Indian women) and their half-blood children, especially the young men grown to maturity.

In 1902, Major W. R. Logan was Indian agent at the Fort Belknap Reservation. His subagent at Lodge Pole, William James Allen, was a former cavalry officer who had married a full-blood Indian woman. Now and then some soldier from Fort Assiniboin would marry an Indian woman after he was discharged from the army, and he and his wife would take up land on the reservation.

Allen, the subagent at Lodge Pole, gradually gained the unenviable status of troublemaker among cattlemen outside the Fort Belknap Reservation. He was a leader among his own special friends, a few of the former soldiers also married to Indian women. During the years prior to 1902, the bitter feeling between Allen and the cattlemen had increased until it threatened to break out in open violence.

One day in March, 1902, Charles Perry, a half-blood Assiniboin who was married to the sister of Allen's wife, rode to the Circle C Ranch to report an almost incredible story concerning the subagent at Lodge Pole. According to Perry, Allen had spread rumors that the Circle C outfit was stealing ID cattle, and he was attempting to persuade a band of Indians to kill the Coburn family and burn out the Circle C Ranch some night. Perry claimed that several Indians who were friendly with the Coburns could testify that what he said was true. Some of the old men had smoked with Robert Coburn and knew that no Indian was ever allowed to leave his ranch empty bellied. The tribal chiefs had met in council to discuss what Allen was trying to persuade them to do.

If the Indians did as Allen told them, they would be rewarded on ration issue days. If they refused, he was in a position to cut them off on ration days and could make trouble for them and their families. Since the old men were afraid of Allen, they had asked Perry to act as their spokesman at the Circle C.

Will and Wallace Coburn were the only members of the family at the ranch when Charles Perry told his grim story. When they asked him if he would face the subagent at a private hearing and accuse him to his face, Perry agreed on one condition—that the

The Allen Killing

meeting take place at the Circle C Ranch, not at the subagency at Lodge Pole where Allen could have him arrested and lock him in jail and lose the key. Everyone agreed to that.

Will and Wallace Coburn met Allen a few days later while riding the range. When they accused Allen of inciting the Indians to kill the Coburn family and burn down the Circle C Ranch, Allen hotly denied the accusation and agreed to a private hearing at the ranch to face his accuser. Allen was told that he was welcome to bring along any witnesses to back up his statement that he was innocent of Perry's accusations. Allen was angered by the supposed treachery of his brother-in-law and threatened to get even with him for the lies he was telling.

The meeting was arranged for March 28, a few days from then. The twenty-eighth was a typical chilly, windy, early spring day. The atmosphere became tense as the small group of horsebackers arrived. The full-blood Indians, the old men with red-powdered

Early-day photograph of Ft. Belknap Indian Reservation Agency.

Montana Historical Society

dust rubbed into their cheekbones and hair roots and with solemn wrinkled faces and a stoical but worried look in their opaque black eyes, formed a separate group as they dismounted and tied their horses to the top pole of the hay corral. The young full-bloods were dressed in cowpuncher clothes and formed their own group. The half-bloods and a small group of white men stayed in another group.

Will Coburn's wife, Vida, their invalid daughter, Alta, and Wallace's wife, Florence, and her first baby were in Robert Coburn's two-storied frame house. A couple of Circle C cowpunchers were posted inside to stand guard.

Will and Wallace Coburn, Pryor Smith, and a couple of Circle C cowpunchers were inside the log office with Charles Perry. Altogether there were about fifteen to twenty men in the gathering of full-blood Indians, half-bloods, and white men. Some of them were friends of Allen, and all, except the old men, were armed with six-shooters.

The log cabin office at the ranch faced south towards the cook house and bunkhouse. There were windows on the east wall, west wall, and south wall near the closed door. From where Charles Perry was sitting inside the office, he commanded a view from all three windows while he awaited the arrival of Allen.

Perry was keenly aware that he was in a tight spot. He was forced into a showdown in which he would have to accuse Allen to his face. Because Allen had threatened his life, Perry was armed with a six-shooter, a fancy pearl-handled Colt .45 that Allen had once given him.

Perry sighted Allen as he passed a window. When Allen knocked on the closed door, someone told him to come in. When he opened the door and stepped inside, Perry saw that his right hand was shoved out of sight under his coat. Perry pulled his six-shooter and fired two shots as fast as he could thumb back the hammer and squeeze the trigger. At that close range both .45 slugs hit a vital spot, and Allen lay dead on the pineboard floor just inside the open door. When his body was rolled over, a six-shooter was found concealed under his coat.

Someone summoned the Indian police who arrested Charles

The Allen Killing

Perry. They examined the six-shooters of Will and Wallace Coburn, Pryor Smith, and the other cowpunchers and found them all fully loaded. Perry's six-shooter had two empty shells in the chambers.

Perry's trial was held at the Fort Benton courthouse on July 23–27, 1902.[1] The defense attorneys were F. E. Stranahan and George H. Stanton, and the prosecuting attorney was Charles H. Pray, who was county attorney at the time. Testimony by witnesses stated that Allen was shot twice by Perry and that when his body was turned over, a gun was found under his coat. At the coroner's inquest Joseph Ganty had testified that Perry had accused Allen of inciting a party of Indians to burn the Circle C Ranch and kill the Coburn family and that the accusation had led to the killing.[2]

Charles Perry pleaded self-defense at his trial, because Allen was armed when he came to the office door. Since Allen had previously threatened to kill him on sight, Perry had decided not to take any chances, and he beat Allen to the draw. In view of the fact that at the coroner's inquest is was proven that Allen was armed, the jury found Perry guilty of manslaughter and the judge sentenced him to serve one year in the state penitentiary at Deer Lodge.

In my opinion, there was no bond of friendship between the sub-agent Allen and the agent at the Fort Belknap Reservation, Major Logan, who was a good friend of the Coburns. The Allen killing in no way changed the friendly relationship between the Fort Belknap agent and the Circle C. As far as I know, Major Logan was an honest man, above reproach in handling the affairs of the Assiniboins and Gros Ventres. The rank of major held by Logan was a true rank he attained in the cavalry before coming to Fort Belknap, whereas Allen's title of "major" was a sort of honorary rank bestowed by the Indian Department.

[1] Case #1632, The State of Montana vs. Charles Perry.
[2] At the coroner's inquest statements were made by Will (W. M.) Coburn, Wallace (W. D.) Coburn, Pryor Smith, William Ball, William Travis, Joseph Ganty, and Peter Wing. State witnesses at the trial were Pryor Smith, Julia Allen, Will Coburn, William Ball, Joe Ganty, and Cecilia Ball. Witnesses for the defense were John Luneberg, Peter Wing, George Bent as interpreter for Peter Wing, Mary Perry, William Travis, Pryor Smith, Grant McGahn, Will Coburn, Wallace Coburn, and James Matt sworn as interpreter for The Capture.

Pioneer Cattleman in Montana

At the time of "the Allen killing," as it was always called, I was only about thirteen years old, too young to pay much attention. Since the details of the shooting were never discussed when I was around, my knowledge of the event is vague. I left the Circle C Ranch in 1916, when the outfit was sold, and never returned. After a lapse of more than fifty years, original information is hard to come by. Most of those concerned at the time of the killing in 1902 are now dead, and those who are living don't want to talk about it.

In 1965 my good friend, E. E. (Boo) MacGilvra, interviewed Mrs. Julia (Allen) Hutchins, daughter of the long deceased William James Allen. She related Charles Perry's version of the killing, and Boo MacGilvra recorded the story, which she signed, for the Montana Historical Society.

Mrs. Julia Hutchins (nee Julia Allen) was born at Lodge Pole in the Little Rockies on Jan. 15, 1901. Her mother was Julia Ball, daughter of Bartholomew Ball and May Ball. Bart Ball was an enlisted man in the U.S. Cavalry and later went to a fort near Wolf Point where he worked as a blacksmith—was later transferred to Fort Belknap in the same capacity. Ball was a white man, Julia Ball was half Assiniboin Sioux and *her* mother claimed she was a sister of Sitting Bull—she died at Lodge Pole in 1932 at age 104.

Major William James Allen was an officer in the Cavalry at Fort Assiniboine near Havre. After he left the Army he went to Fort Belknap as Indian Agent. Here he served several years. Later a Major Logan came to Fort Belknap and the administration of Indian Affairs was split between Allen and Logan. Because Allen better knew these Assiniboines and Gros Ventres and knew the area better than Logan, he, Allen, took charge of the "outside" administration and Major Logan ran the offices at the Fort Belknap Agency.

Being a wide-open range country, both Indian and settler's cattle ran at large. The Circle C ranch on Beaver Creek adjoined the reservation.

As is usual in early range days there was considerable cattle-rustling, each side accusing the other of many depredations. Some Indians accused Bob and Bill Coburn of rustling their cattle. The two Coburns and Major Allen met on the range while riding for cattle and had a discussion relative to the charges. Nothing was settled at that meeting

The Allen Killing

and the Coburns requested Maj. Allen to come to their ranch in a day or two.

Among other workers at the Fort Belknap office was George Cochrane. He advised Maj. Allen not to go alone to the Coburn Ranch and, if he did go, to go armed. Cochrane offered to go with him but Maj. Allen turned him down and said he was going alone and unarmed, leaving his guns on the table with George Cochrane.

Maj. Allen arrived at the Coburn ranch on March 28, 1902. He knocked at the office door and someone shouted "Come in." As he opened the door he was shot and died instantly, never knowing what hit him.

When Maj. Allen failed to return to the Agency the Indian Police were sent to the Coburn Ranch to find him. They returned, bringing the Major's body.

When interrogated the Coburns told this story—that Charlie Perry had shot the Major. All three, Bob and Bill and Perry were asked to show their guns. Bill and Bob's were fully loaded, Perry's had been fired. Perry was taken to the Ft. Belknap Agency.

At the trial the crime was pinned on Charlie Perry and he was sentenced to Deer Lodge where he served seven years before being released, probably on parole. He immediately returned to the Fort Belknap Reservation. Charlie's wife was Josephine Ball, a full sister of Maj. Allen's wife. Charlie was part Assiniboine.

Charlie told Mrs. Allen, Julia's (Hutchins) mother this story—Major Allen was expected at the Coburn Ranch. The Coburns conspired with Charlie and gave him $700.00 to sit in the office awaiting Maj. Allen. When the Major was to knock on the door he was to be asked to come in and when the door was opened all three, Bob, Bill and Charlie were to open fire on him, later claiming self-defense. Apparently Charlie Perry was the only one who did. Charlie also said that Bob and Bill finally got him out of Deer Lodge but Charlie was considerably aggravated with Bill and Bob as he was led to believe they were to be in on the killing too, and he hated to be the goat for them.

Maj. Allen had owned a beautiful pearl handled six gun which Charlie Perry often admired. Finally Maj. Allen gave Charlie the gun and it was with this weapon that the Major was killed. Mind you Charlie Perry was Major Allen's brother-in-law.

Charlie's first wife died and he later married Mary Brown whose folks lived on Lodge Pole. They had several children, Tommy, Ella,

Dora and Jeanette. Jeanette married Rufus Warrior and still lives near Hays, as does Rufus.

Mrs. Allen, widow of Major Allen, died at Lodge Pole in 1951, age 88. After the Major's death she had married George Contway and Pat Contway was their son. Joe Contway, who came up the trail from Texas was a brother of George Contway.

After Charles Perry had served his time in prison, he returned to the Fort Belknap Reservation to take up residence near Lodge Pole. Apparently he mended his fences and made peace with the Allen clan. This seems to be the only explanation for the erroneous story that he told Allen's widow.

First of all, the meeting at the Circle C Ranch was arranged in order to discuss Perry's accusations against Allen, not any cattle-rustling charges against the Coburns. Also, Allen did not leave all his guns at the agency, for it was proven that he was armed when he entered the office. That is why the charge of murder against Perry was reduced to the lesser charge of manslaughter. Court records show that Perry was sentenced to one year of imprisonment, not seven. Therefore it is highly unlikely that the Coburns got him out of prison since he was serving such a short term.

Will and Bob Coburn did not pay Charles Perry seven hundred dollars or any amount to kill Allen, nor did they agree to open fire on him with Perry. If that had been true, it certainly would have been brought out during the trial. Besides, Bob Coburn wasn't even present at the killing. The Coburns who were in the office were Will and Wallace. Perhaps Perry told Allen's widow the story of a conspiracy in order to shift the guilt to the Coburns so that he could return to the good graces of the Allen clan.

The Allen killing did not resolve the question of Allen's guilt or innocence of Perry's charges that he was trying to incite a group of Indians to burning out the Circle C Ranch and killing the Coburn family. On the contrary, it tended to obliterate any chance of determining whether Perry's accusations were true. Two alarming incidents occurred several years later, but whether or not they were related to Allen's death remains unknown.

When new mines in the Little Rockies were opened in 1907,

The Allen Killing

grub-line riders became a problem at the ranch. Strangers, miners, and drifters of all kinds on the stage road from Malta to Zortman and Landusky acquired the bothersome habit of stopping for a noon meal or overnight stay at the ranch. Some of those drifting characters were petty thieves, bunkhouse thieves who prowled the tarp-covered beds and war sacks of the cowpunchers and ranch hands and stable thieves who stole bridles and saddle blankets from the harness room. Anything they could steal they took, and they dropped in at the mess hall at all hours of the day or night expecting to be fed.

This continued until Louis Goslin, owner of the stage line, made a deal with the Circle C to establish a roadhouse on the stage road about a mile from the home ranch and just outside the reservation gate, where the road to the Little Rockies crossed the Fort Belknap Reservation. The large log cabin, with kitchen and dining room, was to be erected on Circle C land adjoining the reservation. Later a log barn and corral would be added.

By fall the cabin was completed. It had a long mess table and benches, kitchen shelves, and cupboards. All was set to move in the kitchen range and the heating stove for the dining room. The kitchen utensils and crockery dishes and tableware were in crates inside the cabin. Louis Goslin was in the process of finding some responsible couple to run the roadhouse that would accommodate all travelers, when the first snowstorm of approaching winter came one late afternoon. Sometime during the night's storm the log cabin was set on fire.

Two five-gallon cans of kerosene, fuel for the lamps and lanterns, which had been left in the kitchen, were used by the arsonists to soak the inside logs and pine-board floors. When set on fire, the cabin had completely burned to the ground.

By daylight the brunt of the storm had passed, leaving a foot of snow on the ground. Later that morning when Will Coburn and Jake Myers, the Circle C ranch foreman, discovered the burned cabin, they rode around looking for signs in the snow and finally discovered the dim tracks of one horsebacker on the stage road leading to Zortman. They followed the horse tracks to town, and after hours of inquiry they located the horsebacker, a sheepherder who was sleeping off a drunk by that time. In his alcoholic daze he staunchly denied having set the fire, claiming the cabin was burning by the time he got there.

It was dark by the time Will Coburn and Jake Myers headed back to the ranch. The storm had spent itself, but the sky was still overcast and the moon and stars were hidden. The men were more than a half mile from the reservation gate when they saw a dull angry glow in the distance, and they knew that the fire was at the ranch. They rode their horses to the limit, and when they got to the ranch, Robert Coburn's two-storied frame house was a blazing inferno. Will's wife and daughter and toddling son were safe in the log mess cabin, as well as the nurse, Margaret Dunlap, and the young half-blood hired girl, Rose Gladeau. Al Taylor and Pete Olsen were the only men at the ranch.

Shortly after Will Coburn and Jake Myers arrived at the fire, a small group of full-blood Indians rode up and dismounted at Wallace Coburn's house which was next to the house on flame. In Wallace's house was a large Indian collection, gifts from the old ones, both Assiniboins and Gros Ventres. The valued collection occupied the entire attic space. Wallace Coburn had, during the years, gained the lifelong friendship of the Indians, and his door was never closed to them.

Without being told what to do, the Indians passed up buckets of snow to scatter on the shingled roof of Wallace's house. Whenever a wind-blown burning ember or live coal landed on the roof, it was quickly extinguished by the snow or beat out with wet gunnysacks. Through the heroic efforts of the Indians, Wallace's new house with its entire contents was saved from complete destruction by fire.

Robert Coburn's house, in which Will Coburn and his family were living at the time, was totally destroyed. Will's courageous wife once told me she expected to be shot down from ambush by the Allen tribe as she and the nurse carried the two children from the blazing inferno and she thanked God that their lives were spared.

The Allen Killing

Pete Olsen and Al Taylor, both unarmed and expecting to be shot down any second, helped the women and children out of the burning house and into the safety of the cook cabin, while the hired girl, Rose Gladeau, scared as she was, gave what assistance she could.

Later that day, when questioned by Will Coburn, Rose Gladeau finally recalled emptying a coal scuttle of hot ashes somewhere close to the woodshed. Whether or not the wind-blown hot ashes started the fire could not be determined. The rumor that one of the Allen relatives, a half-blood youth, had been keeping company with the Gladeau girl tended to add to the mystery of whether the fire was started by accident or whether it was pure arson.

Because of overwhelming evidence, there was no doubt that the newly completed roadhouse had been burned by arsonists. There were a few suspects but proof of anyone's guilt was never found. In view of the fact that the roadhouse fire was purposely set, it was hard to believe that the burning of Robert Coburn's house was the result of a careless accident. It was also highly doubtful that the two fires were a mere coincidence, considering the bitter feeling caused by the Allen killing.

During the dry summer and fall months when there was a constant threat of prairie fire, a wagon carrying filled water barrels, piled gunnysacks, and shovels was kept handy at the ranch. In the Montana cow country there was an unwritten law that whenever a distant cloud of smoke, indicating a fire, was sighted, every man dropped whatever he was doing and joined the fire fighters. Sheepmen, cattlemen, and Indians and half-bloods from the reservation put aside any ill feelings in order to fight the common enemy of fire.

Seldom a dry summer passed without a prairie fire being sighted. With dry brush in the coulees and long draws and sagebrush and greasewood on the bald prairie, an uncontrolled fire could destroy miles of grazing land on a windy day or night and take a heavy toll of livestock, cattle, sheep, and horses, and wild life, antelope herds, smaller animals, prairie chickens, sage hens, curlews, and song birds. A prairie fire left nothing but charred wasteland in its wake.

Cowpunchers automatically stubbed out the short butts of hand-rolled cigarettes. Roundup campfires were smothered under dirt. Sheepherders were doubly cautious. The Indians were taught from childhood about the devastation by fire. Yet, in spite of all the cautions, there were prairie fires. Any man who deliberately set a prairie or brush or forest fire was committing a felony and was subject to a heavy fine and a term in prison. And any man found guilty of setting a fire was no longer welcome in the cow country. Therefore whoever set fire to the roadhouse was wise to keep silent.

During the years following the Allen killing Charles Perry never, to my knowledge, showed up at the Circle C Ranch. In the fall of 1916, I repped with the ID (Indian Department) wagon on the beef roundup. George Contway, the ramrod, had married Allen's widow, although I didn't know it at the time. During the weeks I worked with the ID wagon, George Contway and I got to be good friends. If he nursed any resentment towards the Circle C, he never showed it. Nor did Bill Ball, who worked with the ID wagon that same fall. The Allen killing was never mentioned. Contway chose me as his partner to stand two hours guard every night riding around the bedded beef herd. I was the only white man in the outfit.

When the cattle were shipped to Chicago at the Harlem stockyards, I was broke for town money. George Contway loaned me twenty-five bucks, and I gave him an order on the Coburn Cattle Company for that amount. He and I painted the town of Harlem that night and make the rounds of the saloons along with the other half-bloods. The full bloods were on the "Injun list" at the saloons, so I bought them bottles of whisky and handed them over in the dark alley. If George Contway or Bill Ball had harbored any hard feelings against the Coburns, they could have had me arrested for giving the full bloods whisky, and I would have had to face a stretch in the federal penitentiary.

16.

A New Foreman for the Circle C

A FEW YEARS AFTER THE WAGNER TRAIN ROBBERY, about 1910, Horace Brewster, who had been foreman and wagon boss for the Circle C outfit for as long as I could remember, quit to take a job as chief packer and guide at Glacier National Park.

When he left, I felt that I had lost my one and only friend, because Horace Brewster had been like one of the family. He had been guide, philosopher, and friend in need when a growing boy on a cow ranch actually needed a friend. Brewster, more than my father or older half-brothers or any other man, had taught me whatever I knew about punching cows. More than that, I could confide any of my kid problems to Brewster, and he never once betrayed my confidential talks. So, during my boyhood days at the Circle C Ranch, Horace Brewster had become more than a friend. He was my side partner in all that the term implies and more. The day he said good-by I felt that no man would ever be able to take his place, and I have never had reason to change my mind about him in any way.

I now realize that my father must have felt the loss of his old friend far more that I did. For many long, hard years Horace Brewster had been his staunch and loyal friend. They had faced dangers and hardships together, especially during the Indian trouble. The day Brewster rode away from the ranch on his favorite roan cutting horse, Dixie, my father was left alone. He was fully aware that he had lost the only man he could trust to the end of the line. Proof of that vital loss was destined to come in future years.

From the time the Coburn Cattle Company was formed until the Circle C outfit was sold to the Matador Land and Cattle Company in 1916, my father stood alone with his back to the wall, while the outfit he had built up from his first herd of cows was taken away from him. But even if Horace Brewster had been there to stand back-to-back with him to face the enemy, it would have done little good.

The hardy breed of pioneer, who had braved the dangers of Indian attacks, battled cattle rustlers and horse thieves, and endured the hardships of winter blizzards and summer droughts was powerless against the invasion of the homesteaders who came to Montana by courtesy of Jim Hill's railroad. Even before the homesteader invasion, there were sheep outfits on all sides.

But there was still another far more insidious factor that Robert Coburn had to contend with, now that Horace Brewster was no longer protecting his interests. The more charitable label would be bad management and faulty decision on the part of his sons, although Robert Coburn used the harsher term of larceny to account for his personal cattle losses.

When the Coburn Cattle Company was formed in 1901, for reasons known only to Will and Bob Coburn, they jointly registered in partnership the Bar L brand in their names with the Montana Stockgrowers Association. Their cattle brand was a Bar L on the left ribs and on the left shoulder of the horses.

Wallace Coburn acquired the Four T brand that formerly belonged to Kid Curry. The Four T brand was used on the left ribs of the cattle and on the left shoulder of the horses.

Both the Bar L and the Four T brands were recorded in the brand book under individual ownership, while Robert Coburn retained the Circle C and Half Circle C brands as recorded in the Montana brand book. The Circle C brand was used on the left shoulders of horses, and the Half Circle C brand on the left ribs and left thighs of cattle.

A New Foreman for the Circle C

Then the Coburn Cattle Company bought a sizable herd of cattle in the Rafter T brand which was registered in the brand book as belonging to the company. Later when the Half Circle C brand and all cattle in that brand were sold to Oscar (Spud) Stevens at Lewistown, the Coburn Cattle Company used the Rafter T brand on all cattle in place of the Half Circle C.

Range gossip spread the ugly rumor that Will and Bob used their brand to increase their spring calf crop and that there were

Horace Brewster at Glacier National Park in 1925.

Jake Myers with his wife and daughter Cecil at Pauls Valley, Indian Territory, in the early 1900's.

Courtesy of William Armington, Malta, Montana

A New Foreman for the Circle C

too many dry cows wearing the Half Circle C brand. But it had always been my belief that Robert Coburn had given Will, Bob, and Wallace the Bar L and Four T brands along with a sizable bunch of cows.

There was a lot of wild speculation about who would take Horace Brewster's place as ranch foreman and wagon boss. A lot of top cowhands who had worked for the Circle C were capable of filling Brewster's boots. Among the top hands were Ike Neibaur (later a sheriff), Fred Roberts and his brother Lew, Frank Howe, Pryor Smith, Scott Miller, Puck Powell, Tom McDonald, Letch Lemmon, Charlie Summers, Pete and Beulah Davenport, Charlie Stuart, George Hall, Horace Brewster's brother Charlie, and others too numerous to mention here. They were all good cowhands who knew the country like a brand book. Most of them had at one time or another worked as straw boss or repped for the outfit.

But while Horace Brewster was still running the outfit, Robert Coburn had hired a cowpuncher named Jake Myers from Oklahoma. Jake Myers was a stranger in a strange land and unfamiliar with the Montana cow country. Coburn had always prided himself on being a good judge of men and horses, and he took a liking to the young, handsome, black-haired Oklahoma cowhand and liked the way he handled cattle and men. During the following years Coburn proved he was a hundred per cent right in his judgment of Jake Myers. So, when Horace Brewster left the ranch to take on his new job as guide at Glacier Park, Jake Myers was given the job as ranch foreman and wagon boss.

Jake had left his wife, Janie, and daughter, Cecil, in Oklahoma at his small ranch in what was once called the Cherokee Strip, and when he landed the job of ramrodding the Circle C, he sent for them. The fact that Jake was a married man with a young daughter had something to do with Coburn's decision. A married man who had settled down and had owned his own outfit was likely to be more stable and permanent than a single man without responsibilities. Again Coburn was right, because Jake Myers held his foreman's job until the outfit was sold.

Jake always referred to Robert Coburn as the "old gent," but he used the name with respect. "It was the old gent who hired me in the first place," Jake would say whenever occasion arose. "I shore intend to look after his interests." And he kept his word to the best of his ability. Moreover, he took upon himself the job of riding herd on me, at times a somewhat difficult chore. But there were a lot of times when I thought he worked overtime at it.

It was a hell of a challenge for a rank stranger to come into cow country he did not know and take over a ramrod's job running a big outfit and handling a crew of strange cowhands who had worked for the outfit for years and knew the country like the palm of their hands. But if it worried Jake Myers, he never let anyone know, and although he never traveled on his shape, he was always ready and willing to take his own part. He would give any man under his orders a chance for his taw as far as work went, and he was enough of a cowman to tell if any man was sloughing off.

I had worked on the roundups when Horace Brewster was running the wagon, and I figured I was earning my forty-a-month and holding up my end. I also knew I still had a lot to learn, and right from the start I knew my kid's place around the ranch and on the roundup. A kid did what he was told to do, and if it griped him, he told his troubles to his horse or to the sagebrush. He didn't talk back to the boss, no matter what. That cardinal rule held equally true for any cowpuncher. He took his orders from the wagon boss or quit.

If a cowpuncher put up an argument, he got fired. If he had a chip on his shoulder, the wagon boss had to knock it off and whip him or get whipped. Once a wagon boss let one of his cowhands or any rep working with his wagon whip him, that wagon boss had to draw his time and drift yonderly, because he had lost face for all time.

That's how matters stood for Jake Myers when he started out as wagon boss for the Circle C that fall on the beef roundup. I was too much of a kid wrapped up in my own affairs to think much about the wagon boss job Jake Myers was holding down. Years later I realized the many problems Jake had to contend with. Believe me, Jake had his hands full in more ways than one on his

Top: Mess wagon and bed wagon leaving the home ranch at the beginning of the fall beef roundup.

Bottom: Circle C roundup camp on Beaver Creek with Coburn Buttes in background.

first Montana roundup before the last trainload of beef steers were shipped.

First of all, Jake was handling a crew of top cowhands who were bound to feel jealous because he had been chosen wagon boss over them. Although Jake had been working for the Circle C for a year and had made friends with the other cowhands, there was bound to be a feeling of resentment among the old Circle C cowpunchers, and they were not about to make Jake's wagon boss job any easier or go out of the way to do him any favors.

Jake knew how they felt, and he wasn't about to ask any favors from any man in the outfit. There wasn't an hour of the day or night when Jake wasn't on guard. He kept his ear to the ground to catch any loose talk, and while most of the cowhands were friendly enough, there were a few Jake suspected of making medicine against him.

During the years I knew Jake Myers, I never saw him without a Colt .45 six-shooter shoved in the waistband of his Levis or town pants. He slept with his gun under his pillow, and while he never bragged or even hinted about his gun prowess, Jake let it be known he was ready to back any argument that started.

Jake never ate breakfast. Coffee and Bull Durham cigarettes were his breakfast at the ranch or on the roundup. Breakfast was about four in the morning, a couple of hours before daylight, at the end of last guard when the men started on day herd. While the rest of the cowhands were hunkered down, their tin plates piled with grub, Jake would walk around, as restless as a caged wolf, with a cup of black coffee in his hand and a cigarette in a corner of his mouth, whistling tunelessly through his teeth as he walked in and out of the mess tent. He kept an eye on the grub plates, and when most of the cowpunchers had nearly finished eating, Jake would walk into the mess tent and toss his tin cup into the empty dishpan. That was the signal that the day's work was about to begin.

Jake carried a big, open-faced, silver watch of the make used by railway conductors and locomotive engineers. It was the sort of watch he called a "turnip," a guaranteed and rugged timepiece. He carried it in the watch pocket of his Levis, on a whang leather

A New Foreman for the Circle C

string that was fastened in a metal suspender buttonhole. While the sun did not actually rise and set by Jake's silver turnip, that timepiece regulated the roundup outfit, and the cowhands stood night guard by the watch. Jake would hand it over to one of the cowhands going on first guard at eight o'clock, and the watch would be passed along to the men on second guard, then third guard, and was returned to Jake by the men on last guard when they rode into camp for breakfast.

Jake's watch was the only timepiece in camp, except for the battered alarm clock belonging to the roundup cook, who set the alarm for three-thirty on the dot. That gave him barely enough time to prepare breakfast by four. There were times when the alarm system went out of kilter, and the alarm would not stop ringing until the spring ran down. Sometimes the hard-used and abused clock got balky or tired out and stopped for no apparent reason. Then George L. Bickler, the roundup cook, laid it on its back in a lard pail filled with kerosene. When it had soaked a few hours in the coal-oil bath, it would start of its own accord. Bickler had named the clock "constipation." Each time it stopped, it was reset by Jake's turnip. Jake liked to brag about the accuracy of his watch, saying it was the same brand of watch by which Jim Hill ran his railroad trains. But even a railroad watch, when used as the only timepiece on a roundup and passed from hand to hand on guard watch, was likely to go astray. For instance, some cowpuncher with a leaky slicker on a cold rainy night during third guard time, could, with shivering hands, set the watch ahead in order to crawl into a warm bed in the bed tent half an hour ahead of his scheduled two-hour guard.

There were some who suspected Jake Myers of setting the railroad watch a few minutes ahead each day in order to get his crew in the saddle a little ahead of time. Those few minutes a day added up during the week.

One day while we were eating our midday dinner at camp, the three wagon bosses compared the time by their watches, and Jake's watch was an hour ahead of the other two. From then on, that daylight-saving-time trick was a standing joke at the ranch, along with Jake's reputation as a "coffee cooler." Jake could drink more coffee per day than any other man in the cow country, and he kept it up for years even when his hair was as gray as a silvertip grizzly and he had acquired the name of "Old Griz" among his cronies.

The Circle C roundup wagon, the Long X, and the Milner Square wagons would move camp to Sun Prairie according to the schedule arranged by the Northern Roundup Association. This would let the three outfits, working together for a few days, get a clean work in the broken country of the adjacent Larb Hills and the badlands along the Missouri River.

During the ten days before the pooling of the three outfits, Jake aimed to get a clean work on a part of the Circle C range. Jake had been over the country the year before when Horace Brewster ran the wagon, and any cowhand worthy of the name was supposed to know any country he had ever ridden across, no matter how long ago. Jake figured he knew every foot of the badlands country between the Little Rockies and the Missouri, from the Cow Island Crossing east to Rocky Point and beyond, to the bend in the river at the mouth of the Musselshell, without having to ask one of the old Circle C hands to lead the early morning circle.

When Jake led his men on early morning circle, riding a little in the lead at a long trot, he would head for some high point that overlooked the country, and we would sit and wait for daybreak. Then traveling at that same long trot, Jake would scatter his riders in pairs on the long circle. He would drop off me and my pony Snowflake first, pairing me off with George McNeil, a long-geared, rawboned, black-headed Irishman with the map of the auld sod for a face. George repped for the St. Paul's Mission on the Fort Belknap Indian Reservation. He spoke with an Irish brogue you could cut with a knife and rode a string of big horses sired by a Percheron gray stud. They were gentle, hog-fat, awkward horses that should have been hauling a plow.

George McNeil never used a quirt or spurs, and he was as sorry as a sheepherder at a roundup camp and admitted it. He depended on the wagon boss to brand the Mission calves on the spring roundup and cut the Mission beef steers into the beef herd in the fall. His love for his horses was well known, as were his anecdotes about "me and my brother Pat."

I am sure now that Jake must have dropped me and the Irishman off to get rid of us when he led what the cowhands claimed were forty-mile circles. They were the longest circles in Montana round-up history in the opinion of all the hands, including the reps. Scarcely a day went past without the luckless pair Jake dropped off on the last of the long circle coming in on played-out horses with their cattle drives. Almost always the last men to come in were the ones who had been griping about the outfit and saying Jake was trying to build a rep for himself by getting a week's work out of a man in one day.

Those men were mostly nester ranchers repping with the Circle C wagon, and they had a somewhat unsavory record of swinging a maverick-hungry loop. The only reply they got out of Jake when they started griping was that they rode sorry horses or had played out their horses roping some unbranded calf and running their brand on it with an old horseshoe or cinch ring. Then Jake would add, "Any man working for the Circle C wagon makes a hand or goes down the road talking to himself."

Charlie Stuart, the Circle Diamond rep, was the one-eyed, half-blood son of the pioneer cattleman and historian, Granville Stuart. He wore a square black patch, like a miniature saddle blanket, across the caved-in socket of his blind eye. One night as we rode around the bedded beef herd together he said to me, "If Jake knew the country like the rest of us old hands do, he'd save a lot of wear and tear on the horses and cowhands on them long circles that take in half of Montana. The best cowhands in the world can't round up cattle on played-out horses. It's short circles on fresh horses that gets the job done. Hell, Jake's been lost since we left the home ranch. He's got this crew of hands and reps ringy as bulls pawin' dirt, and unless he stops crowdin' 'em too hard, Jake will have trouble on his hands before the fall roundup's over.

"I hate like hell to see it happen to a man like Jake Myers. He's a hell of a good cowhand and a damn good wagon boss, but he's a stranger in a strange land and he's tryin' his damnedest to hold the job Horace Brewster left behind. But there isn't any way for me or any other man in the outfit to tell him where he's wrong. Jake will just have to learn the hard way."

17.

Trouble at the Circle C Roundup Camp

DURING THE SHORT WEEK the three wagons were working on Sun Prairie, the first streak of the false dawn in the broken skyline of the Larb Hills found each wagon boss with his crew of men gathered on the pinnacles waiting for daybreak. At least seventy-five or eighty riders were scattered on the long circles throughout the badlands, and about ten o'clock in the morning the sight of circle riders fetching in their small drives of cattle from every direction to the designated holding ground was spectacular. They came in from every compass point in the vast Sun Prairie, forming spokes of a rimless wagon wheel with the holdup ground as the hub. When the drives were all in, the herd of cattle was so large a man would have to raise his carbine sights to the last notch to shoot across without hitting a cow brute.

Half of each roundup crew would ride to camp to wolf a bait of grub and change horses, then lope back to relieve the men holding the big herd. By the time the second section of riders ate and came back on fresh horses, the wagon bosses and top hands were already working the herd, cutting out their beef steers into separate cuts, with the cows and their unbranded calves in another cut.

A dozen or more top hands cut out the beef steers, while a dozen pair of riders cut out the cows with unbranded calves, laning them to the edge, where the riders holding up the herd picked up the cow and calf and hazed them out to the cut. They picked up the four-year-old beef steers the same way.

The cowpunchers doing the cutting were among the best cowhands in Montana. They had cow savvy, a knowledge of brands and earmarks, and every man was an expert at his work. They were the cream of the cowhands, with the added quality it takes to ramrod a cow outfit, run a wagon, or act as straw boss in handling a crew of men. Those men rode the best cutting horses in the cow country, which added up to the old saying that the best cowhand that ever lived was no better than the horse he rode.

It was an education just to watch that many top hands forking top horses and working that immense herd without interfering in any way with the other horsebackers as they eased their cutting horses on slack rein through the herd without seeming effort on the part of man or horse. For a novice young cowboy like me it was an absorbing and fascinating sight.

It was part of my job to tend the branding fire, and it was no easy job to keep about twenty-five branding irons red hot for the ropers who dragged the calves up to the fire. Three men did the branding as each roper called out the brand to be burned on each calf. A couple more cowhands did the earmarking and castrating. A man from each outfit kept tally of the branded calves that were burned in his iron.

The testicles from the bull calves were dropped in the hot ashes till the bag was seared and popped open and the mealy-looking nuts were seared brown. These prairie or mountain oysters were a rare delicacy, and because it was part of my chores to pick the testicles up off the ground and drop them into the hot ashes, I got my share. Now and then some cowpuncher holding up the cut would lope over and gather a big handful and go back to share them with the others. There was a bucket of water and a long-handled dipper for the thirsty.

It was hot, dusty, sweaty work for the calf rasslers, and now and then dangerous when a cow on the prod followed her bawling calf as it was dragged to the branding fire. The cow was apt to hook at the calf rasslers who were on the ground holding the calf, and they would have to fight her off with their hats. A cow on the prod was a dangerous animal, as many a mauled calf rassler well knew. Those sharp horns could rip the shirt off a man's back and the sharp-pointed cloven hoofs could be painful, as any luckless cow-tromped calf rassler could profanely affirm.

Usually about sundown or past the branding was done, and the cowboy's long day came to an end. The crew of hungry cowpunchers would ride into camp holding the hot branding irons upwards in gloved hands. The irons were cooled off in water holes or the creek or left on the ground near the bed wagon to cool.

That short week when the three outfits worked together was something never to be forgotten. After supper I'd ride over to the Long X outfit and listen to the campfire talk. Because the Long X was a Texas outfit and most of its cowpunchers came from Texas, their talk consisted of stories of the Texas Rangers and Sam Bass

Branding calves at the Circle C corral.
Frank Howe handling branding iron and Lew Roberts earmarking and castrating bull calves.

and other outlaws who rode the Texas range, yarns about the Staked Plains (the Llano Estacado), and wild tales of the tough trail town of Tascosa. They retold the story of the Alamo, the historic battle with the Mexican army under Santa Anna, and the fence cutters' war between the big outfits and the wire cutters. They talked about the XIT outfit and the brand artists who altered the XIT into the Star Cross and the fabulous King Ranch. When I rode back to the Circle C wagon, my head would be dizzy with countless stories of Texas cattle wars and the Texas Rangers.

Norville Wallace was the Long X wagon boss, although Joe Reynolds, one of the Reynolds family who owned the Long X, was with the outfit. What surprised me a little was that most of the Texas cowhands spoke border Mexican like a native.

With three outfits working together, there was a three-ring circus every day. Long circles and big drives daily brought another thousand-odd head of cattle in the holdup. By the time the calves were branded at the end of the day, the shadows of approaching night darkened the cut coulees and blind canyons in the brakes of the Missouri and the broken country of the Larb Hills. Each morning when the camp was moved, there was a wagon race to see which outfit got the best camping ground.

Humpy Jack Davis, the nighthawk who drove the green-broke, rollicky, four-horse team for the Circle C, claimed he could drive his bed wagon wherever the wagon pilot could ride his horse. In those early morning races he lived up to his bragging, for he was the first to reach the best camp site each day. He drove down steep slants where there never had been a wagon before and where he and the wagon pilot had to rough-lock the hind wheels with chains. Humpy Jack sat on the high spring-wagon seat, one leg braced in front, the other boot hooked on the long foot brake, the four lines in one hand, and his buckskin whip cracking like a pistol shot over the heads of the leaders as he shotgunned the steep slant. He perched like a big bird on the high swaying wagon seat, shouting meaningless cuss words that sent shrill echoes through the clatter of wagon wheels, the clanging of chain harness, and the loud metallic crash of rattling branding irons in the rear compartment.

Trouble at the Circle C Roundup Camp

Humpy Jack Davis was one of the best drivers of a four- or six-horse team in the cow country. He was expert in every detail that required skillful handling of the lines, cold nerve, and timing that made the difference between safety and a pile up of wrecked wagon and crippled horses, between life and death. Humpy Jack was a man who made his own legend in the Montana cow country.

When the roundup was over and the three big outfits split up and went their own ways, the Circle C outfit with its beef herd headed for the shipping point at Malta. They followed the freight road from the old Fort Musselshell Crossing on the Missouri, grazed the cattle along the way, and rode circle to gather more beef steers and branding calves missed on the spring roundup.

When the outfit reached Alkali Creek and camped at the old roundup crossing, we were about five miles from Malta. Jake Myers rode to town that evening after supper to make arrangements with the station master at the Great Northern depot for the cattle cars and to confirm the shipping date.

Charlie Stuart and I were on cocktail guard, along with Old Tex, the beef boss. We had the herd bedded down when Scott Miller and Lew Roberts, the men on first guard, rode out in the gathering dusk to relieve us, and the three of us rode to camp. Stuart and I unsaddled our horses and turned them loose, but Old Tex only loosened his saddle cinch and tied his horse to the bed wagon. The three of us headed for coffee at the mess wagon, where George L. was kneading a big mound of sourdough for morning biscuits.

There were times when George L. was as cranky as the average roundup cook, but that day he was in rare good humor and told us where the pie was.

"Another day," he mused, "another dollar. It won't be long now, another day or two, and we'll be bellied up to the bar. It's been two months since I throwed my lip over a slug of booze." He smacked his lips in joyous anticipation. For George L. Bickler from Philadelphia loved his liquor. That was why Jake kept the vanilla and lemon extract bottles hidden. At the smell of alcohol, the grizzled cook would shed his floursack apron, put on his coat, and head for town, even if he had to walk the distance.

I noticed Old Tex giving George L. a fishy eye as he drank his coffee. When I'd finished a second cup of coffee and got half a dried apple pie under my belt, I headed for bed. Charlie Stuart was unrolling his bedroll nearby when Old Tex came over to augur awhile.

"When the cat's away," Old Tex said in his slow, lazy drawl, "the mice come out to play."

"Meanin' what?" Charlie Stuart asked.

"Jake Myers has gone to town," Old Tex said. "He ain't the only man in this outfit that's pulled out for Malta. There's two, three night horses missin'. Them fellers sorta jumped the gun. Couldn't wait to likker up till after these cattle were shipped." The white-whiskered beef boss walked away muttering cuss words to himself.

"That's how come Ol' Tex didn't unsaddle and turn loose," Charlie Stuart said in a low voice. "He figgers if there's booze in camp there'll be trouble. Wonder who slipped off to town for a bottle?"

It was too dark to tell who belonged to the missing night horses that had been tied up.

"This outfit's been a-feudin' amongst themselves," Stuart went on. "All it needs is a jug of rotgut to bring it to a head. Purty Harry Asher's been bellerin' and pawin' dirt in Big Jim Brown's eyes. If that big Assiniboin gets enough firewater under his belt for a brave maker, he'll climb that spur jingler's frame, and them that's been takin' sides will lock horns and there'll be hell a-poppin'. That's when this gent saddles up and goes on day herd with Ol' Tex, on account of fightin's hard on the eyes, and I aim to keep that one eye I got left from bein' bruised." Charlie rolled a cigarette and lit it, and as he pulled off a boot, using a spur shank for a bootjack, he recited,

> *Him who grins and walks away,*
> *Will live to fight another day.*

Harry Asher was a sort of range dude who wore a red flannel shirt and white angora chaps and packed an ivory-handled Colt .45

he claimed he'd cut his teeth on. He was a good-looking man and a good bronc rider who put up a fancy ride, the angora wool of his chaps rising and falling every time his bronc hit the ground. With his scarlet shirt and high-crowned, wide-brimmed Stetson hat, he looked like one of Buffalo Bill's Wild West Show cowboys. Jake Myers once said that Asher rode a bronc as if he were watching his shadow.

Harry Asher and Jim Brown, a half-blood Assiniboin, had been breaking out about two hundred head of broncs during the summer. While Asher could put up a pretty ride, big Jim Brown was the better hand with a green bronc and the better rider of the two, and there was that jealousy between them.

The half-blood was big, awkward, and slovenly. He wore his shirttail out behind half the time, and his straight black hair always needing cutting. Jim Brown always got the broncs that were hard to sit, and he rode them without too much trouble. He was easy going and never had much to say and kept to himself, unlike Harry Asher who walked with the long-legged swagger of a spur jingler and liked to brag about his bronc riding.

Now and then Asher's talk around camp in the evening ridiculed Jim Brown. He would refer to Jim as a big Injun or a boneheaded gut-eater in a voice loud enough to be overheard by the half-blood. A sullen look would creep into Jim's swarthy moon face, and a calculating glint showed in his opaque black eyes although he never picked up the challenge.

Harry Asher had a side partner named Jim Loughlin. Although Loughlin never came out with it in the course of his conversation, he had a habit of dropping hints that he'd been mixed up in the Johnson County War in Wyoming and a sheep and cattle war in New Mexico.

Charlie Stuart interrupted my thoughts when he said, "Pull off your boots, Kid, and crawl betwixt the blankets. You'll be needin' what shut-eye you can get while the goin's easy. Yonder's Ol' Tex already in the hay, dead to the world, like he hadn't a care in the world."

I had decided to stay awake until Jake got back to camp, but before I knew it, I was out like Nellie's eye and having mixed-up dreams about the trouble that was bound to come between the two bronc riders if they got liquored up in town and brought a jug back to camp.

I awakened hours later to the jingle of horse bells as Humpy Jack Davis corraled the remuda. I was pawing off tarp and blankets when I heard George L. holler, "Come and git 'er."

The lopsided moon was low along the prairie skyline, and the first dirty-gray streak of a false dawn to the east was dimming the stars as I knuckled the sleep from my eyes, pulled on my Levis and boots, and rolled up my bed. Charlie Stuart was up and so were the majority of the cowpunchers by the look of the rolled-up beds and the sound of voices as the men filed into the mess tent to pile their plates with grub and fill coffee cups and go outside to eat.

I was on my way to the mess tent and almost there when the sound of loud, angry voices inside the tent halted me in my boot tracks.

"I been ridin' broncs that you wouldn't go into the corral with," came the deep, mumbling, drunken voice of Jim Brown. "A man gits fed up being called a gut-eatin' Injun. There ain't a horse in my rough string you kin set five jumps without grabbin' leather, you purty, spur-jinglin' tinhorn."

"Looks like this drunk Injun's makin' war talk." Harry Asher's voice was saw edged. "Step outside, Brown, and I'll drag it outa your big carcass."

Jim Brown, who had too much tanglefoot under his belt, staggered out of the mess tent, big and awkward as a Missouri mule. Harry Asher was right behind him. He had shed his cumbersome angora chaps, and the legs of his buckskin-foxed pants were stuffed inside the fancy tops of his high-heeled boots. The crowd of cowpunchers eating outside made way for the two men as they came out of the lantern-lit tent into the pale light of the fading moon.

There was the muffled sound of heavy blows and the jingling of spur rowels as the two men swapped wild punches. The halfblood outweighed the white man by about twenty pounds, but al-

Charlie Stuart in his eighties.
Courtesy of Mrs. Ethel Seaford, Zortman, Montana

though there wasn't an ounce of fat on Jim Brown's big-boned frame, he was clumsy and slowed down by booze. Although Asher was half-drunk himself, he was more active on his feet and could side-step Brown when he charged head down like an angry bull. Asher's fist caught him with an undercut blow that landed in the lowered face with a force that snapped the half-blood's head back. Then as Jim Brown stepped sideways, his feet became entangled in the chain harness alongside the wagon tongue. As he staggered off balance, Asher stepped in close and hit him a couple of times in the belly. Brown grunted and went down. His hat was knocked off, and his head with its thick mat of untrimmed hair lowered against his chest as he moved sluggishly to free his feet from the tangle of chain harness.

Harry Asher took a step or two forward and kicked Brown in the belly. "Git up, you gutless Injun! I ain't done with you yet!"

Jim Brown kicked off the harness as he rolled over, shaking his head sluggishly to clear his brain. Blood poured from both nostrils, and his swarthy face was a blood smear. He got his legs under him, then staggered to his feet, swaying back and forth, a ghastly grin on his face. His black eyes were narrowed to slits, and the blade of his knife was gripped in a blood-smeared fist.

Harry Asher's right hand slid to the ivory butt of the Colt .45 shoved in the waistband of his pants. The two men stood glaring for several long moments, sizing each other up. Then without warning Asher sprang, clubbing the barrel of his gun down across the half-blood's lowered head with a dull, sickening thud. Jim Brown went down like a beef steer knocked in the head and lay motionless.

Asher stood straddling the fallen man on long, widespread legs. "One thing I hate," he said, "is a knife. By rights I should tromp your guts out." He was breathing hard, and sweat slimed his lean-jawed face. "Got enough, Injun?"

"I got a-plenty for now," Jim Brown said, hate in his slivered black eyes. He groaned and rolled over on his belly and began vomiting.

Harry Asher stepped clear and backed away, his gun still gripped in his hand as he looked around him at the cowpunchers who stood in a wide circle.

"Any of you jaspers want to take up where this knife-slingin' Injun left off?" The bronc rider's eyes were narrowed.

No man broke the uneasy silence.

Then Jake Myers and another cowpuncher rode up out of the gray light of dawn.

"What in hell's going on around here?" Jake's flat-toned voice was ominous. His hand was on the black butt of the Colt six-shooter in the waistband of his Levis.

"Me 'n that big breed tangled." Harry Asher slid his gun back in his waistband. "Jim Brown pulled a knife on me. I bent a gun barrel across his head, and that's about the size of it. Without some of his friends want to play his hand out."

"Looks like you're the big rooster on top of the manure pile," Jake said flatly. "But don't crow too loud, mister." Jake reined off and headed for the corraled remuda, the big, rawboned cowpuncher following him.

"Walk slow," warned Charlie Stuart, who was behind me, "and speak easy. Jake's got a horn drooped. Let's get breakfast, such as it is. George L. is drunker'n seven hundred dollars, settin' straddle of his bed with his coat and hat on, talkin' to himself like a locoed sheepherder."

I asked Stuart if he knew the cowpuncher Jake had brought with him from Malta.

"Feller named Jim Swain from Oklahoma," Charlie Stuart said. "Him and Jake growed up together. Swain's part Cherokee. Been workin' for the Circle Diamond."

The grizzled roundup cook came lurching out of the mess tent, his town fedora hat cocked at a rakish angle on his balding head and a pint bottle showing from the hip pocket of his pants. There was a loose grin on his slack-jawed mouth and a few days' growth of gray whiskers on his face. Tears welled in his rheumy eyes. He bumped into a cowpuncher in the dark shadow and mumbled some kind of apology. "The name is George L. Bickler from Philadelphia... best damned roundup cook in Montana... give my kindest regards to Jake Myers when he gets back. Tell him I'm a man of peaceful nature, avoiding quarrels and bloodshed. I'll wait at the Alkali bridge a mile from here until a rig bound for Malta picks me up. Look me up when you get to town and I'll buy you a drink, whoever you are. Mislaid me specs and can't make you out in the dark."

"I'll be proud to deliver your message to Jake," answered Jake from the shadow of the mess wagon, with a hint of a chuckle. "Don't spend your money all in one place," he called after George L. as he stumbled off through the clumps of sagebrush and was lost to view.

The mess tent had flaps that opened at both ends. I followed Charlie Stuart as he entered the tent from the rear. Scott Miller and Lew Roberts were filling their plates and coffee cups. They gave us a sideward grin as we grabbed plates, cups, and eating tools and proceeded to load up with grub. Wash Lampkin, who had followed us in, fell in behind us. Jake and Jim Swain were outside, and the lazy drawl of Old Tex drifted into the tent.

"Two-thirds of your outfit's got a hide full, Jake," the white-whiskered old beef boss was saying. "Them as ain't half stung is huntin' a bottle. The trail betwixt camp and Malta was shore well traveled durin' the night. Them that wasn't comin' back was headin' for town. There's a bottle behind every sagebrush. Looks like they had 'er made directly you was outa sight. When you aimin' to ship?"

"The Circle Diamond's shippin' out today," Jake said in a brittle voice. "Our cars will be at the stockyards' siding at daybreak tomorrow morning. So graze your beef herd to the roundup camp at Bowdoin Lake. We're moving camp sometime before noon, regardless. Me 'n Jim Swain was on the prowl last night in town. When we found half a dozen Circle C horses tied to the hitchracks in front of the saloons on both sides of the tracks, we left the saddles on the ground and led the horses to the feed yard. Them hands that was set afoot ain't workin' for the Circle C no more. And them I find with a bottle in camp goes down the road talkin' to theirselves. Them that's sober enough to make a hand

Trouble at the Circle C Roundup Camp

goes on day herd or gets the can tied to their tails. You're handlin' the beef herd, Tex. It's up to you to keep those cowhands on day herd on the job. Fire any man that's got a bottle, regardless of who he is. That goes for the reps, if I have to fire every man in the outfit." Jake Myers deliberately spoke in a voice loud enough to be heard throughout camp. Then he entered the mess tent whistling that same hungry tune through his teeth, which were bared in a mirthless grin. Jim Swain followed him in.

Jake filled his coffee cup and carried it over and sat straddle of George L.'s bedroll. "I reckon it's up to you, Wash," he told Wash Lampkin, "to do the cookin' for a day or two. Like as not George L. will crawl in behind the sagebrush nearby to sleep it off, the shape he's in. When we get ready to move camp, hunt around the brush and load him in the mess wagon."

Jim Swain was a tall, rawboned cowpuncher with swarthy skin and black hair that showed his Cherokee blood. He was handsome enough in a hawk-beaked, thin-lipped way. He had a Colt .45 with wooden grips shoved in the waistband of his saddle-warped Levis. He filled his plate with grub and his cup with coffee and hunkered down on spurred boot heels alongside the bedroll that Jake sat straddling.

Charlie Stuart had gone outside to eat. I was about to follow him when Harry Asher and Jim Loughlin, his side-partner crony, came in and filled their coffee cups. Asher stood by the cookstove, his long legs spread apart, and Jim Loughlin stood on the opposite side of the stove. If either of them had been hitting the bottle again, they knew how to hold their liquor.

"Tom Ball loaded Jim Brown on his horse," Asher said, a faint grin on his face. "Them gut-eaters are headed for town to finish their drunk. It don't take no mind reader, Jake, to read what's inside your skull, so I'm beatin' you to it. I'm quittin' this outfit here and now. But just to get the record straight before I draw my time, it was Brown who started the ruckus he wasn't man enough to finish. The big gut-eatin' breed had enough booze under his belt to take the chill outa his Injun yellow guts, but he's as big as a skinned mule and clumsy awkward. I knocked him down with my fists, and when I kicked him to his feet, he came up with a knife in his hand. By rights I shoulda gut-shot the sonofabitch. I let the Injun bastard off easy. Me 'n my pardner Jim Loughlin are ready to pull stakes when you write out our checks for what we got comin'."

"I turned my time book over to Bob Coburn," Jake said. "You'll find him at the Great Northern Hotel in Malta."

Harry Asher tossed his empty cup into the dishpan and Jim Loughlin did likewise. When they turned to go, Jim Swain's quiet voice stopped them in their tracks.

"I got just enough Injun blood in me," he said with an Oklahoma accent, "to call your hand, Asher. My mother was a full-blood Cherokee. That makes me one of them gut-eaters you've been runnin' off at the head about." Swain put down his coffee cup and got to his feet, saying, "This gut-eater plays for keeps, tinhorn. You walk out the front of this tent. I'll go out the back. Have that bone-handled six-shooter you cut your teeth on in your hand, because I aim to gut-shoot you, white man!"

"Stand your hand, Loughlin!" Jake said harshly. He was on his feet with his gun in his hand. "Stay tracked and keep your hand off your gun. All right, Asher, play your string out."

I was hunkered down with my grub plate and coffee cup near George L.'s bedroll. Jake motioned with his left hand for me to flatten out behind it, and I did.

Harry Asher was moving crab-wise as he left the tent, and his gun was in his hand. Swain backed out the rear opening into the gray light of dawn.

"Don't shoot to'ards my horses!" Humpy Jack Davis shouted in his shrill cackling voice.

"Don't shoot!" Asher shouted in a hoarse voice that sounded like an echo. "I throwed away my gun!" He stepped back into the lantern light of the mess tent, both red-sleeved arms held high over his head and both hands empty.

"How's about it, Loughlin?" Jake spat out like a bad taste. "You aim to play out the hand that this spur jingler throwed into the discard?"

"Not this hombre," Jim Loughlin grinned, lifting his hands to the level of his shoulders. "I figgered this fancy bronc rider was tough from the way he talked, but if it's all the same with you, Jake, I'll stay on the payroll. Me 'n Harry Asher's done split the blankets."

"Take it up with Ol' Tex," Jake said coldly. "He's the beef man. He figgers you're sober enough to make a hand, he'll put you on day herd. You got a bottle hid out, smash it. Clear out before I change my mind."

Jim Loughlin gave his erstwhile side partner a withering look as he passed him. Jim Swain came into the mess tent the way he had gone out. He had his forefinger hooked through the trigger guard of the bronc rider's six-shooter. His opaque black eyes had a dangerous look as he swung the Colt.

"For a man who's cut his eye teeth on this white-handled gun," the Oklahoma cowpuncher said contemptuously, "you shore part with it easy."

The two men stood at opposite ends of the twenty-four-foot tent. Wash Lampkin, who was tying on a clean floursack apron, backed out of the line of fire. Jim Swain began spinning the gun, thumbing back the hammer with each swift whirl, then letting the hammer down, with the barrel pointing at the bronc rider's belly. The rapid double-click of the cocked six-shooter was the only sound that broke the tense silence in the tent.

Harry Asher's clean-shaven face had a sickly, yellow color that matched the fear in his bloodshot pale eyes. He had bragged more than once how he had filed the spring down to what was called a "hair-trigger." Now his life hung in the balance of that boast and the split-second timing of the swift-spinning gun. A slip of Swain's thumb, and a soft-nosed, lead .45 slug would tear through the guts of the man who had called Jim Brown and all half-bloods gut eaters.

Swain's thin-lipped mouth was twisted sideways in a contemptuous sneer, and his squinted black eyes were fixed with cold hatred on the luckless spur jingler. The spinning gun was a pinwheel of blued steel, and the rapid click-click sounded like the fast ticking of George L.'s alarm clock.

After what must have seemed an eternity to the bronc rider, who stood tracked like a frozen cottontail, the rapid clicking stopped, and Swain tossed the gun the length of the tent. It landed between Asher's widespread feet encased in alligator boots.

"Pick up your gun, mister," Swain said coldly. "Have it in your hand next time we meet in town."

Harry Asher picked up his gun and shoved it into the waistband of his pants, his eyes still glazed with fear. Then he turned and walked out with the shambling gait of a sleepwalker. It was broad daylight now, and the crowd of cowpunchers made way for the bronc rider as he walked to where his private horse stood saddled with the bridle reins dropped. He gathered up the reins and mounted without bothering to pull on the white angora chaps that lay across the saddle. Gone was his customary saddle swagger as he rode away, round shouldered as an old man.

Jake came out of the mess tent and stood hipshot facing the crowd of cowpunchers. "You fellers who slipped off to town last night," Jake said in a flat-toned voice, "fork your horses and head back to Malta to finish your drunk. You're fired. Don't get the idea you're leaving me short handed for a damn minute. I can manage." He paused for a long moment, then added, "Another thing. Ride them Circle C horses straight to the livery barn in town. Bob Coburn will be on the lookout for any horses tied to the hitchracks. Any of you cowhands that belong to them horses don't get paid off till I get to town and these cattle are shipped, and by God, you have me to whip before you draw your time. I got a bellyful of your janglin' since this outfit left the ranch. That goes as she lays." Jake walked back into the mess tent and filled a cup with black coffee.

Now that it was daylight a bruise on his cheekbone and the beginning of a black eye that partly closed one of his eyelids showed, and swollen knuckles on his left hand were raw where the skin had peeled off. I figured Jake had taken care of a few of the drunken cowpunchers he'd found in Malta the night before.

18.

Shipping Time at the Malta Stockyards

CHARLIE STUART AND I RODE TOGETHER to where Old Tex and half-a-dozen reps were grazing the beef herd off the bed ground to let them water along the creek.

"That Jim Swain's proud and haughty about his Cherokee blood," Stuart mused aloud as we rode at a running walk. "Like me. I'm proud I have Injun blood. Just as proud as I am that Granville Stuart was my old man. Take Jake Myers on the other hand. Judging from Jake's straight black hair and high cheekbones, I'd say offhand that he had a little Cherokee blood, but he has never said so, one way or another, and it ain't for this halfbreed to ask. But that Jim Swain sure broke Purty Harry Asher from speaking outa turn, I'll tell a man. That spur-jingling bronc rider will quit the country, traveling at a high trot, looking back over his shoulder like a scared coyote."

When we got to the grazing beef herd, Old Tex was giving his travel orders.

"Let them steers scatter out, boys. Graze 'em every foot of the way. Trot one of them steers and you're on your way to town. We'll water the herd at Bowdoin Lake around sundown. When we bed 'em down on cocktail, the steers will be swole up like they had gas balloons in their paunches. I've been two weeks puttin' taller on their ribs, and I don't want you cowhands knocking off an ounce by chousin' 'em." Old Tex's faded blue eyes had deep sparks of light when he added, "Them as has a drink left in a bottle, go easy, Mable. It's going to be a long day, so save up for that town drunk tomorrow night, and I'll help you boys paint Malta redder'n war paint. After the roundup is over, I'll be doin' business at the same old place at Rocky Point. Drinks on the house for you boys who treat me right. Handle these beef steers like you owned them, and there'll be no holler comin'."

It was a mighty long speech for the old, white-whiskered beef boss, spoken in his lazy drawl as we sat our horses. By the time he'd finished and whittled off a corner of chewing tobacco and tongued it back like a lump-jawed old bull, the scattered steers had finished watering and were spreading out grazing at a slow walk.

There was no disputing the fact that the Circle C outfit was short handed. Those who had gone to town were drifters who worked for a different outfit each roundup time, young cowhands not ready to settle down, a restless breed who moved from state to state.

The sun was two hours noon high, and the slow moving beef herd was still in distant view of yesterday's camp when we saw the two wagons and the remuda heading along the dim roundup road for the next camping ground on Bowdoin Lake, a mile or so from Malta.

Jake and Jim Swain and several more cowpunchers rode a little ahead of the wagons and just behind Joe Contway who was piloting the wagons. I recognized Frank Howe among the riders. Howe had been away repping for the Circle Diamond wagon. He must have showed up at camp after I had left with Charlie Stuart.

As the wagons and remuda passed out of view, Frank Howe and four cowhands came riding over to the beef herd. I had not seen Howe for a month, and he was a sight for sore eyes.

When Horace Brewster had run the wagon, Frank Howe and I had stood night guard together, and I could still hear his gravel voice singing his bagful of songs—sad cowboy laments and old English, Scotch, and Irish folksongs, with limey accents, a Scottish burr, or the brogue of old Erin, sung in the whimsical, husky voice of a true ballad singer. Wherever and however Frank Howe learned

Shipping Time at the Malta Stockyards

such ancient folksongs I had no way of knowing, but they brought light and happiness and laughter to many a lonesome cowpuncher at roundup camps and winter bunkhouses. Howe had made his own legend as he rode his careless way. His habitual good nature and his sense of humor had gained the big, homely, towheaded cowhand more friends than any man in any walk of life I have ever known. Frank Howe had been my lifelong friend since my kid memory began. He was forking a long-legged, deep-chested brown gelding called Treasure Box, one of his string of top horses.

"I ran into your brother Bob in Malta," Frank told me after we had shaken hands. "He said Jake was in a tight and sent me out to the outfit to lend a hand. Looks like Jake got himself in a jackpot, half the outfit in town drunk and what's left of this shorthanded crew cussed out and ready to quit at the drop of the hat."

Jake Myers and Frank Howe had had some sort of a run-in right after the spring roundup was over. It was one of those mixed-up deals. Jake figured Frank was jealous because he had gotten the

Malta, Montana, showing north side (top) and south side (bottom).

Courtesy of J. J. Sullivan, Malta, Montana

ramrod job instead of an old top hand like him, and Howe figured Jake was handing him the dirty end of the stick and pouring it on till he'd get fed up and quit. There was more truth than poetry on both sides, and Frank Howe was ready to draw his time when he was sent over to rep with the Circle Diamond at the same top hand, straw boss wages of seventy-five a month that he'd been drawing down for years. There was no love lost between Jake Myers and Frank Howe, but it behooved both men to bury the hatchet and make the best of a deal neither one of them liked.

Howe rolled a cigarette and set fire to it and let the smoke drift lazily from his nostrils as he spoke. There were times when Howe could swell up with self-importance and assume an air of dignity like a banker or senator. All this change from a cowpuncher into an important dignitary was illusionary, because there was no outward change in his appearance. Nevertheless, the big, homely cowhand gave that impression.

"I told Bob Coburn I'd be willin' to help Jake out in a tight," Howe said. "But it was your old man I had in mind. I was workin' for old man Robert Coburn before you were born, when he had his outfit on Flatwillow—repped for him with the DHS wagon. It's to pay off somethin' of the obligation I owe him that I'm here."

At the crack of dawn the following morning the fat four-year-old beef steers were being crowded into the plank corral at the Malta stockyards. Horsebackers cut off a bunch and worked them into smaller pens. Men on foot moved along the slanted catwalk on either side of the long chute with poles to prod the cattle into the cars.

The beef herd had been cut in half, the first half penned while the second half grazed along the flats on the shore of Lake Bowdoin under the wary, watchful eye of Old Tex. When the bulk of the first section of steers were loaded into cattle cars, the remaining steers were shoved into the large corral at the stockyards.

It was hot, dusty, and sweaty work for all hands. Only the seasoned cowpunchers were on horseback in the cattle-crowded pens, handling the steers with as little chousing as possible. Being a kid, I was handed a long prod pole, and I walked the slanted catwalk

Shipping Time at the Malta Stockyards

along the loading chute, prodding the steers along, until there were blisters on both heels.

My father and brother Bob were at the top of the chute with pencils and tally books, and the reps took turn tallying the cattle in the irons they represented. George Hall, the stock inspector, was also there.

People in top buggies, buckboards, and light spring wagons came from town to watch the loading. Several saloonkeepers had cases of beer covered with wet sacks on the floor of their buckboards. Prostitutes holding parasols against the hot sun came in top buggies and spring wagons.

The powdery manure dust rose in a huge cloud and hung in the air. Cowpunchers and spectators alike were powdered with the fine dust. The air was filled with noise—the continuous bawl of cattle, the thud of cloven hoofs and the shod hoofs of the cutting horses ridden by the cowhands working inside the pens, and the shouts of the prod-pole wielders along the chute. There was seldom a pause in the loading, except when a cattle car was filled and the slotted door banged shut and fastened by a steel bull bar. Then after a few minutes respite, the next empty cattle car was "spotted" by shouted calls and hand signals from the freight conductor and brakemen to the locomotive engineer who slowly moved his train.

During these brief intervals quart bottles of beer were passed along to the working cowpunchers as come-on gifts from rival saloon men. Jake Myers had sent out word to the saloonkeepers that no whisky would be allowed, and he passed word to the shorthanded crew of cowhands that there would be no break for noon dinner.

It was midafternoon when the last steer was loaded in the long train of cattle cars. Frank Howe, in charge of the cattle train to Chicago, waved his hat in a farewell salute from the rear platform of the caboose as the cattle train got under way. The dusty, sweat-soaked, and weary cowpunchers were headed for camp for a delayed noon dinner and a change of horses to ride into town.

Robert Coburn had ridden out to the yards in a hired rig from the livery stable which had left him and returned about the time the last car was being loaded. The last thing he told me before he headed for Malta was to get to town in time to take a hot bath, get into my town clothes, and be at the station in plenty of time to catch the midnight westbound train for Great Falls, where I would enter school the next day.

My father and brother Bob were going to Chicago for the national stockgrowers' meeting, and their eastbound train left about nine-thirty that evening. Bob had ridden out on horseback. It was only about four in the afternoon, but my father, a stickler for being on time to catch a train, was already in a lather fretting about missing the train as Bob talked to Jake about hiring new hands to replace the men Jake had fired.

"The thing to do now, Jake," Bob advised, "is to move the wagons back to Alkali tomorrow. Lay over a day or two. That'll give your men plenty of time to blow in their wages and get drunk. A couple of days and they'll be sick and hung over, broke and ready to go back to work."

"I'll manage, Bob," Jake said. "I done weeded out most of the ones that were causin' the trouble."

My father was having some kind of a medicine talk with the stock inspector and kept looking at his watch every minute or two.

"The old gent's rarin' to go back to town by the way he's clockin' you, Bob," Jake said in a low voice.

"Lead my horse to camp, Jake," Bob said. "I'll ride back with him in his hired rig. If I'm not at the hotel eating supper when you get to town, you can locate me at the depot. I'll be there walking the platform or inside asking the station agent if the eastbound's on time. That goes on every five minutes when you travel with Father. If the train's fifteen minutes late, he'll start a tirade about the delay and wind up cussing Jim Hill for the high shipping rates the Great Northern charges for a load of cattle. He's apt to blame Jim Hill if the price of cattle is down at the Chicago market."

"Come along, Bob," my father called out, watch in hand. "If

Shipping Time at the Malta Stockyards

we expect to eat supper and catch our train, you got no time to waste talkin' nonsense. I heard every damned word you said."

"There's times like now," Bob laughed, "when that busted eardrum of his hears like a fox. See you later, Jake. Be sure to see that the kid gets aboard that midnight train for Great Falls. His school starts tomorrow."

19.

Mutiny at the Circle C Ranch

THE NEXT FALL there were about half-a-dozen cowhands at the home ranch, and Al Taylor was doing the cooking. Vince Fortune was the bookkeeper, and he bunked in the large, square, log room that had been added onto the back of the office that summer.

Bob and Wallace Coburn were both in Helena, and my father was staying at the ranch with Will Coburn's family. Jake Myers was in Malta getting his family settled in town so that his daughter could go to school. During Jake's absence Will Coburn was the ramrod, and with winter just around the corner, he and the cowpunchers had been gathering cows that had dropped late calves and were throwing them into the big pasture. Come a snowstorm, the cows and calves and any cattle that needed feeding could be gathered in a few hours and fetched into the large cattle shed and hay yard.

Besides the crew of cowhands, there was Pete Olson, the big Swede who tended to the summer irrigation, milked the half-dozen range cows, and did odd jobs around the ranch. Pete was as honest and trustworthy as any man and he had become sort of a permanent fixture, like Al Taylor, the ranch cook.

Will Coburn's house was a good hundred yards from the mess house and bunkhouse, and the office was about halfway between.

One evening when Swede Olson brought the pails of milk to Will's house, he told Rose Gladeau, the hired girl, that the cow-

Mutiny at the Circle C Ranch

punchers had somehow gotten hold of a gallon jug of whisky and there was a poker game in the bunkhouse. Rose had passed on the information to Will's wife, Vida, who had in turn told Will about it. My father had a long-established ruling against drinking or gambling among the cowpunchers.

That night about nine o'clock Will, without telling my father about the booze and gambling, decided to look into the matter. He told Vida he was going to the office to go over the books with Vince and drink some of Al's roundup coffee. He shoved his six-shooter into the waistband of his pants and put on a heavy wool coat, and left the house. A cold night wind was blowing down from Canada, and the sky was overcast as if there might soon be a storm.

"I'll be back inside of an hour," Will told Vida as he went out into the dark night.

But Will's lame excuse hadn't fooled his wife, and when it was a quarter to eleven by the mantel clock and Will had not returned, Vida awakened my father who always bedded down before nine. She told him what had happened and said she was sure Will had gotten into some kind of trouble. My father dressed hastily and got the hammerless Smith and Wesson .38 pistol from his dresser drawer. He told Vida not to worry, but to lock the door when he went out.

The green roller blinds on the office windows were pulled down, and threads of lamplight showed through the sun-cracked blinds. My father tried the door and it was locked. He rapped on the door with his gloved hand and called Vince's name in a low voice. There was no answer. There was nobody in the room behind the office. My father picked up a wagon spoke used to prop open the door and proceeded to the bunkhouse. The windows there were covered with gunnysacks or old blankets, and only a faint light showed through. Listening at the window, he could hear the sound of men's voices in a drunken argument. He listened in vain for the sound of Will's voice. Then he headed for the cook cabin. No light showed in the mess hall, but he could see lamplight inside the kitchen. When he peered through the window, he saw no sign of Al Taylor moving about.

He left the window and headed for the door into the mess hall. As he moved cautiously in the dark, he stumbled over somebody lying alongside the door. He squatted down and lit a kitchen match. Holding the cupped flame in his gloved hand, he saw that it was Will.

Will's hat had fallen off. Sticky blood matted his thick black hair, and his forehead and face were covered with blood that oozed from a long scalp wound. He looked dead enough to bury.

My father slowly got to his feet and stood there for a short time to figure out his next move. Then he walked cautiously back to the door of the bunkhouse. The black doorknob turned in his hand, but the door wouldn't budge when he tried to shove it open. It was blocked from within. He thought of pounding on the door with the heavy wagon spoke but decided against it. He'd lived too long in the lawless frontier country to make that foolish mistake.

He stood alone against the half-dozen cowpunchers. As far as he knew, they had killed his son. So he stood there listening as he held the wagon spoke in his left hand, his pistol in his right hand. From what he could hear of the drunken talk, the men were planning to take over the Circle C outfit. One of them admitted hitting Will over the head with a six-shooter barrel. Putting the old man out of the way would be an easy matter, a voice said. With those two Coburns out of the way and Jake Myers in Malta and Bob and Wallace Coburn in Helena, the coast was clear. There were over two hundred saddle horses in the Circle C remuda in the big pasture. There would be a ready market for those horses in Wyoming where no questions would be asked. They could haze the remuda to hell and gone before daybreak, and they'd be long gone and across the Wyoming line by the time a sheriff's posse followed their cold trail.

My father thought he recognized the whisky-bragging voice as Jim Loughlin's, but he couldn't be sure. Whoever it was was commenting about how the dude bookkeeper had run like a scared coyote. They had gotten Al Taylor half drunk, and he was sleeping it off among his pots and pans, and they had Swede Pete inside the bunkhouse, scared to death.

Mutiny at the Circle C Ranch

My father flattened himself against the log wall near the door. He could hear the noise as something heavy was dragged from behind the door. Then the door opened and a man stepped out. My father hit him as hard as he could over the head with the wagon spoke and dropped him like a beef hit on the head with a sledge hammer. Then he stood back in the shadows and gave his orders to the others inside the bunkhouse.

He told them he had them dead to rights there in the lantern light and ordered them to raise their hands. He told Pete Olson to take their six-shooters and throw them out the back window that faced the creek, and the big Swede did as he was told. Then he told Pete to go over to the mess hall and carry Will to his house while he held the cowpunchers prisoners in the bunkhouse. He kicked the door shut and told them to stay there and said that he'd kill any man who came out.

Al Taylor had awakened about then and helped Pete carry Will to his house. Al and Pete returned to the bunkhouse to help.

Will, his head bandaged and feeling groggy, woke up before daylight. He got up, and using the telephone that had been connected between the ranch and Malta, he got in touch with Jake Myers. Will told Jake to hightail it back to the ranch as fast as his horse could travel, but not to call on the law for help—that between them they could handle the deal.

The best horse Jake could find was a quarter-horse mare that belonged to the man who ran the livery and feed barn in Malta. She was a racing mare with a big suckling colt. Jake said afterwards that the mare must have broken all records traveling the forty-mile distance.

By the time Jake got to the ranch, the trouble-making cowpunchers were long gone, including the man my father had hit over the head with the wagon spoke. They had saddled up and vowed they would quit the country.

The scared bookkeeper had walked ten miles to the Veseth place, which was then used as a winter line camp. Jake trailed him there and fetched him back, but the bookkeeper drew what time he had coming and went back to Great Falls. Vince Fortune was a well-fixed and prominent society bachelor. He had taken the bookkeeping job as a sort of vacation spent on a cow ranch and had gotten a bellyful of the wild and woolly West.

Al Taylor wanted to quit, but Will talked him out of the notion. Al was sparking a Miss Dunlap at the time, and a few years later they were married and ran a boarding house at the B & M Smelter at Great Falls. The last I heard of Al Taylor, he was mayor of the mining town of Neihart, Montana.

Thus ended the trouble that began when Harry Asher gun-whipped big Jim Brown and climaxed in the abortive attempt by half-a-dozen cowpunchers to take over the ranch and steal the remuda. Those were the cowhands Jake had hired to replace some of the other regular Circle C cowhands who had quit when Jake took over the ramrod job.

Most of the old-time Circle C cowpunchers showed up to go into winter line camps, and everything was peaceful and quiet at the ranch. Jim Swain had gone back to Oklahoma. Jim Loughlin and his would-be tough companions were gone forever. And Jake Myers was undisputed ramrod of the Circle C.

20.

"One of Ourn"

JAKE MYERS WAS A FIRM BELIEVER in the old frontier adage that a cattleman never ate his own beef. During the years he ramrodded the Circle C outfit, Jake initiated me into what I now term the fraternal brotherhood of the O.O.O., coined from "One of Ourn," Jake's pithy term for the big four-year-old beef steer about to be butchered.

The secret order of the O.O.O. had only two members, Jake Myers and me. Old Black Dog and his wife were the uninitiated and innocent accessories to the crime of butchering another outfit's beef. Old Black Dog's participation consisted only of driving his team and wagon to the place where the shot beef lay on the ground, with its jugular vein cut and the brand and earmarks already cut from the hide and head. If that old Assiniboin Indian ever had any inkling of what went on, he never gave any outward indication of it in any way.

In the big pasture at the east Coburn Butte there were always about fifty or a hundred head of cattle scattered out grazing in the coulees and on the rolling hills and ridges. Among them were about half-a-dozen stray cattle that wandered in probably because the wire gate had been left open or a rotted fence post had fallen over to leave a gap in the fence.

In the summer we usually butchered the beef in the cool of the evening, and in the winter in late afternoon before the early dusk of the short day set in. Sometime during the morning of the butchering day, I would ride to Black Dog's camp on the Fort Belknap Reservation and tell him to come with his wagon that evening at a designated time, which as a rule was a little before suppertime. I'd put a rolled-up meat tarp and a big dishpan and an ax in his wagon under the seat with the washed rolled-up gunnysack Black Dog's wife had made ready to hold the paunch and entrails.

When I returned to the ranch, Jake would be saddled up and ready to go, and we'd ride out ahead of the slow moving wagon with a hound pack trailing. Once we were out in the big pasture, there was no need to tell that wise old Indian which direction to take. He'd keep us in sight.

Jake and I both carried skinning knives, and Jake carried an old Mauser carbine in his saddle scabbard and a pair of field glasses he always carried in a leather case strapped to the cantle of his saddle. That day Jake would have already spotted the bunch of cattle that held the beef steer to be butchered.

While I stayed back a short distance with the hounds, Jake would ride slowly among the grazing cattle with the Mauser across his saddle in front of his belly. When he had eased his horse close enough to the steer he would shoot the critter behind the ear, and the explosion of the gun would scatter the bunch of cattle. By the time I reached him with the hounds, Jake would have the steer's throat cut and the ears with the telltale earmarks cut off. He'd toss the whittled bits of hairy ears to the hungry hounds.

By that time the steer had finished bleeding, we would roll it on its back, twisting the neck around and the head up and shoving the horns into the ground to brace the carcass. In less than a minute we would have one-half of the hide (the branded side) skinned off. Another few seconds and Jake would have the brand cut out and whittled into tiny bits, small enough to be gulped down by the hounds. As Jake would remark, "it would take a live-wire stock inspector a hell of a long time to hand pick a hundred dog turds scattered to hell and gone."

It was Jake Myers' contention that without a brand to show as evidence, the prosecuting attorney didn't have a foot to stand on

"One of Ourn"

in court. "Let a stock inspector or some nosy sonofabitch ride up on us while we're butcherin'," Jake would say, "all we gotta do is claim the beef for 'One of Ourn' and to hell with it." Then Jake would put a grin on his face.

"If ever me 'n you are ketched butcherin' a beef," Jake often cautioned me, "keep your trap shut. Leave the talkin' to me. Thataway there'll be no need of us ever makin' horsehair bridles in the Deer Lodge pen."

Nevertheless, there were times when Jake would hand me the Mauser and a handful of cartridges and send me on horseback to some hogback ridge as a lookout. "Any horsebackers show up,"

Black Dog, Assiniboin chief, at roundup camp on Beaver Creek.

Jake would tell me, "all you got to do is drop a couple of shots near enough to kick up dust, and the nosey bastard will high-tail it for home."

Black Dog and his wife never took part in the skinning of the hide. Only after we had dragged the bulging, grass-filled paunch from the carcass and put the heart, kidneys, liver, marrow guts, tongue, and brains in the dishpan would Black Dog's woman go to work. She would slit the paunch with her skinning knife, cut the entrails in three-foot lengths, strip them clean of watery manure, and sack them, while old Black Dog sliced the liver and dipped it in the yellow gall from the slit bladder and ate it with relish as he squatted on moccasin heels.

Jake would split the head in two, the upper half with the horns and severed ears going to Black Dog, as well as the neck. The four hoofs, the front legs severed at the knee joints, and the hindquarters below the hocks also went into the Assiniboin's gunnysack. When the quartered beef was loaded in the wagon and covered with the meat tarp to keep off the blow flies, the job was over and done. When the wagon pulled out for the ranch, all that remained on the ground was a pile of moist grass from the paunch and a pool of drying blood.

Then Jake would cut the hide lengthwise down the back, and each of us took half of it and rolled it hair side out to carry it across the saddle in front of us.

In the upper field at the ranch there was a large dam across Beaver Creek where it coursed between two high cut banks. The thirty-foot cut banks on each side made a reservoir lake about two hundred feet wide and approximately that long. On each end of the dam was a deep ditch spillway that allowed the surplus water of the dammed creek to flow back into the natural course of Beaver Creek. The reservoir was used for irrigating the field of bluejoint hay and for cutting ice blocks in winter. As a rule Jake and I dumped our rolled hides in the lake. We tossed them in separate places, and they would sink in the deep water and lodge in the mud.

Sometimes we would dump the hides in the beaver dams in the lower pasture called the Mitch Field, so named because it had been

"One of Ourn"

the homestead of Jim (Mitch) Mitchell, a roundup cook and cowhand, and the Circle C had bought the land from him. The beaver cattail swamps were wide and boggy, and we would drop the rolled-up hides in the black mud and shove them out of sight with long willow poles chewed by beaver teeth and used by the busy beavers for riprap on their dams.

Because Black Dog's Indian pony team always traveled at the same, slow, whittle-dee-dig trot, we would get to the ranch before his wagon pulled up at the meat house. This gave us enough time to see if there was a livestock inspector waiting to take a look at the beef hide. If there was, Jake would keep the unwanted lawman occupied in conversation in the mess cabin or office while I lugged the quartered beef into the meat house and sent Black Dog and his wagon on their way.

During the summer months, when there was the lambing crew and the haying crew to feed, we butchered an average of one big four-year-old beef steer a week. Jake was bold and seemingly loose and careless about the whole deal during all the five or six years it went on.

During those years we had several narrow squeaks. One time when I sighted a horsebacker coming and dropped a couple of warning shots to turn him back, the rider turned out to be Charlie Beard, justice of the peace in the Little Rockies. Another time when we returned with "One of Ourn" in Black Dog's gut wagon, stock inspector George Hall was in the office. In former years George Hall had punched cows for the Circle C. He was a big man, a sort of range dude and ladies' man, and quite a josher who liked to rib a man. Later on that evening when he and Jake were drinking coffee and shooting the breeze, Hall told Jake that he would like to take the fresh hide belonging to the beef in Black Dog's wagon along with him to make a rawhide rope. Jake said he should have spoken up sooner because he had given the hide to Black Dog's squaw to make winter moccasins. But, Jake said, if he wanted to make a rawhide rope, he had just the hide Hall needed. It was a bullhide in the barn which was used to drag out the manure. The hair was already worn off, and the hide was limber as a dishrag, just right for braiding a rope. Jake told Hall he was welcome to it as the flowers in May, but the stock inspector politely declined the gift.

It was the law that the hide of a butchered beef be kept hung on the corral fence for a given length of time, the stock inspector went on to explain in a careless give-a-damn manner. He advised Jake to keep the bullhide handy, just in case some nosy bastard happened along. Both men grinned at each other.

As Jake Myers often said, the only crime attached to the butchering of another man's beef was getting caught, and he didn't aim to get caught with his pants down.

It was all in a day's work, and if Jake got paid a bonus from the company, he never said so. Jake's one fear, he told me, was that if the "old gent" ever found out, he would get the can tied to his bushy tail right away. But my father never got wise, and he never knew that I got callouses on my right hip from packing a Colt .45 shoved in the waistband of my Levis.

A cowhand had to pack a gun to travel the route with Jake Myers during the years he was ramrod of the old Circle C outfit.

21.

Tales of South America

THE PERIOD OF TIME when Jake Myers was foreman of the Circle C Ranch formed a new era, an era that was destined to see the passing of the free range of the old-time cow country and a decline in the cattle industry which preceded its fall.

Robert Coburn, along with the rest of the owners of big outfits, the so-called "cattle barons," had long foreseen the beginning of the end. There were too many outfits grazing large sheep bands across the free range claimed by the big cattle spreads. The sheep left a comparatively barren wasteland behind, unfit for the grazing of cattle or horses. In some places, where bands of sheep grazed during the summer, the following year would bear a goodly crop of fast spreading locoweed, the first to sprout green after the warm chinook winds in the spring had melted the snow. Once the locoweed, with its pale purple blooms that died and left seed pods, got hold, there was no way of stopping the scattered growth. When the range horses, hungry for the first green growth, ate the deadly locoweed, they grew gaunt and sick and eventually went crazy and died. Like a human dope addict, a horse craved the insidious, fatal locoweed.

Once the large herds of sheep grazed on the free range, it was no longer cattle country. It became sheep country.

After the sheep, the homesteaders came to plow up the sod and plant wheat. They built barbwire fences to protect their grain fields against the grazing livestock, and the cow country was no more.

For long weeks and months Will, Bob, and Wallace Coburn talked of South America and about selling the Circle C outfit. Sheep outfits were crowding in on the free range that was the cattleman's domain. Other cattle outfits from Texas, Colorado, and Wyoming were moving in, and it was only a matter of a few years before the range was overstocked with cattle and sheep.

Because of Jim Hill's misleading propaganda about absurd profits to be made overnight by dry-land farming, the homesteaders were coming in with their families and all their worldly goods by the trainload from the Middle West.

Soon the name of Jim Hill became a dirty word among the pioneer cattlemen and the Montana Stockgrowers Association. There were lawsuits galore filed against the cow outfits over water rights and claims to school sections leased on long terms by the cattlemen throughout the entire state. Without the benefit of free range to graze their cattle, the big outfits would go under. The free range was their lifeline. The homesteaders were stringing barbwire across the old roundup trails. The sod was being turned under by plows and leveled by discs and harrows and seeded in flax and wheat. Water holes and creeks were being fenced off, and the thirsty cattle were being driven off the unfenced creeks by the farmers' mongrel dogs.

In many instances bands of sheep were being driven across the cattle range on their way to summer range, and there was no legal way for the cowmen to halt the sheep invasion, short of violence and bloodshed and the carnage of open range war.

Cowhands from the southwest spoke of the bloody Lincoln County war in New Mexico, where Billy the Kid first gained his fame as a ruthless killer. In Arizona the Graham-Tewksbury sheep and cattle war in Pleasant Valley and the Tonto Basin was taking heavy toll of human life. The law officers were summarily told to keep away, for neither faction wanted any law interference. In the southern part of Montana on the Wyoming line there were rumors of another bloody range war in progress.

Tales of South America

These matters were discussed at a meeting of the Northern Montana Roundup Association, and all the cowmen agreed that the handwriting was on the wall. After the meeting John Survant and Will Coburn talked about going to South America. According to all reports, the vast *Pampa* land in Argentina and Brazil could be had for a few cents an acre on long term leases if a man knew how to deal with the politicos and bankers. Since neither Survant nor Will Coburn had any knowledge of the Spanish language, they knew they would be handicapped from the start, as a couple of strangers in a foreign land. They needed to take along a man who could speak fluent Spanish, and they decided on Abe Gill, who was well educated and had a thorough knowledge of the language. So when they departed for South America, Abe Gill accompanied them. His services as a guide, philosopher, and friend proved invaluable, for Gill had the breeding of a gentleman and scholar and the charm of a born diplomat. He was also a splendid companion throughout the trip, and his natural diplomacy in meeting the politicos gained them the red-carpet treatment in Buenos Aires where they were wined and dined in lavish style.

Will Coburn and John Survant were promised all the land they needed in the vast *Pampa* country on long leases at cheap rates. Argentina welcomed the North American cattle industry with open arms.

Abe Gill stayed in Buenos Aires while Will Coburn and John Survant went inland by train to look over the great *Pampa* country. When they reached the last town at the end of the railway line, they decided that John Survant would remain there while Will Coburn went farther inland with a pack outfit to get a first-hand knowledge of how the Gauchos worked cattle, how they handled beef herds that they trailed for hundreds of miles to the shipping point on the railroad, the breed of cattle they raised, and many other things about cattle raising in this foreign land. By the time Will Coburn worked cattle with a few big outfits and was ready to return to Buenos Aires, he had learned about all there was to know about the cattle industry in South America.

Upon their return to Montana, Abe Gill went back to his ranch where he remained until he disappeared in 1906. Both Will Coburn and John Survant were completely sold on South America. Bob Coburn went along with the idea of selling out the Circle C and moving to South America, and Wallace Coburn was anxious to go, mainly because he wanted to hunt big game in the Andes.

But Robert Coburn threw cold water on the talk and arguments that went on. He said he had spent a lifetime building up the outfit, and he was too old to pull up stakes and move to a foreign country. If his sons were bound to head for South America, there was nothing to stop them. If they wanted to sell the Circle C, he was willing to go along with the deal, but he wasn't about to sell out cheap. If they could find a buyer with enough cold cash to lay on the line, it was all right with him. He said he was getting sick and tired of all this South America talk, and as far as he was concerned, all Will had to show for his South American trip was a mean-tempered, ornery, squawking parrot that couldn't talk which he had brought back in a wire cage.

That settled the argument for all time, and after a few months when no buyer showed up, the plan died a slow death. And during the following years Robert Coburn's prophecy came to pass. There was only the raucous sound of the green-feathered parrot to show for Will's trip to Argentina—that and a paragraph in Joseph K. Howard's book, *Montana: High, Wide, and Handsome*.

> The Kid [Kid Curry] moved on [after the train holdup at Wagner] finally to Patagonia, South America. There one of the Coburns, operators of the Circle C outfit, was said to have visited him several times years later. Some stories say the Kid died there. One Montana friend of the outlaw says he died in Denver. Others insist that he still lives.[1]

I have no way of knowing where Howard got the information that Will Coburn paid a visit to Kid Curry at Patagonia, South America. For all I know, Will might have visited the Kid when he made the pack trip into the vast *Pampa* country. I was a kid at that time and too young to share in any confidential talk among my three half-brothers, who were fifteen to twenty years my sen-

---
[1] Page 141.

iors, but I do vaguely recall that Will did see Kid Curry on his trip.

Another kid recollection is that one of the reasons why Abe Gill remained in the city of Buenos Aires was his fear of being killed by Kid Curry, who was said to be in the interior. There were rumors that Butch Cassidy and Harry Longabaugh (alias the Sundance Kid) owned a sizable cow spread in a remote part of southern Argentina, near the tip of the horn. A group of Confederate soldiers, all of them die-hard rebels, had settled there after the Civil War, and any outlaw from the United States who had a price on his head was welcome among the self-exiled outcasts.

So, guided by the old maxim that discretion was the better part of valor, Abe Gill chose to remain in Buenos Aires, although he was a man of known courage and at times brave to the extent of being foolhardy. The very fact that Gill consented to go to South America with the foreknowledge that Kid Curry was somewhere in South America was proof of his courage. Will Coburn and John Survant, on the other hand, had nothing to fear from venturing into outlaw country in quest for new range where Kid Curry, Butch Cassidy, and the Sundance Kid supposedly had gone with their South American stake from the Wagner train holdup to go into the cattle business in the firm conviction that they were safe from the long arm of the United States law. Whether or not the outlaws were safe from extradition was a moot question.

During those years there were plenty of rumors and tales about Pinkerton operatives following the cold trail of the Wild Bunch to South America. For example, one story told around the roundup campfires was that a top Pinkerton detective was sent to Buenos Aires under the guise of a gambler to open up a high-class casino. He had a dozen or more crated slot machines and roulette wheels on the steamer he booked passage on. In Buenos Aires the Pinkerton man, supposedly a high-stage gambler, frequented the saloons and gambling houses where Butch Cassidy and the Sundance Kid and his lady friend, Etta Place, liked to spend their evenings under assumed names. He bought drinks and passed out membership cards to his exclusive gambling club. Before the shank of the evening was over, he had found Butch Cassidy and the Sundance Kid and bought them champagne with a lavish hand. They were feeling no pain when the gambling man ordered a cab and took them to the waterfront to see the crated slot machines and roulette wheels on the dock where the steamer was tied up, due to embark the next morning for the return trip to New York.

The disguised Pinkerton operative perhaps entertained the idea of single-handedly capturing the two outlaws that night and marching the handcuffed pair up the gangplank of the boat to claim the large reward. Beyond all doubt, Butch Cassidy and Harry Longabaugh were both drunk from countless shots of whisky with champagne chasers, while the detective had surreptitiously emptied his whisky into brass cuspidors during the evening.

It was in the early hours before dawn when the gambler showed the two outlaws the crates piled on the dock. As he bent over to pull off the tarp covering, he felt the jab of a six-shooter in his back and heard Butch Cassidy's chuckling voice say, "Dump them goddamned slot machines into the water, Mr. Detective." The Pinkerton man did as he was told under the silent threat of the gun.

They then ordered him to go into his stateroom, and they kept him company until time for the early morning departure of the boat. Butch Cassidy had a quart of whisky and invited the detective to "drink hearty" and to pour the booze down his gullet instead of the cuspidor. The outlaws reminded him that he was lucky to be dead drunk instead of dead enough to bury in the watery grave of the harbor. When the detective had passed out drunk, they hogtied him, and when the ship's whistle sounded at dawn to warn all visitors to go ashore, the two outlaws marched down the gangplank and waited on the dock until the New York–bound steamship was under way.

Whether or not the story was true I have no way of knowing. I have heard much the same story told in detail about a certain bounty-hunting United States marshal instead of a Pinkerton operative. So pay your money and take your choice.

In recent years Jim Thornhill told me that Kid Curry, Butch Cassidy, and the Sundance Kid had gone to South America to go into the cattle business. They had decided to go straight, and they would have, except the bounty-hunting law officers kept on their trail like bloodhounds until they gave up their honest way of living and started out on the outlaw trail in South America.

There were two sides to the coin, the glitter of a tin star on one side and the tarnished side belonging to the outlaw who gambled his life for a South American stake. The outlaw with a bounty on his tough hide couldn't win for losing. His fate was a long stretch in the pen or an unmarked grave.

The days of the cowhand-turned-outlaw have long since passed. Only the legend lives on in the memory of the few old-timers who knew that breed of man in his true light and called him friend. The passing of the outlaw marked another milestone in the passing of the Old West.

22.

The Circle C Enters the Sheep Business

AFTER WILL AND BOB COBURN spent a couple of years looking over different cattle outfits in New Mexico, Arizona, and California, they finally located on the San Carlos Apache Indian Reservation in Arizona. Not long after that the Circle C outfit went head over boot heels into the sheep business.

Meanwhile I had graduated from Great Falls High School and had spent a year at Manzanita Hall preparatory school in Palo Alto, California, to bring my grades up to the standard required at Stanford University. My diploma from Manzanita Hall in 1910 was all I needed to enroll as a freshman. I was all set and raring to go, and my room was ready at the fraternity house to which I was pledged while in prep school. But the week before I was due to head for college, Bob Coburn called me into the log office at the ranch for a medicine talk. From the way I sized it up, Bob and my father had already had a discussion before they talked to me.

Bob, who divided his time between the Arizona cow outfit and the Montana Circle C spread, still retained his interest in the gold mines in the Little Rockies. He said there was no sense in my going to college in California. The Circle C outfit would foot the bill for my tuition and pay all my expenses if I would enroll at the Butte College of Mines. I was to study mining engineering, and during the summer vacations I would work at the Ruby and Alder

The Circle C Enters the Sheep Business

Gulch mines in the mill and the assay department to gain experience.

When Bob finished talking, I spoke my mind. I had gotten through algebra, geometry, and trig by the skin of my teeth and would last as long as a snowball in hell at the Butte College of Mines. I said I wasn't going to work at any job at Ruby and Alder Gulch—I was going to stay right here at the ranch. I would rather herd sheep than work in the mines or mill or assay office. I had been brought up to make a hand as a cowpuncher, and that was all I knew or ever wanted to know. As long as there was a Circle C outfit, I said, I'd make a hand there, or I could hire out as a cowhand with the Circle Diamond, the Long X, the Bear Paw Pool, or the Milner Square if I had to.

When I finished sounding off, there was an ominous silence. Then I heard my father clear his throat.

"By God, the boy's right, Bob," he said. "If he wants to stay here on the ranch, that's fine. After all, he will be working for his own interests. You'll be pulling out for Arizona before long, and

Ruby Gulch gold mine mill, Zortman, Montana.
Courtesy of W. J. Nankeman, Malta, Montana

Jake Myers will need somebody he can depend on. I don't see the need of him going away to college."

"You wrote your own ticket," Bob said as he looked at me with a sideward grin. "It's up to you to play your hand out." That was all the signal I needed to get the hell out of there.

Bob sure was right. I had made out my own ticket, no doubt about that, and dug my own grave so far as going to Stanford was concerned. So, what the hell, I'd hang and rattle, regardless.

My father was leaving the next week for San Diego, California, where he had already bought a home. My mother and younger brother, Harold, were already living there. Our home in Great Falls had been sold.

The previous fall Oscar (Spud) Stevens at Lewistown had bought most of the cattle and the Half Circle C cattle brand. The big herd had been delivered at the Rocky Point Crossing and tallied out as they crossed the wide Missouri to be thrown on Spud Stevens' range on the Red Barn Ranch at the head of the badlands on the south side of the Big Muddy.

Will and Bob Coburn had already sold their Bar L brand and all cattle in that iron to Spud Stevens. Wallace Coburn's 4T brand and cattle were sold at the same time.

What cattle remained at the Circle C Ranch were in the Rafter T brand. It was a sizable herd that was large enough for a man to go into the cow business in a small way. I had always been led to believe that someday, when I reached the legal age of twenty-one, the Rafter T would be registered on the brand book as mine and the cattle in that iron would belong to me as my rightful share of the Coburn Cattle Company. But nothing had been said about it since the previous fall, and I took it for granted that the deal was off—another bitter pill for me to swallow.

The morning after Bob had thrown the monkey wrench into my plans for going to Stanford, he pulled out for Arizona, and my father went to California. Wallace had left for New York with Charlie Russell to see about having a book of poems he had written published. Russell had done the western illustrations.

Jake Myers and I were left alone with ten bands of sheep still

The Circle C Enters the Sheep Business

on summer range. Around October they would have to be moved along to winter quarters that had formerly been used as line camps to winter cattle.

Jake Myers took the sheepherding job in his cowpuncher stride. Too proud to seek any advice from big sheepmen like B. D. Phillips, who was eager and willing to help put him onto the ropes, Jake bulled his way through the sheep handling.

"Forty years a butcher and never cut a gut," was one of his pet sayings. While Jake made mistakes at the beginning, he never made the same mistake twice.

The first thing Bob Coburn did when the Circle C entered the sheep business was to hire an experienced sheep boss, a short, stocky Mexican by the name of Frank Núñez, who was kind and understanding when handling his "sheepies," as he called them. There was always a sort of inner smile on his clean-shaven, swarthy, moon face. His love for animals, his sheep, his saddle horse and buckboard team, and the sheep dogs that followed him everywhere was a part of his nature and at times a little pathetic. On a cold drizzly day during lambing season I have seen Frank take off his yellow slicker and use it to cover a newborn lamb until the gut wagon came along to carry the ewe and lamb to the large, tin-roofed, lambing shed that was divided into small pens.

Frank and I were in Malta one day to pick up a sheepherder and his dog and bed and haul them out to the ranch in the little tin Lizzie. We were walking along the wide sidewalk in front of the Great Northern Hotel when the hotel door suddenly opened and two tall, blonde-haired, rosy-cheeked girls about sixteen years old came running out and threw their arms around the little Mexican, hugging and kissing him, laughing and crying at the same time, while tears of joy welled in his dark eyes.

"These are the tweens," Frank said pridefully as he acquainted me with the two girls who looked alike as peas in a pod.

Later I learned that they were the twin daughters of Angus Dunbar, a sheepman whose range was north of Milk River, close to the Canadian border. Frank Núñez had been herding sheep for Dunbar and staying at the ranch when Dunbar's wife gave birth to the twins. Since it was a forty-to-fifty-mile ride to the nearest doctor, there just wasn't enough time to summon him, and Dunbar and the Mexican had to deliver the babies. Because of some mysterious ailment, the mother died when the babies were a few weeks old. Frank Núñez figured out a formula combination of ewe's milk and condensed milk to bottle feed them, and no children in the country were ever healthier.

The twins were in their early teenage when the spring blizzard of 1907 hit Montana. All of Dunbar's money was invested in the bands of sheep. There was little or no chance of their survival, and the hardy Scot stood to lose everything he possessed. There was nothing on earth he could do to save the sheep that huddled for shelter under the roof of the sheep sheds. The stacks of winter hay were gone, and it was only a matter of a few days before the sheep would pile up and die.

Against the protesting of Angus Dunbar and the twin girls, Frank Núñez, with his dogs, his bed, and meager supply of grub, threw the three bands of sheep together and drifted them with the storm.

A month or more passed, and the delayed chinook wind had melted the winter snowdrifts. Dunbar had long given up ever seeing Frank Núñez again, and he and the girls mourned his death.

Then one bright, sunny day in June a large band of sheep appeared on the rolling prairie horizon. The little Mexican sheepherder and his two Scotch collie dogs had come home with more sheep than they had started with.

Small wonder then that in the eyes of the Scot and his flaxen-haired daughters, Frank Núñez had attained a somewhat saintly stature given to few men on earth.

Now it was largely due to Frank Núñez and his knowledge of handling sheep that the sheep operation at the Circle C Ranch was successful. Jake Myers knew nothing about the sheep business; nor did the few cowhands at the ranch, including me. The first lambing season at the home ranch was a fair example of our inexperience.

A large frame lambing shed with a corrugated, galvanized, tin

The Circle C Enters the Sheep Business

roof had been erected on the hill near the pole corrals and branding chute. The inside of the lambing shed was divided by a series of pine-board panels held together by baling wire. Each pen held a small number of ewes with newborn lambs.

A carpenter had constructed a gut wagon about twenty-five feet long, with pens large enough to hold a ewe and lamb or twin lambs. The gut wagon was divided down the middle, and the two small pens had hinged gates that opened outward and were fastened with a wire hook and eye.

The large "drop" band of pregnant ewes of nearly two thousand head were scattered out on the wide benchland, held by a sheepherder and his dog. Because of a slipup by the bookkeeper or the forgetfulness of Frank Núñez or the ignorance of Jake Myers, the necessary sheep hooks had not been ordered.

Sometimes when a ewe gave birth to a lamb, she would let it lie in the afterbirth and go back into the band. Then the scattered dozen or more men, called "lamb lickers," armed with long handled sheep hooks, would snare the hind leg of the deserting ewe and let the newborn lamb suckle its mother. Then they would place the ewe and lamb in the pen of the gut wagon. Once the ewe licked off the slimy afterbirth of the lamb, she would claim it.

Instead of a dozen lamb lickers with sheep hooks scattered on foot around the outskirts of the grazing ewe band, Jake Myers had half-a-dozen or more scattered cowpunchers on horseback, with loops cocked to rope the young ewes that deserted their newborn. Among the cowhands were Frank Howe, Rawhide Dan, Joe Holt, Tom Gordon, Charlie Summers, Walt Sizer, and me, and Joe Contway, Roy and Abe Long Knife, and Jesse Iron Horn from the Fort Belknap Reservation, and Jake Myers ramrodding the sheep roping.

We were doing a fair-to-middling job of heeling and head roping the fugitive ewes in late morning when the sheepman, B. D. Phillips, showed up in his brass-lamped fire-engine red, White Steamer automobile with his chauffeur. There was a twinkle in his eyes as he watched the unorthodox procedure.

Jake loped his horse over to where the car was stopped on the stage road. He was whistling a hungry tune through his white teeth bared in a wide grin. B. D. Phillips had promised Bob Coburn that he would drop around to see how Jake was managing his first lambing.

"With a lot of them ewes having twins," Jake boasted, "I reckon I'll lamb out over 90 per cent, Ben."

"You'll have about 40 per cent loss of ewes," B. D. warned, shaking his head, "when that sheep-roping contest is over."

"How come, Ben?" Jake asked suspiciously.

"Those aren't calves you're roping and hogtying, Jake," B. D. explained. "Riding through a band of sheep only chouses them up, and you're apt to break a hind leg or neck. Your men should be afoot with sheep hooks."

"Set those cowhands afoot," Jake argued, "they'll quit right now. I had a hell of a time as it was getting them that close to a band of sheep."

"A cowpuncher has no business around a band of sheep, Jake," B. D. said. "Hire yourself about a dozen lamb lickers in town and give them all sheep hooks. Frank Núñez will tell them what to do."

"Sheep hooks," Jake said, puzzling over the strange words. "So far as I know there are no sheep hooks on the place. Frank Núñez is over yonder at the lambing shed where he belongs."

B. D. Phillips explained the situation and told Jake the best thing he could do right then was to hire a dozen lamb lickers. He said there were a lot of homesteaders and half-blood kids who would be glad to earn a few bucks and get free meals. He advised Jake to tell his cowpuncher crew to coil up their ropes if he didn't want a lot of good ewes crippled and in the hospital band.

There were a couple of tin Lizzies at the ranch, and Jake sent me to Malta to get the sheep hooks and pick up a few herders with sheep dogs. He took the other beat-up jalopy and headed for the homesteaders and half-blood camps.

That evening about fifteen lamb lickers, mostly teenagers, sat down to supper at the ranch. I had picked up three sheepherders and their dogs during the three round trips I had made to Malta, as well as a bull cook and dishwasher to help the ranch cook.

The Circle C Enters the Sheep Business

There was enough work for the handful of cowpunchers—cattle to round up and calves to brand. Jake sent Joe Contway to rep with the ID wagon. Will Coburn had wired for Charlie Summers to come to Arizona to work, and he lost no time rolling his bed and sacking his saddle. Glad to get away from the blatting sheep, he left on the stage the next morning when Ruel Horner, the stage driver, pulled in at the office from Zortman.

Joe Holt, Tom Gordon, and Roy Long Knife went back to breaking broncs. Will Coburn had shipped two carloads of unbroken four- to five-year-old stags that had run as range studs, and they were pretty rank to halter break and hard for a bronc rider to sit.

Up until lambing time I had been helping halter break the rough string and hazing for the bronc rider when he rode outside the corral and out across the flats. But with Frank Núñez busy at the lambing shed, Jake put me at his camp-tending job, much to my disgust. But I had dealt myself the cards and it was up to me to play my hand out.

23.

Bucking Range with the Sheep Outfits

THE SHEEP CAMPS WERE SCATTERED from hell to breakfast—from Big Warm, Little Warm, and Beaver creeks to Sun Prairie, bordered by the Larb Hills on the east; along Beauchamp and Fourchette to Slippery Ann and Rock creeks on the west; from the vast prairie land between the ranch and the Little Rockies to the edge of the badlands north of the Missouri River.

My job was to make the rounds of the sheep camps on horseback and pick up the grub lists of the sheepherders. Then I would travel by buckboard, drawn by a gentle team and loaded with the grub for the sheep camps, with my saddled horse tied behind the rig.

Each band of sheep had to be moved to a new location on an average of every two weeks. I would hook my team to a sheep wagon and move it to the next camp where the grazing was good. Then I would unhook the team and mount my saddled horse and lead the harnessed team to the next wagon. This continued until I had moved the last sheep wagon to its new location. It took me the better part of a week, and whenever I stayed overnight at some sheep camp, it was part of my job to do the cooking.

Sometimes when I camped the herder on a dry camp a mile or so from a creek, it was my job to haul the water. There was a water barrel lashed to the buckboard behind the seat, and I would fill it with a bucket by driving into the middle of the creek and then filling the two twenty-gallon kegs that hung on both sides of the sheep wagon.

Near the end of the lambing season, only a few days before Frank Núñez would take over my job, I ran into what looked like trouble. I was on horseback making the rounds of the sheep camps to pick up the grub lists. I had picked up the last grub list from the sheepherder camped on the Big Warm and was on my way back to the home ranch. As I rode near the Parrot place, a ranch Robert Coburn had acquired in the early days from a rancher named Parrot, I sighted a large band of sheep that I knew did not belong to our outfit and a canvas-topped sheep wagon camped on the creek near a small bridge on the stage road.

Part of the band of wethers were grazing on the Circle C fenced-in hay meadow and more were coming. When I rode down along the fence, I discovered that between a few dozen fence posts the lower strand of barbwire had been raised and fastened to the upper wire by short lengths of baling wire to allow sheep to enter the hay meadow.

My first notion was to unfasten the tied baling wire, but that would have left several hundred sheep trapped inside the fence. I sure was hot under the collar when I headed up a small hill where the herder and his dog sat watching the grazing sheep. I was fit to be tied by the time I got there.

The herder's tow-colored hair needed cutting, and a bushy yellow beard covered most of his face. What skin showed on his cheekbones and nose was sunburned and peeling. He showed white teeth in a friendly grin, and his pale china-blue eyes under bleached brows were guileless. His big black and white shepherd dog stood up and wagged its tail as a greeting.

The sheepherder was young, in his twenties. He was a tall, broad-shouldered six-footer dressed in a clean, faded-blue cotton shirt and faded bib overalls. He wore a pair of rusty work shoes and a hayseed-farmer, wide-brimmed straw hat. His belt was a leather harness strap from which hung a canteen of water. A fancy, engraved, silver-handled knife was in a silver scabbard fastened to the strap belt.

Before I could open my mouth to cuss him out, he took a round metal box of snuff from the pocket of his overalls, removed the top, and held it towards me. His friendly grin put a smile into his blue eyes. I shook my head. If the box of snuff was a peace offering, I wanted no part of it. I wasn't about to be fooled by the friendly grin. The sheepherder looked bigger than a skinned mule, but the Colt .45 that I had shoved in my waistband was an equalizer.

"What the hell's the idea of letting your woollies graze in that hay meadow? That hay belongs to the Circle C Ranch. Don't you know it's against the law to herd sheep across fenced land?" My voice sounded dry and choked with anger.

The sheepherder shook his head from side to side and laughed. It wasn't a loud laugh, and it had a friendly sound. Then he began to jabber.

"No speak English. Yust Swenska," he explained, pointing a thumb at his chest and laughing at himself. He was friendly as could be and acted glad to see me and happy for my company.

I tried sign talk, pointing to the sheep then to his wagon, trying to make him understand that he and his sheep were trespassing. He shook his head and grinned. He pointed one of his arms and his forefinger along the road to Malta, then towards his sheep and camped wagon. Then he held up three fingers.

"Three more bands of sheep? Three more sheep wagons coming from Malta?" I questioned aloud. The big Swede nodded his head and grinned up at me, while the dog wagged its bushy tail.

I motioned him to follow me as I rode back to the fence. Then I motioned for him to get the sheep out of the hay meadow and pointed to the tied-up wires. He finally got the drift, nodded his head, and motioned his dog to round up what sheep were inside the fence. He jabbered Swedish and shook his head vigorously as he pointed to the fence and then to his chest to indicate that he was not responsible for the tied-up wires. Then he scowled thoughtfully for a minute and suddenly smiled.

"Harmon!" he cried out excitedly. "Boss man!"

The painted black brand on the sheep belonged to the Hansen brothers, a comparatively new sheep outfit that had bought up

Bucking Range with the Sheep Outfits

a couple of small nester outfits south of Zortman and west of the Gill place and the Jim Thornhill ranch. Frank Harmon was their sheep boss and head camp tender.

When the shepherd had rounded up the sheep and driven them back through the fence, I got down from my horse and proceeded to unwrap the short lengths of baling wire and allow the barbwire strands to fall back into place.

The friendly smile was now gone from the herder's face as if he had a notion to stop me. I kept watching him out of the corner of an eye, and when I had put the fence back in place, I forked my horse and rode away at a long high trot without looking back. I pulled up on a high benchland that commanded a view in all directions. Sure enough, I could make out three bands of grazing sheep and three canvas-topped sheep wagons camped a mile apart, just off the stage road to Malta.

That told the story. I hightailed it for the ranch to break the news to Jake. It was suppertime when I got there. I found Jake in the office with his tally book and stub pencil, quoting figures to the bookkeeper who sat behind the roll-top desk. Frank Baker, a tall, rawboned individual who until recently had tended camp for the Phillips sheep outfit, sat sprawled in one of the old barroom chairs, his long legs stretched out.

Frank Baker had built up sort of a tough reputation for himself in the Little Rockies country, where he had matched more than a few drunken fights at Zortman and Landusky. Sober, he was good natured and easy to get along with and as good a sheepman as there was. Drunk, Frank Baker was apt to be ornery and treacherous, handy with the knife he packed along with a sixshooter. Baker had locked horns with Fatty Jones, Phillips' foreman and sheep boss, and had either quit or been fired.

I waited until Jake finished quoting the day's lamb tally and the bookkeeper had gone to the cook cabin. Then I told him the bad news about Frank Harmon moving three bands of sheep across land that belonged to our outfit. I told him about the big Swedish herder who spoke no English and the tied-up wires that let the sheep into the hay meadow at the Parrot place. I explained that

I had used sign language to communicate with the big Swede and he had gotten his sheep out and I had lowered the wires and hightailed it for home.

Jake had never met Harmon. According to Frank Baker, Harmon was big and hard to handle. He traveled on his big shape and packed a six-shooter. Baker figured that Harmon would have a camp tender with him to move the sheep wagons each day, and the camp tender probably packed a gun and was tough in his own right.

As Jake walked the floor, he said he could handle Frank Harmon when the play came up if Baker would keep the camp tender off his back. Frank Baker grinned and declared it would be his pleasure.

"You're running this outfit, Jake, but you're a green hand when it comes to knowin' the ropes. I don't aim to butt in, but I'm an old hand at the game when it comes to handlin' a deal like this," Frank Baker said.

"If you got any ideas, Baker," Jake said grimly, "lay them on the line and we'll make medicine."

"This outfit owns the Rollin' M Lake," Baker said in measured words. "Them three bands of sheep Harmon is trailin' in to the Hansen ranch has to water at that lake. The lake is fenced in, so padlock the gates and charge Harmon a cent a head for waterin' his sheep. Have a couple or three horsebackers ridin' Winchester guard along the fence, and Harmon will have to pay through the nose."

"You got somethin' there, Baker," Jake admitted.

"That ain't the half of it." Baker rubbed the wire stubble of his jaw with a calloused hand. "Directly the sheep are done waterin', Harmon will move 'em on. This time of year, before shearin', you'd be surprised at the number of sheep with the brands wore off since they was branded last June or July." Baker spat a sodden cud of tobacco into the gaboon.

"What's that got to do with it, Baker?" Jake asked, puzzled.

"Between the Rollin' M Lake, where Harmon pays for waterin' the sheep, and the Hansen ranch is a week to ten days travel. You

Bucking Range with the Sheep Outfits

got four bands of wethers camped on water on that range Harmon has to cross. All your sheepherders have to do is to graze their sheep close to Harmon's and dog 'em into a merger. Accordin' to range law, the mixed bands have to be put in a panel corral with a long chute and a dodge gate leadin' into an empty corral big enough to hold a band of sheep—Hansen's sheep! The dodge gate puts your sheep in the open.

"Now, Frank Núñez keeps all your sheep freshly painted with black paint, but chances are that a third of the Hansen sheep have worn off brands you can't read. So the sheep that shows no brand that can be read is, by law, divided between the outfits, with a tally man from each outfit there at the dodge gate. And if you're wise, Jake, you'll have a couple of men handy, one with a sheep hook to snare the unbranded sheep, the other with a bucket of black paint and a short-handled brandin' iron.

"I'm willin' to bet a month's wages that you'll come out a hundred sheep ahead each time the three bands of mixed sheep are cut at the dodge gate. You'll be at least three hundred head of big wethers ahead when the dust settles, mebbe five hundred if that sheep boss Harmon is as careless about keepin' his sheep branded up to date as I figger he is. With the price of wethers like she is now, Jake, you'll make money on the deal, and it'll break Harmon from moving his sheep on another man's range."

"You won't be losing nothing, Baker, if it works out. I'll make it right with you if you handle the whole thing," Jake promised.

"You got a deal, Jake," Baker said. "Keep Frank Núñez at the ranch. He's too damn honest for a Mexican. Let me and my young brother, Aleck, handle it, but you be on hand in case of any argument. Have plenty of panels nearby to build the corrals with and enough baling wire and long stakes. I'll rig up the dodge gate and handle it personally. We'll mix the bands before sunrise. By the time you have the corrals set up, we'll have the sheep ready to pen and have the job done by early afternoon. All shuffled and dealt. Me 'n Aleck is old hands at this range buckin', Jake," Baker bragged.

Just about then the supper bell rang.

"We'll talk about it after supper," Jake told Frank Baker. "Come over to my house where that scissorbill bookkeeper won't have his big ears to the ground."

Some Malta real-estate shark had located a St. Paul bookkeeper named Cordray on Alkali Flat where nothing but greasewood would grow. Cordray, in his late thirties, was a sod widower whose wife had died a few years earlier. He had sunk what money he had in the dry-land homestead and was broke when Jake hired him as bookkeeper. Cordray had once worked for Sears, Roebuck in St. Paul, and he knew how to save the Circle C money by ordering groceries and clothing by the carload lots. But he had a tenderfoot's curiosity about the wild and woolly West, and he had big listening ears. What Cordray didn't know, Jake figured, he couldn't gossip about.

So Jake and Baker made their war medicine at Jake's house behind drawn window blinds. When Jake showed up about midnight at the mess cabin for coffee, he was all keyed up like a tightly wound clock, judging from the way he paced the floor, sipping coffee and talking aloud to himself.

Jake had never met either of the Hansen brothers or their sheep boss, Harmon, but they were asking for trouble and Jake aimed to give them a bellyful. Jake told me to get hold of Walt Sizer and be at the Harmon sheep camp the next morning before sunrise.

Sunrise the following morning, when Harmon and his camp tender showed up to move the Swede's sheep wagon from where it was camped in the lane at the Parrot place, Jake and Frank Baker were there waiting for him. Harmon was on horseback, and his camp tender drove a light spring wagon.

The big, whiskered Swede had grazed his band off the bedground and was a half mile from camp when Walt Sizer and I rode up on him. He carried a Winchester .30-.30 saddle carbine in the crook of his arm. His friendly smile was gone, and his china-blue eyes had a cold, suspicious look. Walt Sizer was a husky five foot eight and had the build of a welterweight. He, too, had built up quite a reputation as a rough and tumble fighter in the Little Rockies, and it was our job to keep the Swede on ice.

Bucking Range with the Sheep Outfits

Before the sheepherder knew what was happening, Sizer drew down on him with his six-shooter. Somewhere in his travels around mining camps, Sizer had picked up a few words of Swedish, which he now jabbered to the herder, backing his words with a motion of the gun. The herder nodded and laid his Winchester on the ground. Then, a scared look in his eyes, he picked up the sheep dog and held him in his arms.

I had been trying my best to see what was happening down below at the sheep wagon and at the same time keep an eye on Sizer in case he needed help or to prevent him from going too far. At the ranch Jake had warned me to keep Sizer from gun whipping the harmless sheepherder. When the Swede picked up his dog, I knew it was time I put in my two-bits worth, because I could tell by the look in Sizer's eyes that he intended to bend the barrel of his gun across the herder's head.

I crowded my horse between them and told Sizer to lay off— that Jake had said there was to be no rough stuff. Sizer shoved his gun back in the waistband of his Levis and put a twisted grin on his face. He muttered something about just throwing a scare into the lousy herder. I told him he had already done that and the herder did not want his dog hurt.

About then we heard a gunshot from the sheep wagon below on the creek. We could see Jake and Harmon wrestling around on the ground, while Frank Baker sat his horse with a six-shooter in his hand. The camp tender was on the seat of the wagon with his hands in the air. Jake straddled Harmon and worked the sheep foreman over with the barrel of his six-shooter. Harmon hollered he'd had enough, and Jake got up and stepped back with his gun in his hand and told Harmon he had let him off easy.

Harmon got to his feet and stood wiping the blood from his face with his shirt sleeves as Jake proceeded to chew him out to a fare-thee-well. He told him to get the Hansen brothers' sheep off the Circle C range and said it would cost him a cent a head to water the sheep at Rolling M Lake.

Harmon agreed to pay the watering fees, and Jake had him put it in writing. Jake had sent Joe Holt, Tom Gordon, Doc Corrigan, and Rawhide Dan to ride herd on the Hansen sheep. So we all spent the rest of the day riding Winchester guard on the moving sheep. It was dark by the time we got back to the home ranch.

Jake managed to get one of the Hansen brothers on the telephone at Zortman, and he agreed to pay the watering fee. The way Jake hollered over the telephone, you could hear him cussing as far as the Little Rockies. That's how the telephone between the ranch and Malta, with branch lines to the Phillips and Hog ranches, acquired the name of the "Whoop and Holler Line."

In the course of the following weeks Frank Baker's plan for mixing the bands of sheep was put into action. But, as Frank Núñez argued later, chousing the sheep at the cutting pens did harm far greater than any profit gained. Thus Jake Myers learned the hard way another lesson about handling sheep.

24.

A New Routine at the Circle C

LATER ON IT CAME TO LIGHT that Aleck Baker and some of his shirttail kin had driven a bunch of range horses at daybreak through the lake where the bands of sheep were camped, riling the shallow water into a mud hole, which rendered it unfit to water the sheep. Shortly after Frank and Aleck Baker handled the mixing of the sheep bands, they drew their time and went back to work for the Phillips outfit.

Castrating buck lambs differed from castrating bull calves. The cords attached to the lambs' testicles were not severed by the sharp steel of a jackknife, but were severed by the teeth of the docker. It was believed that the whetted blade of a stock knife would injure the lambs and cause blood poisoning.

The dockers customarily wore short jackets and pants of oiled yellow rubber. At the end of the day's docking, the slicker jackets and pants would be covered with spurted blood and the remnants of dried lamb testicles, which had to be washed off by the wearer.

Frank Núñez did most of the docking and castrating. Jake had watched the little Mexican get the job done, and one evening after supper he began talking about how easy it was for any man who could stand the taste of blood. All a docker needed, he said, was a chunk of chewing tobacco in his jaw and a set of strong teeth. Jake finally coaxed Bob Coburn into a fifty-dollar bet, suckered the cowhands at the bunkhouse into betting, and left for town in the tin Lizzie. By the time he returned, he had a list a mile long of bettors—Joe Brown, Dutch John, the Dewar brothers, Buster Moran, Sam and Luke Deniff, George Heath, Louis Goslin, and others. The total town and ranch bets added up to four hundred dollars and two Stetson hats. Not only that, Jake had made an offhand bet of one hundred dollars with B. D. Phillips that he would lamb out 90 per cent at docking time.

After the next day's docking Jake had won all bets, and he split his winnings fifty-fifty with Frank Núñez because it was owing to the little Mexican's experienced skill that the bulk of the twin lambs dropped were saved.

For instance, when a lamb was born dead, Frank would skin the hide off and tie it to one of the twin lambs born that day. He would make the ewe that had given birth to the dead lamb suckle the twin lamb and would rub her nose in the fresh afterbirth on the tied-on hide the lamb wore. He would keep the ewe and lamb in a separate pen that night and the following day to make sure the ewe would claim the overcoated lamb for her own.

On other occasions, when a ewe had insufficient milk in her udder to feed twin lambs, Frank Núñez would bottle feed one twin from a mixture of cow's milk and condensed milk. He would have twenty or thirty bottle-fed lambs in a separate pen he called his "orphans."

When Núñez was too busy to bottle feed his orphans, it was the cook's job. As a result, every morning and evening at feeding time there would be a dozen or more hungry, blatting lambs at the screen door of the kitchen. The orphan lambs were both pets and pests around the ranch. If the door of the bunkhouse was left open, the orphans would make themselves at home, leaving their droppings on the floor and tarp-covered beds.

At docking time the tails of the bottle-fed pets were left long for markers in the big bands of sheep on the range. Their long tails were easily spotted by the herder for a range count on an evening when the band was grazed to the bed ground. The long-tailed sheep, the black sheep, and the belled sheep were tallied each evening. If any were missing, it meant that a small bunch

A New Routine at the Circle C

of sheep were also missing and the herder and his dog had to find them.

The pet sheep were also used especially for lead sheep when a band crossed a bridge or entered a chute. The herder would tie a rope around the pet sheep and lead it, and the rest of the band would follow. Thus there were times when the pet sheep more than compensated for the bother of being bottle fed, and the little Mexican had a right to be proud of his orphans.

The Mexican shearing crews followed the seasons from California, Arizona, Nevada, and New Mexico into Colorado, Wyoming, Idaho, Montana, and the Dakotas. The shearing season in the Southwest varied by a few months from the season in the northwestern states. At one time Frank Núñez had been a high roller boss of this itinerant shearing crew who used hand shears.

He supervised the conversion of the log machine shed and adjoining cow barn at the Circle C Ranch into a sheep shed. Using the pine-board panels held together by baling wire, he made the shearing pens large enough to hold ten sheep and two shearers. These pens were equipped with panel gates that opened out into a lane the width of a panel. A large panel pen just outside the open front of the shed was used to hold about two hundred head of unsheared sheep at one time.

In the morning every sheep shearer counted out the long cord strings used to tie each sheared fleece. One hundred strings was the average that one shearer could handle. The high rollers could shear 150 sheep in a day. In the evenings after supper the shearers were kept busy at the grindstone and whetstone sharpening the shears. Usually each shearer sharpened two or three sets of shears at a time.

The sheep shearers sang a Mexican song about a strong back and a weak head, much tequila and marijuana. There were other ribald verses lauding the virility of the high-rolling sheep shearer who sweated all day in the shearing pens and bedded down at night with a different *puta*. Sung to the lilting tune of *Ay Tulipán*, it had endless verses.

Shearing sheep by hand blades was gruelling, back-breaking

work that required a strong back and shoulder and arm muscles and strong wrists and hands to work the stiff spring of the large steel blades. The shearers labored from sunrise until noon. During the noon hour after dinner they worked at the grindstone and whetstone, then went back to the shearing pens until six o'clock suppertime when the first bell rang at the cook cabin. The second bell half an hour later gave them time to wash up and hit the jug.

For the first time on record at the Circle C Ranch since 1886, Robert Coburn was forced to allow whisky and gambling. Each time the stage from Malta rolled in at the ranch, there were half-a-dozen jugs of whisky aboard which had been ordered by Frank Núñez from Phil Castleberg's Hotel Annex Saloon. It was well-aged barreled whisky.

Each sheep shearer had his own jug under his bunk at the bunkhouse, and without exception they all consumed at least a quart a day, then sweated it out at the shearing pens. And there were always a couple of poker games going at night.

The Mexican shearing crews varied in age from seventeen to a few with a sprinkling of gray in their coarse black hair. Peralta, the high roller boss of the crew, who tallied daily the most strings at the shearing pens, had iron-gray hair. He was a quart-a-day man and banked a high-stake poker game at night. When the shearing season was over, Peralta worked as sheep boss for a big sheep outfit in northern California, in the grape vineyard and wine country.

Some of the shearers mixed marijuana with their cigarette tobacco. Now and then when a shearer hollered "sheep out" at the pens, he took time out to roll a smoke, and the peculiar odor of marijuana would be noticeable.

Outside the log cow barn, in the corral, was a high plank scaffold where the wool fleeces were sacked. The cow barn was divided into stalls, and each stall had a window without glass. A solid pine board covered with rawhide hung from the top and was held up by a hook. The open windows were used to shove the cord-wrapped fleeces outside to be gathered up by the sacker's helper, tossed up on the platform, and covered by canvas wagon sheets to protect them

A New Routine at the Circle C

from rain until they were picked up by the jerk-line freight wagons and hauled to the Malta warehouse.

As the sheared sheep were driven out of the pens and into the alley, Frank Núñez, using a bucket of black paint he had made from lampblack, and coal oil, branded each clipped sheep with a short, wooden, stamp branding iron. Our outfit branded the Hat which was a half circle with a bar attached to each end. The converted cow barn would have a peculiar pungent odor, a mixture of oily wool and human sweat, and despite the breeze from the open windows, the air was always hot and humid.

It was my job to tally the sheared sheep out of each pen and give each shearer full credit on the time book. I would be on hand to open a panel gate when they hollered "sheep out" and let the sheep drift of their own accord into the open corral with the other sheared sheep. The gate served a dual purpose as both exit and entrance. It was the wrangler's job to have ten sheep waiting the minute the pen was emptied, and as a rule he was Johnny-on-the-spot. Only on rare occasions did an unsheared sheep balk at the entrance to the small shearing pen. When this happened, I would help the wrangler by grabbing the sheep and carrying it bodily into the pen.

At the end of each day's work I would go down the line with the total tally of each shearer and compare my figures with each man's tally that he kept by his bundle strings, so there was never much chance for an argument.

A red-bearded Scotsman named Andy Cameron, called Scotty, was sheep wrangler at the shearing pens. He owned a pair of Australian sheep dogs, a male named Bruce and a bitch named Bonnie. Scotty used Bruce inside the shed and left Bonnie out in the corral with the unsheared sheep. Scotty seldom spoke commands to the two trained sheep dogs, because the Mexican shearers were constantly jabbering back and forth between the pens or singing ribald songs. Scotty had his own method of signaling to Bruce with his arm. Believe it or not, the dog would cut off ten head of sheep and get in behind the cut and herd them to the shearing pen, nipping gently at the woolly rumps of the drags. If a sheep turned back,

Bruce would head it off and shoulder it back into the bunch like a cutting horse. Then Scotty would motion to Bonnie out in the corral, and without any barking or fuss she would gently nip enough sheep into the winged chute that led to the shed to replace the penned sheep.

Scotty claimed, and he spoke without bragging, that his pair of Australian sheep dogs could understand every word of his Scottish burr, and no man who ever watched while Scotty talked to his dogs at the sheep camp would argue to the contrary. Scotty was as sparing of words as he was thrifty of pennies, but at camp or sitting on some hill while his band of sheep were spread out grazing, he would talk to the dogs as he'd talk to a human. The dogs' ears would be cocked forward as they listened to his every word with devotion in their eyes. Only God and Scotty and the two dogs ever knew the nostalgic stories he told of the highlands and lowlands and lakes of Scotland, where he had spent his boyhood.

Even my father, who disliked the sheep business in all its varied forms, would watch the red-bearded Scot work his dogs in the shearing shed and corral with reluctant approval.

My father had wintered in California and returned to the ranch in May during the height of the lambing season. He came from Malta by stage and sat on the driver's seat with Ruel Horner, the stage driver, who had brought him up to date on the change-over to the sheep business at the ranch. But even with Horner's somewhat vague description of the changes that had taken place during his absence, the gray-bearded, pioneer cowman must have been shocked by what he saw. Now, instead of grazing cattle, small bands of ewes and young lambs, each with its bunch herder, were scattered grazing as far as the reservation fence. Near the ranch were the big "drop" band, the long, wood-sided gut wagon, and the corrals filled with sheep. The large frame sheep shed with its corrugated, galvanized, tin roof caught the reflection of the lowering sun and gave off a blinding glare. It was a sheepman's monstrosity, an ugly eyesore, and an abominable object in the eyes of a cowman. The distant, constant blatting of the sheep which

A New Routine at the Circle C

disturbed the hushed silence of a balmy evening sunset and contained a dismal mockery of shame and defeat greeted the return of a once proud cattleman to his lost domain. The soft evening breeze, steeped with the obnoxious stench of sheep, clogged the old cowman's nostrils, and he took a large, white, silk handkerchief from his pocket and blew his nose vigorously in a vain attempt to rid himself of the oily, sickening odor. But the sheep stench was destined to remain, clinging like an invisible fungus to the old, sod-roofed log cabins.

There was an edge of sadness in the return of Robert Coburn which showed in his long brooding silences as he sat in his old barroom chair in front of the log office.

Sometimes when my day's work was done, in the long evenings after supper he would tell me to saddle Reader, and I would ride with him out into the big pasture on East Butte where the cattle grazed and no sheep were allowed. We would get a range count on the Rafter T cattle and see what shape they were in, see if the calves had been branded on the spring roundup and get a range count on the Rafter T bulls. Then we would ride through the Indian camps along Beaver Creek, where the tipis of the old men were located, and stop to visit a short while with Black Dog, Iron Horn, Watch-His-Walking, Old Thunder, and others. My saddle pockets would be bulging with packages of pipe tobacco to pass out while shaking hands. I had a fair-to-middling knowledge of the Assiniboin tongue and I acted as interpreter. Invariably the talk of the old men concerned early days, the buffalo days before there were any reservations to fence them in. On the ride back in the moonlight I knew without being told that those visits to the old men lifted my father's spirits for a few brief hours.

"The smell of an Injun camp," he once remarked on our way home, "takes away the sheep stink for a while."

I remember one day when my father and Jake Myers rode out to the "drop" band where they were lambing at Big Warm Camp. One of those sudden thunderstorms came up, with a regular cloudburst and the chain lightning popping close. The two men had no saddle slickers, so they got off their horses and crawled under the gut wagon for shelter. A bolt of lightning struck too close for comfort, and my father crawled out from under the shelter and stood clear of the wagon in the rain.

"Let 'er pop!" he called out to Jake, his teeth showing in a grin. "I'm damned if I'll be lightning struck under a damned sheep wagon."

Another time Wallace Coburn brought a group of men and their wives out from Malta to watch the shearing. Joe Sklower was taking photographs, and he wanted a picture of my father sitting on top of a pile of wool sacks. My father flatly and profanely refused and threatened to bust the camera over Joe's head. His irate outburst was good humored, but he meant every word he spoke.

The bottle-fed lambs that hung around the back door of the kitchen and let out a chorus of blatting every time the door opened were a constant irritation to my father, who was in the habit of dropping in at the kitchen for a cup of coffee.

Al Taylor, the ranch cook for many years, was long gone, and a number of cooks came and went, including a Chinaman. Nigger Bob was an old-time roundup cook who drew the line at feeding lambs, and finally a character named Deadwood Jones was hired. He had cooked a few seasons for Buffalo Bill's Wild West Show and talked about it until my father, fed up with his talk, voiced his low opinion of Buffalo Bill as a government scout and buffalo hunter. He called Buffalo Bill a drunken windbag and then fired the talkative Deadwood Jones. Jake then hired Charlie Wingate who had been chief cook at the Ruby Gulch boarding house. He hired Wingate away at twice the pay he'd been getting, and the hungry miners who worked the graveyard shift were forced to eat at Biddy Moran's restaurant while Wingate cooked breakfast for the lamb lickers. Jake had connived with Biddy and her son Buster, who owned a saloon next to his mother's restaurant, to shanghai Wingate, who was gambling in the back room of Buster's that night. He persuaded them that the grizzled mining-camp cook was gambling away his hard-earned wages to the tinhorns.

My father and Wingate got along first rate. Wingate cooked his favorite rice and custard puddings and saved the choice top sir-

A New Routine at the Circle C

loin and porterhouse steaks for him, and his cooking was equal to Al Taylor's. But it just wasn't the same anymore and never would be the same again.

While my father never uttered a complaint, he seemed to have lost his appetite. But he doggedly stuck it out throughout the lambing season until the lamb lickers and sheep shearers had gone. The few cowhands moved back into the bunkhouse after Doc Corrigan and Rawhide Dan had deloused the place with coal oil and cattle dip.

The bottle-fed lambs had long since been distributed to the sheep bands, and the nearest sheep were the hospital band at the Veseth place, ten or twelve miles below the ranch. The ten bands of sheared sheep were on their way to summer range, and all was peaceful and quiet at the home ranch. The rains had rid the ranch of the offensive sheep stench, and at last my father could sit in front of the office and read his newspaper in quiet, while the meadowlarks warbled their evening song and the familiar odor of wild roses along Beaver Creek sweetened the air.

25.

Hiring the Sheepherders

JAKE MYERS WAS RAPIDLY LEARNING all the ins and outs of the sheep business. Although Frank Núñez was the sheep boss and Jake never interfered with his way of handling the sheep, it was Jake who worked the over-all strategy.

Jake was well aware of the fact that B. D. Phillips was in the habit of trailing several bands of sheep north to summer range after shearing. So when Peralta took his shearing crew to the Phillips ranch, Jake made his first move. He asked Núñez which bands of sheep they should trail north. Núñez suggested he send three bands of wethers, and Jake heeded his advice.

While the Phillips sheep were in the process of having their wool sheared, Jake had the wether bands on the move northward. Frank Howe was in charge, and he was accompanied by a camp tender, a light wagon loaded with a grub supply, and the camp tender's team to move the three sheep wagons.

Frank Howe knew every foot and square mile of that country as far as the Canadian line, and the country north of Milk River was the summer range Jake had in mind. Up until recent years the land had been the unfenced free range of the cattlemen, but the homesteader invasion had taken over, and fenced-in, dry-land farms were scattered far and wide on both sides of the Milk River.

Jake told Howe that Frank Baker and Fatty Jones had been trailing Phillips' bands of sheep north almost to the Canadian bor-

Hiring the Sheepherders

der in spite of the homesteaders. Baker had told Jake his method of getting through, and Jake passed it on to Frank Howe for what it was worth. All he had to do was to give an occasional homesteader one or two of the sorefooted drags, and he would let the sheep cross his worthless parched land. When Frank Howe returned a month or two later with his three bands of sheep which averaged two thousand head to the band, he told how easily he had handled the homesteaders who demanded sheep for allowing them to cross their lands.

"All I got is wethers," Howe said he told them, passing himself off as B. D. Phillips, the wealthy sheep owner. "I got three bands of fat ewes following. Keep two of the ewes from each band. All you homesteaders will need is one buck between you to breed the ewes to." Howe said he would write out an order to the camp tenders to give each homesteader the promised ewes, and he would sign the order with the forged signature of B. D. Phillips.

"Fatty Jones was trailin' three bands of ewes," Howe said with a chuckle. "When Fatty balked about givin' up the ewes, the homesteaders got hostile. Armed with pitchforks, half-a-dozen scissorbills surrounded that fat bastard, and he had to give in or get his big gut punctured. I come back by a different route and pulled the same trick, and it cost Fatty Jones twenty or more ewes before he got back home. The hell of it was Fatty didn't dast tell B. D. about how he'd been jobbed, or he'd got the tin can tied to his bushy tail."

Meanwhile, during the summer Jake was bucking range with the Hansens and two or three other sheepmen whose bands were edging onto the range between the Little Rockies and the Missouri River. Thanks to Frank Baker, however, Jake was digging into the bag of tricks used by the wily camp tender.

Jake used Walt Sizer and me to move the sheep wagons when necessary to new grazing land where creeks were located. Every night we would split up and each stay at a different sheep camp, wherever there was likely to be trouble. Two or three sheepherders were packing Winchesters under the pretense of shooting coyotes.

Jake and Harmon settled their differences and shook hands on it,

Pioneer Cattleman in Montana

but for all their outward shell of apparent friendliness, there was an inner core of enmity.

Every few days Jake would make the rounds of the scattered sheep camps with his pack of hounds, and usually he would have some cowpuncher along, just in case of trouble. Coyotes and prairie wolves were plentiful, and Jake usually had a couple of fresh coyote and wolf hides to show for the trip. But what Jake was actually doing was riding line on the strung-out sheep camps as a mounted, armed, patrol rider and trouble shooter, in case there were any arguments with the camp tenders or sheepherders who were crowd-

Jake Myers, left, and Bob Coburn, right, with part of the hound pack.

Hiring the Sheepherders

ing our range from all sides. News of Jake's run-in with Harmon had spread to other sheep outfits and built up his tough reputation, and word got around that the big, black-haired Oklahoman was a good man to leave alone. Consequently, the thinly veiled threat of Jake's frequent appearances had the desired effect, and we had very little trouble bucking range.

The Circle C sheep were strung out from Sun Prairie and the Larb Hills to the Cow Island Crossing on the Missouri, over a fifty-mile stretch as the cow flies. The sheep wagons were spotted five or ten miles apart, depending on the terrain and water. If possible, the wagons were camped on patented land belonging to the outfit or on school sections. So, while the sheep wagons were camped on land owned or leased by our outfit, the sheep grazed on free range that belonged to Uncle Sam but had been a part of the Circle C range since 1886.

The few scattered homesteads in that area had been taken up years earlier by nester cowmen. The Circle C had long ago bought those small ranches, along with their cattle and brands, and used them as line camps. There would be a log cabin and horse barn and fenced-in haystacks of wild hay that had been mowed down in the coulees, where in good seasons the bunch grass touched a rider's stirrups. The line camps and the school sections under long lease, red inked on the blueprint map at the office, had the appearance of a large checkerboard.

In other words, the Circle C outfit was claiming that free range to run sheep. Jake had given Sizer and me orders to hold that range. If the Hansen brothers or any outside sheep outfit moved a band of sheep on that fifty-mile stretch, one of us would take the word to the home ranch, and Jake would take it from there.

Most of the sheepherders were Mexicans hired by Frank Núñez, and they usually spoke and understood enough English to get by. Mac Bracamonte was the best educated of them, and he herded sheep for the outfit until it was sold. Jack Conley, Scotty, and a black Irishman named Brian Donahue were the only non-Mexican herders at the sheep camps Sizer and I worked with that summer. Frank Howe had three non-Mexican herders, Rattlesnake Jack (so called because he saw snakes in his boots when he was drunk), Pete Hilforts (a big Dane), and Two Dog Moore. Howe's camp tender was a former cowhand named Clay Hill.

Although Frank Núñez was Sizer's and my camp tender, we would see him only once a week when he fetched out grub in his spring wagon. His black saddle horse, Nig, would follow the wagon without a lead rope, and Frank's saddle and bridle would be in the wagon. The fat, gentle Nig would graze along the way, sometimes a mile behind the rig.

Núñez drove a buggy team called Injun and Sundown. Injun was a dark bay and Sundown a sunburned brown. Both horses were fat and lazy, and they had but one road gait, a slow, steady dogtrot. All three horses were biscuit eaters and never wore hobbles at camp. They would show up at mealtime, morning and night, for the biscuits Núñez fed them and for the oats in feed bags fashioned of gunnysacks. Jake had long since given up the argument that the horses had no need of the grain Núñez carried in the spring wagon when the grazing was good in the summer.

Injun and Sundown were strictly a one-man team. If any other man than Frank Núñez hooked the rank-spoiled horses to a sheep wagon that needed moving, they would lay back their ears and balk without tightening the slack chain tugs. But they would pull their hearts out hauling a loaded wagon for Núñez, who never used a buggy whip.

Wherever Núñez went, he took at least one sheep dog. More often it was two, one older trained dog and a half-grown pup he was training.

Teddy Roosevelt had sent Wallace Coburn an Airedale pup to be used for breeding with the wolfhounds and greyhounds that made up the hound pack at the ranch. For some reason the big, shaggy pup got the habit of following Frank Núñez around, and when he would start out in the wagon, the Airedale, called Teddy, would follow behind the rig with a female shepherd called Fannie. On a hot, sunny, summer morning they would travel in the shade under the wagon, and long before the noon sun got hot, the little Mexican would have both dogs in the wagon. For some reason

Hiring the Sheepherders

known only to Núñez, the Airdale pup's name was changed from Teddy to Don. Núñez said Don was inclined to be a little rough handling a sheep band, and so eventually Don went back of his own accord to the hound pack and served his purpose as stud dog and a member of the pack.

The usual procedure for hiring herders was for Jake to telephone Phil Castleberg at the Malta Hotel. The Malta Hotel was north of the tracks, and the barroom had long ago become the headquarters for sheepherders, ranch hands, cooks, and others. So the ranchers usually telephoned or sent word to Phil whenever they wanted to hire ranch hands.

Jake did the telephoning and Frank Núñez would stand by in case the herder the hotel man had available on his list was Mexican. Núñez had a dread fear of the wall telephone. He would take off his hat and drop it on the floor and grab the receiver in both hands. "Hello, Mr. Telephone! Hello, Mr. Telephone! Who is there, Mr. Telephone?" Núñez would yell at the contraption on the wall. After a short silence he would jabber Spanish with a grin on his swarthy face, and when the conversation ended, he would shove the receiver into Jake's hands as if to rid himself of a hot potato.

I happened to be at the ranch the day when the stage pulled in with the Mexican sheepherder and his dog the only passengers inside the coach. Frank Núñez had told me about the new herder he had talked to over the telephone the day before. His name was José Guerrero, but he was called Pepe, a colloquial pet name. Pepe Guerrero, a half-blood *Indio,* was born in Sonora. His mother was a full-blood Yaqui and his father a Mexican goatherd. Pepe knew no English. He was a peon who had never gone to school, never learned how to read or write, and he now had white in his hair.

Frank Núñez had first met Pepe when he was boss of the Mexican shearing crew that Peralta now ran. They were shearing in Nevada, near Reno, when Pepe fetched in his band of sheep. During that few days while the sheep were being sheared, he and Pepe had become friends. Pepe Guerrero, Núñez explained, carried much sorrow and bitterness in his heart. He had suffered many hardships and had known violence and was a silent man of brooding nature. Because Núñez had been left an orphan at the age of ten, he, too, had been alone and lonely, and he and Pepe had many things in common.

Pepe had told Frank over the telephone that Peralta had told him how to locate Núñez when he got to Malta and that Castleberg had called him by telephone. It had been many years since their last meeting. Pepe had given Peralta the money to buy a ticket for him to Malta, Montana, but when the railroad would not allow his dog on the train, Pepe had torn up the ticket, and he and his dog walked the long road from Reno, Nevada. Now Frank Núñez was waiting to greet his old friend.

Núñez stood a few paces back from the stagecoach, and a strange smile on his round face crinkled the corners of his eyes. I was standing nearby to witness the meeting of the two friends.

On the back seat of the stage sat the ugliest dwarf-sized human being I ever laid eyes on. A shock of iron-gray hair that had never known comb or brush covered his large head like a shaggy fur cap. He had a frog-like mouth, a swarthy skin the coarse texture of charcoal, and a wide-nostriled, dished-in nose. A pair of beady black eyes peered through the fringe of hair that covered the low sloping forehead, and he looked for all the world like the primal ape man. He wore a clean, faded-blue, cotton shirt, nearly new Levis, and a pair of homemade huarachos on his big bare feet.

Beside the dwarf sat the most handsome, brown-spotted, white collie that was ever benched at a high-society dog show. Man and dog sat frozen on the seat as if afraid to move until Frank Núñez untracked himself and called a greeting in Spanish. Only then did the strange, neolithic, human figure show signs of life by emerging from the coach with the dog in his arms.

Pepe Guerrero stood there on short, bowed legs and let the collie down. The plume of the dog's brushed tail waved as he stood alongside his lord and master with dog-like worship revealed in his brown eyes.

"*Amigo!*"

"*Compadre!*"

The little Mexican and the half-blood Yaqui went through the

Hiring the Sheepherders

motions of Latin *embracio*. Tears welled in Núñez' eyes as his arms went around the other man who was in the throes of deep emotion, while the dog whined uneasily as he circled the two men, not knowing if his master was in danger.

The ape-like sheepherder wore his shirttails hanging outside, and during the affectionate *embracio* the shirt slipped up to expose the wooden butt of a Colt six-shooter shoved in the waistband of his Levis.

The *embracio* over, the two men stood back, eying and smiling at each other. The collie between them reared up on his hind legs, front paws on the shoulders of the dwarf-like figure, his nose nuzzling the monkey face and shock of wild hair.

"Bobo!" the shepherd said proudly, showing big white teeth in a wide grin. "Bobo!" he repeated like a father introducing his son.

Frank Núñez and Pepe headed for the bunkhouse. The big collie took time out to hoist a hind leg on a clump of sagebrush.

Ruel Horner stepped down from the driver's seat and shook his head as he motioned to the dog.

"About time that dog emptied his bladder," the stage driver said. "That Mex sheepherder and his dog have been sittin' there inside the coach since six this mornin'. When we stopped at the Hog Ranch, I tried my damnedest to get the herder out to eat dinner. But no savvy. I had the cook make some beef sandwiches and fill a bottle with coffee. The Mex ate the bread and drank the coffee and fed the meat to the dog. With that monkey face he shore looks like the wild man from Borneo I once seen at Ringling Brothers' side show.

"Once we got rollin'," Ruel Horner went on, "I heard this music, a sorta twangin' sound. So directly I looked over to see inside and there sat the dwarf, cross-legged, whanging away at a jew's-harp, with the dog's ears cocked listening. And I'll tell a man that freak of nature can play shore sweet music, the likes of which I never heard before."

When the stage pulled out, I headed for the barn to tend to my barn chores. When I got there, Frank Núñez was hooking up his team to the spring wagon, and Pepe and the dog were sitting on the seat. Núñez said he was taking Pepe to Rattlesnake Jack's sheep camp on Rock Creek below the Gill place and he would bring Rattlesnake Jack back in time to catch the morning stage to Malta. Frank had found enough sugans left behind by the lamb shearers to fix up a bed for Pepe.

Frank told me that the Nevada sheepman raised his own breed of Scotch collies and had given a pup to Pepe. Bobo understood only the Mexican language, and Pepe loved the dog as he would a son.

Pepe had told Frank that because of his monkey face and dwarf size, since boyhood the children in the little village near Nogales, where he had been born and raised, had made fun of him. The small boys threw rocks at him, and the older boys tied a rope tail to his pants and made him wear it.

"Pepe told me that a few months ago he went to this town in Nevada, bought a jug, and got drunk by himself," Frank went on to explain. "He was sleeping it off in the brush when a big white man with a sheriff's badge dragged him off to jail. Next morning the judge sent Pepe to a crazy house. When the Basque sheepman he worked for found out about it, he got Pepe out and took him to his ranch. But Pepe was afraid the policeman would come back and put him back in the crazy house, so he came here, knowing I would give him my protection. He knows I am his friend, his *compadre*. It gives me a great pleasure to help the man who has no friends."

When the team was hooked up and ready, I watched them as they drove away. I had a hard, aching lump in my throat that came from a knowledge that I basked in the reflected glow of a kind and charitable gesture, along with its bountiful reward, between two men of humble peon heritage.

26.

The Little Yaqui Sheepherder and His Collie

SOME WEEKS LATER I happened to ride to where Pepe was camped with his sheep at the edge of the brakes, where Frank Núñez had moved his sheep wagon. It was rough country, spotted with a sparse growth of scrub pine, but grass was abundant. Núñez de-declared that if a herder was not experienced with that kind of rough country, he could lose the sheep that strayed off into cut coulees and draws. But it was the kind of terrain Pepe had herded sheep in as a boy in Mexico, and he had the savvy that was needed.

It was one of those bright sunny days in early October, and I was on my way back from the Rock Creek ranch on the Missouri, traveling the old wagon trail in late afternoon. The band of sheep were scattered out and grazing. The occasional tinkle of a sheep bell was the only sound that broke the lazy silence. About a mile away the white canvas top of the sheep wagon showed at the spring, and beyond was the open rolling prairie of the antelope country. But there was no sign of the Yaqui sheepherder or his dog.

Then I heard the sound of music coming downwind with the evening breeze. I had played a jew's-harp as a kid and knew what it was. I rode off the trail and up a small hogback spotted with scrub pines, and when I sighted the herder, I reined up where I was, hidden from view.

Down below about a hundred yards was a wide flat where the

bulk of the sheep were scattered out. At one place there was a wide patch of dark-green swamp grass and a clear gypsum spring that was bitter as quinine. The mud around the spring was black as tar and surfaced by a crust of white alkali.

At the edge of the swamp grass was the monkey-faced, bowlegged dwarf. He was stripped to the waist and barefooted, the legs of his Levis rolled up to the knees. The jew's-harp was in his wide frog-like mouth, and his blunt thumb was whanging away. He was dancing around on the tromped swamp grass in cadence to the high pitched music that had a weird, barbaric sound, and the collie dog, its long hair carefully brushed and combed, was leaping like a young pup around the man.

When the performance ended and the music stopped, the herder held the dog embraced in both arms and spoke to him in soft words of endearment, while the collie's soft whimper gave answer. Then the dog stood on all four legs, his long bushy tail waving back and forth.

Pepe knelt down on the bank of the spring and shoved his head and shoulders in the water to wash off the sweat from his shock of iron-gray hair. Then he dried himself with his shirt. He picked up the six-shooter that lay hidden in the grass and shoved it into the waistband of his Levis. Putting on his rawhide huarachos, he stood up and put on his shirt. One long arm made a circular motion, and the dog trotted off in one direction and Pepe in the other to gather the sheep that had strayed from the main band into a cut coulee.

The sun had lowered to meet the ragged skyline of the badlands, and I waited until the herder was out of sight, then headed for the home ranch. No barking of the collie, no music broke the evening silence as I rode away with the notion that I had just witnessed some strange Yaqui ceremonial dance by a man who shunned any overtures of friendship.

Sometime in late October, Frank Núñez moved Pepe's sheep wagon to an advantageous campground on the creek about a mile from the Gill place that now belonged to the Circle C. The old, thatched-roof log shed that had in former times been used to

The Little Yaqui Sheepherder and His Collie

shelter cattle that needed feeding was now used as a sheep shed. In case of a snowstorm Pepe could easily drive his sheep there for shelter. If it looked like a storm was brewing in the morning overcast, he could drift his band northward. If the storm came up during the day, he would have the north wind at his back and could make the shelter of the shed without any trouble.

Pepe's sheep wagon was camped on the creek bank a quarter-mile above the old road crossing that led to Landusky. Nearby was the sandstone rimrock country with its scattered growth of scrub pine. The winds of time and rains had eaten the sandstone into countless shallow caves under the rimrock capping, and scattered places in the sandstone had blackened spots caused by smoke signals, for the Indians had once used them for lookout points.

On several occasions in recent weeks our sheepherders and the Hansen herders had had heated arguments regarding boundary lines. Despite the fact that the Circle C and the Hansen brothers were on semi-friendly terms, Jake Myers and Frank Harmon, Hansen's sheep boss, had had another run-in at Zortman. It was a heated, wordy argument that never climaxed in violence and ended by their shaking hands and having a drink. The sheepherder quarrel had been between Nick González and Rattlesnake Jack, the Circle C herders and the Hansen brothers, and the argument had been settled by the two camp tenders, Frank Núñez and Harmon.

Hansen's big Swedish herder was camped with his band about a mile west of Pepe's camp. Frank Núñez had camped overnight with Pepe and had told him about the arguments, warning him to be careful not to mix his band with the Swede's band because then it would be necessary to herd the mixed bands to the cutting corral.

"If that big gringo sheepherder," Pepe told Núñez, "mixes his band of sheep with mine, there will be bad trouble. I have seen that herder with the yellow hair all over his face. He carries a rifle on his back. I do not like that big gringo. If he comes near my sheep, I will shoot him in the gut with this pistol I had when I was a soldier in the Mexican army. Then the gringo police will put me in the crazy house. I would rather be dead than locked up in that *casa de locos* without windows to see the stars. Promise me, *compadre,* that you will look after Bobo if I am taken away."

Frank Núñez gave his solemn promise, then tried to explain to the frightened man that there was no need to shoot the big Swedish sheepherder, who was friendly and kind to his dog, and that the Swede carried his rifle to kill coyotes and wolves. He made the Yaqui promise that he would not shoot the gringo herder or any other man.

Two days after Núñez' long talk to Pepe a saloonkeeper at Zortman got Jake Myers on the telephone at the ranch. He told Jake that some cowpuncher had ridden past the Gill place on his way to town and reported that he had sighted a band of sheep scattered from hell to breakfast and that a bunch of coyotes were among the sheep. The cowhand had emptied his six-shooter and scared the coyotes off and had spent an hour or more trying to locate the herder who was nowhere to be seen.

Jake rounded up three or four cowpunchers and me, and we got .30-.30 carbines from the gun rack in the office and headed yonderly with the hound pack. Jake blamed the trouble on Frank Harmon and cussed him out to a fare-thee-well as we rode along at a high trot. We picked up Frank Núñez at a sheep camp along the way.

The cowpuncher had spoken the truth when he claimed the sheep were scattered from hell to breakfast. While Núñez on his black gelding Nig rounded up the sheep, the rest of us scattered out in search of Pepe. It was a fruitless search that lasted all day, and it was getting dark when we rode back to the Gill place.

Frank Núñez had bedded down the sheep near the sheep wagon, and Jake sent me over to spend the night with him. For the first time since I had known the little Mexican sheep boss, there was no smile on his face. His warm brown eyes were sad, misted over with a film of unshed tears. He stayed outside while I cooked supper on the little sheet-iron camp stove inside the covered wagon. He kindled an outside bonfire, and after we had eaten supper, we sat hunkered down at the fire.

The coyotes had killed half-a-dozen sheep and filled their empty

The Little Yaqui Sheepherder and His Collie

bellies. About twenty-five more had been hamstrung or chewed up, so we had been forced to cut their throats. The rest of the band were in good shape.

Núñez was worried sick about the missing Pepe. We drank coffee and smoked while he voiced his worried thoughts. Pepe was dead, Frank repeated over and over. He had to be dead, and his sheep dog dead. Otherwise the sheep would never have been scattered, and no coyote would go near them with Bobo there.

There was a slight possibility that Pepe had a broken leg, so on the chance he might sight the blaze of the campfire and crawl to it, we kept feeding it with dry sticks and stove wood to keep the blaze alive. But the only sound that broke the silence of the chilly night was the crazy yapping of coyotes.

The first streak of the false dawn was showing in the east when the mournful howl of the dog came downwind.

"Bobo!" Núñez cried out in a strange, hoarse voice as he scrambled to his feet. "Pepe is dead!"

I told Frank to wait there by the fire while I rode to the Gill place. It was getting daylight when I rode back with Jake and the other cowhands and the hound pack. The tip of the sun was showing when we finally located Pepe and the dog. Pepe was lying on his side under a shallow cave of the rimrock ledge, his Colt .45 still gripped in his hand. The back of his skull was blown in a ragged mess. Bobo was crouched close to the body, his big white fangs bared in a snarl as he guarded his dead master.

Jake told me to take the hound pack off a ways, and I did. Then he sent one of the cowpunchers to Zortman to fetch Charlie Beard, the justice of the peace and acting coroner.

It took time and patience for Frank Núñez to get close to the collie. The little Mexican talked in soothing low tones for a long time as he edged closer until finally he had Bobo cradled in his arms. After a while Frank put a rope around the dog's neck and lifted him up and brought him out. He buried his head in the collie's ruff, and we could hear the sound of muffled sobs and the fitful whining of Bobo as they mourned the death of the shepherd. Even the hound pack seemed to recognize and understand the collie's whimpering grief as they lay down where I sat on my boot heels.

When Charlie Beard arrived, he swore in Jake and all of us as a coroner's jury. It was the verdict of the coroner that Pepe Guerrero had placed the barrel of the Colt .45 in his mouth and pulled the trigger.

Near the entrance of the cave Pepe had butchered a sheep and skinned the carcass and removed the entrails to provide food for the dog until his body was found. Since Pepe had never learned how to read or write, there was no farewell message to reveal the reason for his suicide. In Frank's opinion, Pepe killed himself because he was afraid he would kill the Swedish sheepherder if he bothered the sheep, and he was afraid if he did that, someone would put him in a crazy house. That seemed to supply the motive.

Judge Beard asked Frank Núñez about the dead man's relatives and was informed that Pepe Guerrero had no relatives. He had left Sonora, Mexico, as a youth and never returned. Frank asked if Pepe could be buried in the little grassy park just beyond the rimrock lookout from which he had watched the sheep, and it was there the grave was dug. I helped Frank make a coffin from the pine-board panels stacked at the Gill place. We wrapped the body in a clean blanket shroud and placed the jew's-harp in Pepe's shirt pocket. After the coffin was placed in the grave, we gathered boulders for a monument to keep the coyotes and wolves from digging the mound of fresh earth, and Bobo kept a close watch.

For more than a month the big collie was Frank Núñez' constant companion, but for days on end refused to eat anything except what the little Mexican could force him to eat from his hand. It took Bobo that length of time to slowly grieve himself to death.

I was with Núñez at the Gill place the night Bobo died where he slept in the sheep boss's arms. We wrapped Bobo in a blanket and tarp, laid the shrouded dog on top of the box coffin, and covered the grave again with earth and boulders.

That night Frank Núñez uncorked a brown jug of whisky he had cached in a manger, and we held a quiet sort of Mexican wake for the Yaqui-Mexican outcast and his collie dog.

27.

Misadventures in a Tin Lizzie

AN IDAHO SHEEPMAN named Grinnell was due in Malta in September, 1915, to dicker for the five bands of Circle C sheep. It was my job to drive to Malta to pick him up, then drive him around to where the sheep were camped at the scattered-to-hell-and-gone sheep camps.

I had all day to put the tin Lizzie in shape, put new tires with new inner tubes on all around and put in a new set of spark plugs, new clutch, and brake lining. Everything I needed was in the storehouse, except a new radiator to replace the one that had sprung a couple of leaks. Bill Kearns, the ranch bookkeeper, had telephoned the Ford garage at Malta, but they were all out of radiators. However, they sent out new hose connections and two spare wishbones for the steering mechanism.

Besides my other chores, it was my job to keep that rattletrap tin Lizzie repaired and keep a spare casing or two in the car, along with a couple or three quart cans of motor oil, a big can of hard grease, and a grease gun in the tool box and a couple of five-gallon cans of gasoline, a bucket to fill the leaky radiator, and a tow rope. A .30-.30 carbine in a scabbard was strapped to the steering wheel shaft in case a wolf or coyote was sighted.

There was no way to repair the leaky top except to buy a new one, and if a man wanted to keep dry during the rainy season, he threw a saddle slicker in back. The back end of the flivver was piled high as a junk wagon with square two-by-twelve blocks to rest the jack on, as well as other odds and ends. Repairs were made wherever and whenever the car broke down on the road or open prairie.

There were times when Jake Myers and I would put the three hounds in the back of the flivver—Old Brin, the mixed Dane and wolfhound pack leader, the big Airedale Don, and a fast greyhound called Spinner—to head the coyotes and wolves off. We would take out across country until we sighted a coyote or prairie wolf. Then we would let the hounds out and open the throttle to the last notch, and the race would be on, over bunch grass and prickly-pear cactus and boulders, down steep-slanted brushy coulees and ridges and prairie-dog towns, and at times through barbwire fences with the car wide open. We would yank down our hats, duck our heads, and shut our eyes, and let 'er rip. By the time we got back to the ranch, the windshield would be cracked, the headlights would need new lenses, and the bumpers straightening. There would be slow leaks in all four cactus-pierced casings and inner tubes that had to be repaired with cold patches. The battered tin Lizzie, with a wolf or coyote pelt tied on the back of the rear seat, went wherever we could travel on horseback.

This morning after breakfast I ran the flivver into the blacksmith shop and jacked up all four wheels, blocking the car solid, and went to work. It was sundown and half-past suppertime when I finished the overhaul job. The garage in town had shorted us on the brake lining, so I screwed the plate back in place and called it a day. Having no brakes offered no serious problem. When the brake lining was gone, we used the reverse floor pedal for a brake until we had time to reline the drumheads.

That evening after I ate supper, I filled a galvanized tub with hot water from the tank attached to the kitchen range and lugged the pails of hot water into the cabin where I lived. My hide was smeared with grease, and I did a clean-up job with a bar of strong-smelling laundry soap and a scrubbing brush. It was ten o'clock by the time I got into my clean clothes and went to the office to get my final instructions from Jake Myers. The tin Lizzie was shod

Misadventures in a Tin Lizzie

with new tires, the motor was running like a clock, and I was rarin' to get going to town. But Jake held me up for an hour or longer with last minute instructions.

I was to meet the train at Malta at four A.M., and if Grinnell was hungry, I was to take him to the Chinaman's restaurant for breakfast. Whatever that sheepman wanted, I was to get it for him and charge it to the company. If Grinnell was a drinking man, Jake said as he grinned and winked an eyelid, so much the better. I was instructed to get him a quart of whatever he was drinking at the Great Northern Hotel bar and charge it.

I was sitting high on top of the world when I gunned the motor and left the ranch like a bat out of hell. The next day was Saturday and there was a dance at Malta. If all went well and Jake closed the deal for the sheep with Grinnell and the sheepman wanted to get back to town to catch the midnight train, I sure would get him there and take in the Saturday night dance.

It was a chilly night, and an overcast sky was spitting rain. I had on a heavy, blue flannel shirt and my sheepskin-lined canvas coat, and there were two new saddle slickers in the car, one for me and one for Mr. Sheepman Grinnell. If he bought the five bands of sheep (the other bands had already been sold to the Hansens and B. D. Phillips), there would be no more stinking, blatting sheep on the Circle C range. I was ready to celebrate if Jake made the deal and I got Grinnell back to Malta in time to take in the dance.

Many and many times since I have wished I had stayed on as rep with the ID wagon and let Jake Myers meet the sheepman, but it wasn't in the cards. If I were to hang for it, I can't seem to recall the exact date of that fateful Saturday, but the details of what actually happened are still fresh in my memory.

By the time I got to Malta a little after midnight, they had already taken in the sidewalks, and the town had the deserted look of a ghost town. Dim lights showed in the saloon windows. The bartenders on shift were dozing in armchairs, and the swampers were cleaning brass gaboons and mopping floors. At the Great Northern Hotel, Joe Sklower, who was on shift as night clerk, was asleep on a cot behind the desk, so I wandered along the deserted streets and into the Chinaman's restaurant where I ate a bowl of noodles, drank coffee, and smoked cigarettes. Then I rambled around the town on both sides of the tracks in a futile search for some cowhand to talk to. Nobody was around, so I went into the deserted hotel lobby and, being careful not to wake Joe Sklower, sat down in a chair facing the plate glass window, too keyed up to get any shut-eye.

At three-thirty A.M. by the big clock that ticked off the minutes I got up and went over to the depot and walked up and down the platform. The first excitement and anticipation of being in town for the first time in months had fizzled out like a damp firecracker. I had drunk too much coffee and smoked too many cigarettes, and the letdown was setting in. The long day's grease-monkey work was catching up. I was tired out and leg weary, and I couldn't conjure up any bright dreams to shake off that dismal feeling.

At four o'clock the westbound train pulled in and a medium-sized, ruddy-faced man with gray in his black hair, dressed in unpressed tweeds and gray flannel shirt and work shoes, came down the train steps. He had a sheep-lined canvas coat slung over his shoulder and carried a shabby tan leather satchel. I walked over and told him who I was, and we shook hands as he introduced himself.

I picked up his bag and told him that if he felt like eating breakfast, we could go to the Chinaman's restaurant, but he said he wasn't hungry at this hour. As he put on his coat, he said he felt like he had a cold coming on and what he would like was a little brandy to ward it off. So I led the way to the hotel, and Joe Sklower took us into the bar and broke the seal on a bottle of Three Star Hennessey, which Grinnell said was his favorite brand of hard liquor. He didn't like to drink alone, so Joe and I each drank a shot. When Grinnell offered to pay for the bottle, Joe told him that Jake Myers had arranged for the Circle C to take care of his room, meals, and bar bills. This seemed to please the Idaho sheepman, who had a few more shots of brandy and helped himself to a

Misadventures in a Tin Lizzie

couple of cigars from the box Joe took from the glass case and set in front of the sheepman.

Grinnell said he hoped to catch the midnight train out, if he could get his business deal tied up in time. Joe corked his bottle and put it in a brown paper bag along with another sealed quart, then handed the sack to Grinnell, compliments of the Great Northern Hotel. I carried his satchel, deposited it in the back of the flivver, and climbed in behind the wheel, and we were off to the ranch.

It didn't take me long to realize that Grinnell was a drinking man who knew how to handle his liquor. By the time I pulled up in front of the office, where Jake was impatiently waiting, the Idaho sheepman had lowered the contents of the opened bottle halfway down. When Jake asked him if he would have something to eat, Grinnell said he seldom ate any breakfast. He would eat a noon dinner at the sheep camp. He and Jake sat in the back seat talking sheep as I drove to the first camp.

It was one of those rainy days when black-lined thunderheads scudded through the pale blue sky. Whenever the sun came out, it was warm. When hidden behind the clouds, it was cold, and a chilly wind was blowing and spitting rain. The Idaho sheepman was warding off an attack of the grippe, and Jake helped him fight the enemy. But whenever Jake tilted the bottle, I knew without looking around that he was going through the motions and faking it by taking small swallows. Jake wasn't much of a hand at hard drinking. He had a job to do and he did it.

I had already told Grinnell before we reached the ranch that my father frowned on any drinking I did, especially when I had a job to do, and that went double for Jake Myers. Grinnell had grinned and nodded understandingly. He was quiet, sort of grim looking, and a little standoffish, hard to get acquainted with, and he had no sense of humor. I laid it to the fact that he was a dyed-in-the-wool sheepman and let it go at that, so we got along first rate. He could sure as heck hold his liquor, and it showed up at the first camp we stopped at. When he and Jake got out, he glommed onto a short-handled sheep hook, and as he walked through the band, he would hook a sheep by the hind leg, examine its mouth and hoofs for sores, and probe its thick wool with his fingers. After less than half an hour of this, we would be on our way to the next sheep camp, and Grinnell would reach for the bottle.

The rattle of the tin Lizzie as I drove across country with the hand throttle wide open made such a racket I couldn't hear what Grinnell and Jake were talking about, but I knew they were dickering on the price. About noon we pulled up at the third sheep camp, and when Grinnell had finished looking the sheep over, Jake suggested eating some hot food at the covered sheep wagon. But the Idaho sheepman said he wasn't hungry because of the cold he felt coming on, he reckoned. So he pulled the cork on the second quart while Jake and I drank hot coffee and ate hot grub.

At each sheep camp I filled the leaky, steaming radiator with water. The beat-up flivver drank more water than a Stanley Steamer, but the four cylinders were popping like popcorn and I was using the reverse pedal for a brake. All was well and the goose hung high.

It was four o'clock by my trusty dollar watch when I pulled up in front of the log office at the home ranch. We had come directly from the fifth sheep camp. Jake and Grinnell went into the office for the Idaho sheepman to make out his check. Jake had sold him the five bands of sheep at top prices. They shook hands and had a drink of Hennessey to bind the bargain.

I gave the thirsty Lizzie a bucket of water to cool her steaming innards, and with Grinnell in the front seat beside me, we headed for Malta over the hills and far away at top speed. Grinnell kept taking a pull at his cold-cure medicine.

We would get to Malta in plenty of time for me to take a hot bath and change into my best suit of clothes and white shirt I had in my war sack under the back seat. I would make it in plenty of time to dance every waltz and two-step on the score card. I was the Barney Oldfield of Montana; I had the throttle wide open and was hitting the mud holes in the stage road at full tilt. All I needed was one of Grinnell's cigars to chew on and swallow the spit.

Misadventures in a Tin Lizzie

The radiator was throwing steam like a locomotive when I topped the ridge a couple of miles from the bridge at the School House Coulee, so I eased the throttle back to the last notch and kept my foot on the reverse pedal. I braked to a stop near a water hole and climbed out with my bucket. The sky was overcast again and it was spitting a little rain when I unscrewed the radiator cap and stepped back in time to escape the boiling water that geysered up like Old Faithful. When it died down to an ominous growl, I trickled the cold water in from the bucket and screwed the cap back in place. When I went to throw the bucket behind the front seat, Grinnell was sitting behind the wheel with a cigar stuck in the corner of a give-a-damn drunken grin.

"All day long, boy," the sheepman joshed me, "you've been cutting fancy didos with this tea kettle. Kid stuff, strictly amateur. Now let a man show you some real driving. Henry Ford's an old pal of mine. Crank 'er up, kid, and hop aboard. Casey Jones is at the throttle."

I didn't like the sarcastic tone of his ribbing, but after all, Jake had sold him five bands of sheep, and there's the old saying about the customer always being right.

The old-fashioned Model T Ford had two dinguses attached to the steering post. The lever of the hand throttle was on the right, the spark adjustment on the left. I told Grinnell not to touch the spark adjustment or the gas throttle while I spun the crank or it might kick back and break my wrist or arm. I informed him also that the hand brake was worn out and the lining of the brake drums shot.

The cracked windshield was spattered with dirty water from the mud puddles I'd hit, and I figured I would wipe it off after I got the car cranked. I warned Grinnell again not to touch the spark and throttle and not to release the hand brake. I didn't want to get run over or wind up with a busted arm. But I doubt that he paid any attention. He spat out the half-smoked cigar and tilted the bottle straight up, draining the last drop of the potent Three Star Hennessey. I waited until he threw the empty bottle out into the sagebrush before I reached for the crank.

Any man who ever drove one of those old tin Lizzies for any length of time was leery about "twistin' 'er tail." You didn't close your fist tight but gripped the crank in your bent fingers to give her the first spin. That was what I did when I reached down and shoved it in the notch and came up with a quick jerk. As the motor backfired, it spun the crank backwards with an eggbeater whirl that would have broken my wrist if I had been foolish enough to have had a tight grip. Even so, the sudden kickback sent a sharp pain into my hand and up my arm to my shoulder. As I stepped back, the motor caught with a firecracker roar. That damned sheepman had both spark and gas throttle halfway down.

I was fit to be tied when I opened the right door and slid into the seat alongside him, but I kept my trap closed and banged the door shut. Grinnell had the flivver wide open and under way before I had time to close the door. The road was straight, but the gumbo clay was slippery and the road filled with mud puddles. The chains I had put on the rear wheels threw chunks of wet gumbo in all directions.

There was a fairly steep slant down from the benchland prairie into the long coulee and towards the bridge which spanned the creek at the foot of the hill and had heavy bridge timbers for uprights on both sides.

Grinnell had the flivver wide open when he started down the slant. When his foot pressed the brake pedal, it slammed against the floor board without braking power.

"Hit the reverse!" I yelled. "Close the throttle!"

But he had a grip on the wheel like he was scared to death, and I hung on with both hands during that split-second wild ride. Even then we might have had a long chance of getting safely across the bridge if Grinnell had kept his head and closed the throttle and hit the reverse. But he didn't, and the front end of the Ford hit the upright bridge timber with a sickening crash that upended the car and flung it sideways into the boulder-strewn creek twenty feet below. The sudden impact must have thrown Grinnell out over the door, because he landed on the bridge.

The next thing I was aware of, I was in three feet of water with

Misadventures in a Tin Lizzie

the upturned car on top of me, the front wheels still spinning. Luckily the huge boulders kept the weight of the car off me. I was a little shook up and sopping wet when I crawled on hands and knees between the boulders and up on the muddy bank to a grassy place on solid ground.

I looked up as I heard a wild shout from Grinnell, and there was the Idaho sheepman trotting back and forth with a limping gait as he hollered. "My leg's busted! I've got a broken leg! My leg's broken!"

I was sitting on the grass coughing and spitting out muddy water, blowing hard, and looking myself over in a sort of dazed manner. My legs were stretched out in front of me, and I figured I had come off lucky until I saw my right foot that was bent over above the ankle joint at right angles to my leg. Dazed as I was, I knew that my leg was broken somewhere above the ankle.

Grinnell was still giving up head about his busted leg as he pranced up and down on the bridge. The first thought that entered my head was that I would miss the Saturday night dance, and all of a sudden I was fighting mad.

"You got nothing on me," I shouted at Grinnell, "you drunk sheepherder sonofabitch!"

There was a homesteader shack near the bridge and the homesteader, his wife, and a son about my age were standing outside watching the show. A jerk-line freight outfit was camped there for the night. It was Frank Whitmore's outfit, and Whitty and his son Frank came running to where I sat cussing the sheepman with every foul name I could lay my tongue to. But when Whitty and Frank showed up, I put a sorry sort of a grin on my face and pointed to my leg.

When Whitty asked me if my leg hurt, I shook my head and told him no, and I wasn't lying because it was still numb. I told Whitty to get me a carbine from the flivver so I could shoot the howling sheepman who had wrecked the car and crippled me. But Whitty told me to take it easy and said he would get me a drink of whisky from his freight wagon.

He told young Frank to saddle his wrangling horse and hit a

lope for the Phillips ranch and tell them to get Doc Clay at Malta on the phone and have him come out to look me over as soon as he could. Then the homesteader and Whitty carried me to the house and laid me on the bed. By that time the busted leg was giving me unshirted hell. My foot had swollen considerably, and Whitty had to be careful when he cut the leather to get my boot off. The broken shinbone had come through the skin and the splintered end showed through my sock.

I had drunk enough whisky to ease the pain and was passed out cold by the time Doc Clay and Wallace Coburn, who was living in Malta at the time, arrived in Wallace's new Willis-Knight automobile sometime after dark. When I finally came alive, I found I was in bed at Wallace's house. Doc Clay had given me a hypo, and Wallace said I had vomited all the booze I'd had in me back at the homesteader's place. They had put the Idaho sheepman, unhurt from the accident, on the train at midnight.

My leg remained in wooden splints for a week before Doc Clay put the foot and leg in a plaster cast. He had set the broken leg, which he called a "compound fracture," about three or four inches above the ankle joint. He said he had lined the big toe up with my knee joint to set the splintered shinbone before he had put on the cast. Doc Clay had no X-ray machine in his cowtown office. An X-ray photograph would have shown that all the anklebones were broken, as well as the shinbone.

As soon as the cast was on, I moved to the Great Northern Hotel on crutches. Some weeks later, when Doc Clay sawed off the cast and lined up my big toe with the knee, he declared I would be dancing cakewalks, running foot races, and riding broncs in no time.

I was crippled sometime in September. By November, I was back at the ranch but still on crutches. Sometimes I used only one crutch or a heavy cane to limp through the snowdrifts. I packed the crutch or cane in my saddle scabbard in place of the Winchester carbine and did my best to make a hand around the ranch.

There were no more sheep on the Circle C range, and the outfit had been sold to the Matadors, but they had not taken over yet.

Misadventures in a Tin Lizzie

Jake Myers and I were holding down the outfit with a skeleton crew, feeding some cattle at the home ranch and the Gill place. The Rock Creek ranch on the Missouri, used as a line camp, had been sold to Tommy Robbins, who had bought the UL Ranch at Big Bend near the Old Fort Musselshell Crossing on the Missouri. Jake and I spent a lot of time with the hound pack catching coyotes and wolves.

Doc Clay had been over-optimistic in predicting I would be dancing cakewalks, running foot races, and riding broncs. Cakewalking, hell! And that went double for foot racing and bronc riding. But I derived a certain amount of satisfaction from the fact that the minstrel, black-faced cakewalk had gone out of fashion, that I had never been much of a foot racer anyway, and I was a sorry bronc rider. I was satisfied to ride gentle cow horses. Astraddle a good horse I felt at home, and I tried to make a hand in spite of hell and high water, snowdrifts, and a game leg.

Once I climbed aboard a horse, I would lean over and twist my right stirrup around to get my foot socked in the stirrup, and I was all set to make a day's ride. I grabbed for the saddle horn if I lost the right stirrup and stayed aboard until the horse quit pitching. Only after a long day's ride when we came home and I swung down on the ground would I pull up lame and reach for the crutch or cane. After supper I would ease my boot off and soak the ringboned ankle in hot water and Epsom salts and rub it with horse liniment.

A year after the accident I visited the Mayo Clinic at Rochester, Minnesota, where an orthopedic surgeon told me I had come too late. The broken anklebones had welded together to form solid adhesions that could not be broken down for the bones to be reset. The Mayo surgeon said I would have to learn to live with the crippled ankle and the pain as long as it lasted, which turned out to be a long time, the remainder of my life. But I've got no kick coming on that score. The hand of fate deals the cards and you play your hand out, and I've sure held some lucky hands during the years.

28.

Windup of the Old Circle C Outfit

IN THE SPRING of 1916 the final negotiations for the sale of the Circle C Ranch to the Matador Land and Cattle Company were completed. The necessary papers had been signed in the Great Falls law office of Fletcher Maddox, who was married to my oldest half-sister Jessie. Will Coburn had come up from Globe, Arizona, and Bob and Wallace were also there to sign with my father. For some reason I cannot recall I happened to be in Great Falls that week.

For old-times' sake and because my father was an old friend of the owner and manager, Dan Tracy, he and I had rooms at the old Park Hotel, while Will, Bob, and Wallace stayed at the new Rainbow Hotel. The night the papers were signed we had a sort of last family reunion in the dining room of the Rainbow. The next morning Will left for Arizona, and I took the train back to Malta.

Jake Myers and I were left to pick up the loose ends at the ranch, gather the remnants of the Rafter T cattle, and lend a hand until J. M. (Matt) Walker, the new manager for the Matadors, got onto the ropes. I would stay on until September to rep with the ID wagon on the Fort Belknap Reservation to gather the Rafter T beef steers for shipment to the Chicago market. When Jake finished up at the Circle C, he was going to the B. D. Phillips ranch as foreman.

Windup of the Old Circle C Outfit

Matt Walker had been staying at the ranch for a month or so. He had brought some of his cowpunchers with him from the Texas headquarters Matador ranch and a remuda of saddle horses and mules. The day before I arrived at the ranch, Matt Walker had taken his roundup crew to Malta, where a couple of trainloads of beef steers shipped from Texas were due to unload at the Malta stockyards in about a week.

My father and brother Bob were coming to the ranch for a few days to pick up the company books and clean out the safe with its old files and records. Bob was going to pack his personal belongings at his house while my father rode around the ranch on a sentimental farewell tour of the outfit he had built up throughout the long years.

A year earlier the automobile had replaced the old four-horse stagecoach for carrying the mail and passengers on the stage route between Malta and the Little Rockies, so Bob had fetched his father out to the ranch in his new air-cooled Franklin.

I had my father's big brown gelding Reader brushed and curried down slick as a seal. In his prime Reader was the best all-round cow horse in the country. Now Reader was crowding twenty, but he was still sound as a dollar and sure-footed. I was going to accompany my father on his daily rounds. I had discarded my crutch and cane, and I limped like some stove-up old cowhand. But on horseback I was as able-bodied as any man, and I rode good cow horses, which made up the difference between a sorry ringboned cripple and a cowhand.

Robert Coburn was now in his seventies and prided himself that he could still make a hand wherever a top cowhand was needed and run a roundup wagon if need be. Because the years had stiffened his joints, he walked with a cane, taking his time and walking without the trace of a limp. He never wore spectacles except when reading a newspaper, and he still had a heavy shock of snow-white hair.

After breakfast we would ride out together, our horses traveling at a running walk across the rolling prairie. There were still a few cattle left to ride through, but nary a band of sheep to be seen.

Pioneer Cattleman in Montana

The heavy spring rains had brought up the grass and in spite of the grazing sheep that had close-cropped the range, the hills and coulees and long ridges and benchlands were carpeted green. The range was in better shape than it had been in years, and there was wild hay in every coulee. The Circle C outfit would be a cow ranch once more as soon as the Matador cattle were turned loose on the range to fatten, and that was some consolation.

On our morning rides we visited the nearby camps at the Big Warm and the Parrot place and the Little Warm and the Veseth place on Beaver Creek, getting back each day in time for noon dinner and a long rest in the afternoon. Sometimes in the cool of the evening we would ride out in the big field through the grazing cattle, but never once did my father ride up the slanted trail that led to the summit of the timbered east Coburn Butte as he used to do when he would point out with pride his vast cattle empire that extended as far as the human eye could see towards the badlands north of the Missouri River and to the east to the outline of the Larb Hills beyond Sun Prairie.

Now as he talked of how the range was in better shape than it had been for many years and the prime condition of the cattle, there was an edge of sadness in his voice. The pride of ownership was gone, and the spark of life in his puckered blue eyes was no longer there. For the first time he sat his saddle round-shouldered and bent over as if he had grown weary at last of carrying the heavy burden throughout the long years and had reached the end of his trail.

I remember clearly the last evening we rode out in the big pasture with the fire glow of the sun dropping behind the ragged skyline of the Little Rockies. Streaks of red and yellow war-painted the sky which slowly faded to deep purple that stained the two scrub-pine timbered Coburn Buttes, and with the coming of night the dark shadows that crept across the sky were gray as the ashes of old forgotten campfires.

My father rode in brooding silence, lost in memories of his pioneer days when he and Horace Brewster in 1886 had turned

Windup of the Old Circle C Outfit

loose the cattle in the shadow of the two buttes to water on Beaver Creek. A cowman's paradise he had called it then.

When we got back to the ranch, Jim Thornhill's buggy team, a pair of matched, black Morgan geldings, were in adjoining stalls in the barn. Old Jimmer distrusted automobiles and clung with quiet stubbornness to the horse-and-buggy days and all that went with it.

My barn chores done, I went over to the office where my father and Old Jimmer sat talking outside in the old, battered, barroom chairs. My father told me to go hunt up Bob and tell him that he was riding to Malta the next morning with Jim Thornhill. I could see the old spark of life back in his Irish blue eyes as if anticipating, like some kid, a buggy ride behind a good team of horses and in the companionship of his old friend.

"Tell Bob I won't be riding to Malta with him in his new-fangled automobile tomorrow," my father said. Then he added, "A horse fetched me here in the first place, and by God, I'm leaving here the same way, in Jimmer's top buggy, behind as good a team of horses as ever traveled the road." There was a chuckle in his voice.

Robert Coburn would be long gone when Matt Walker and his Matador cowhands took over the Circle C Ranch the next week.

The next morning after breakfast I helped Old Jimmer harness his team and hook them to his top buggy. My father had given Jimmer his horse Reader to put with some old, pensioned-off cow horses. Never again would Reader be saddled up, for Jim Thornhill was sentimental as a woman when it came to pensioning off the cow horses he had ridden when their time came.

Later I stood alone in front of the office as they left. My father, proud of his horsemanship, held the taut lines in his gloved hands, and a white-bearded grin spread across his face as he drove the rollicky, high-spirited team, leaving a cloud of dust in their wake in the first rays of a crimson sunrise. This was his farewell to the Circle C outfit, and a lump came into my throat as I watched them drive out of sight.

I saddled my horse a few hours later and rode up the slanted trail to the summit of the east butte, an old Indian lookout point, where the rocks were blackened by the ancient smoke signals of the Indians. I dismounted and squatted there. I was all choked up on account of the many things that had been building up inside me. I had watched my father die a little each day for the past week as we rode together in silence, knowing that he was visiting each place for the last time. Often I had seen a film of mist clouding his eyes, but he never uttered a single word to betray his heart-broken feelings. But he knew that I could read his thoughts, and a strange understanding grew between us which had never been there before. I had never been close to my father, as some sons are. He was fifty-three years old when I was born, and he was away most of the time from our Great Falls home. But a certain honor and respect had taken the place of a son's love for his father, and I knew full well that he had an unspoken love for me. He had chosen me as his riding companion on his final tour of farewell, and he knew that I understood his feelings about not riding up here to survey for the last time the vast cattle empire he no longer owned.

So I had come here in his stead. I stayed all day to build a sort of monument to my pioneer cattleman father. I gathered small boulders and piled them in the center of the circle of rock blackened by smoke signals that were made before the coming of the white man. When the rock monument caught the last rays of the sunset, I swung into my saddle and rode slowly down the trail.

I never went back to the rock monument I had erected in honor of Robert Coburn, because somewhere within that pile of rocks I had buried all my kid dreams and hopes of ever attaining my rightful heritage in the cattle empire of the Circle C.

Below in the golden afterglow, spread out like some small Montana cow town, were the log houses of the Circle C Ranch that had been my home. There were the old sod-roofed log buildings that had been the old DHS Ranch—the small cabin called the "White House" where I lived, the mess cabin alongside it, the old DHS horse barn converted to a cow shed for the milk cows, and the old blacksmith shop where the spring rains had sprouted tall weeds and grass on the sod roof, making a green covering. And on the

Top: Malta to Little Rockies six-horse stagecoach leaving the Circle C Ranch.

Bottom: Part of the log buildings at the Circle C Ranch. Left to right: barn, storehouse, office, meat house, and Bob Coburn's house.
In background are mess cabin and bunkhouse.

other side of the White House cabin were the long, sod-roofed, log bunkhouses, and across from them the carriage shed, the icehouse and square-blocked meat house, the log office, the long warehouse, the big barn, and the machine shed where the mowing machines and iron-wheeled hayracks and bull rakes were stored. Beyond were the two-storied, shingled, log houses belonging to the different Coburn families.

Near the houses was the windmill tower and high storage water tank. There were two more windmills, one at the cow barn and one behind the cook house. A large corral adjoined the horse barn, and there were four corrals and a branding chute on the small hill where the old stage road passed and made a wide lane between the ranch buildings. Across the log bridge over Beaver Creek and almost hidden from view by the tall willows were the long, thatched-roof cattle sheds and feed pens, and a quarter-mile below was the long, narrow lake formed by the backed-up waters of Beaver Creek, with a dam half a mile below. In the summer the reservoir lake was used

Blacksmith shop at the Circle C Ranch.

Windup of the Old Circle C Outfit

to irrigate the truck garden and hay meadows. In winter it furnished ice blocks that were packed in sawdust for the icehouse and meat house. Tall willows and wild berry and rose bushes lined the creek banks, and there were giant old cottonwood trees scattered along the banks. The home ranch was landmarked by the two high-timbered buttes called Coburn Buttes, a part of the Little Rockies.

This had been my summer home since memory began, where I had spent my summer vacations from school and where I'd done my best to make a hand. When our home at Great Falls had been sold a few years earlier, the Circle C Ranch had been the only place I called home. My young taproots were planted there when I was a yearling and they had sunk deep during the years. I was now in my middle twenties, and the taproots of early boyhood had sent out a wide network of thousands of branch roots that now covered every foot of the entire ranch.

The original sod-roofed cabins and corrals were steeped in pioneer legends, and I had watched the other buildings being erected by half-blood Metis. The history of the Circle C, with all the bunkhouse tales I had heard from the time I was six years old, had been a part of my life since the day I was born.

The day Robert Coburn left the Circle C Ranch for the last time, driving Jim Thornhill's matched trotting team like he owned them, marked a radical change in the atmosphere of the ranch. For one thing, none of the old Circle C cowpunchers were left. Frank Howe had gone to Arizona to work for Will and Bob Coburn at their San Carlos Reservation spread at Globe. Even Pete Olson, the chore hand who had milked the cows, split wood for the cook, did the irrigating, and kept the windmills running, had pulled out for Arizona.

Jake Myers had already hired out to B. D. Phillips as manager of his big sheep outfit, but had agreed to stay on until the fall roundup was over to help Matt Walker out until he knew the ropes. It was my job to stay on and help Jake. When the fall roundup started, I would rep with the ID wagon on the Fort Belknap Reservation to gather the remnant steers that belonged to the Circle C and ship them to Chicago with the ID beef.

Pioneer Cattleman in Montana

Wallace Coburn had organized a motion picture company to film *Yellowstone Pete's Only Daughter,* one of the poems from his book *Rhymes From A Roundup Camp,* in which he played the lead. His movie outfit was on location at the Rocky Point Crossing on the Missouri River. When the shooting of the picture was finished, Wallace was going to move with his family to Hollywood to begin a career as a producer and movie cowboy actor. It was the era when William S. Hart, Tom Mix, and Hoot Gibson were basking in the glory of being movie cowboy actors and making money hand over fist.

My father and mother and younger brother Harold had moved to Southern California, and when I finished up at the ranch in a month or two I would be heading for Globe, Arizona, to work as a cowhand for Will and Bob Coburn. All I owned at the Circle C Ranch were my two private horses and bedroll and the clothes in my war sack. My homestead claim that lay between the home ranch and the Fort Belknap Reservation fence had been included with the rest of the land sale.

Now I knew how the Assiniboins and Gros Ventres felt about being fenced in. I knew full well that I could never be rid of the uneasy feeling that I no longer belonged here. I was a stranger among aliens who had taken over my homeland, but I would hang and rattle gathering our remnant cattle until I quit Montana for good.

Instead of riding to the barn and putting up my horse, I rode on to the Fort Belknap Reservation. When I reached old Black Dog's lodge, I swung down and sat with the circle of old ones, among them Old Iron Horn, Watch-His-Walking, Long Knife and Black Dog. Every year since I was six years old, Black Dog's wife had made me a pair of moccasins, but never before had she made me a pair of ceremonial moccasins like the ones Black Dog now gave me. Black Dog had named me "Ocksheebee" which meant "boy." Since he had no children, for him Ocksheebee had a special meaning—adopted son.

"You are a man now, Ocksheebee," Black Dog said. "Someday you will marry. These are your marry moccasins." He spoke in

Windup of the Old Circle C Outfit

the guttural tone of the Assiniboin tongue, and his gnarled old hands moved in sign talk which I understood.

After we had smoked and I had shaken hands with the old men, I rode slowly back to the ranch, the sadness gone from my heart. I was young, in the beginning of youth, the best years of my life ahead. I had sat and smoked with the old ones, once brave warriors. Still brave at heart, they set an example of splendid courage. It was up to me to pattern the ways of my life after my pioneer father and after these old ones of the Gros Ventres and Assiniboins, once bitter enemies but now living in peace together. Theirs was a far greater sorrow than mine, because I was at the beginning and they were at the end of the trail.

The best any cowhand could do was to make a hand wherever he was put, regardless of whatever range he found beyond the skyline. And a cowhand's reckless, carefree code was as good as any man's way of life on the long circle to the end of the trail.

Those were my thoughts as I rode back to the Circle C Ranch that moonlit night when the stars in the Montana sky came down within reach. The cowhand's way has been my way, even now when the end of the long trail is in sight.

Appendices

APPENDIX A

Great Falls Tribune, Sunday Morning, January 20, 1935

TRUE STORY OF PIKE LANDUSKY BETTER THAN BEADLE'S BEST THRILLER

JOHN RITCH, EARLY SETTLER, TELLS HOW CURRY KILLED HIM
Uncontrollable Temper and Vindictiveness Toward Those He Disliked Caused Pike Plenty of Trouble, Tribune Writer Asserts

JEW JAKE, CRIPPLED BARTENDER, THOUGHT MURDERER SHOT HIM
Curry's Cronies Guarded Crowd in Saloon While the Kid Mercilessly Beat Landusky, Whose Gun Wouldn't Fire at Time
BY JOHN B. RITCH, *Tribune* HISTORICAL WRITER

SHOULD YOU JOURNEY on the Great Northern railway from some eastern point towards the west coast, as your train moves westward along the Milk river valley, in northern Montana, when you reach the little town of Dodson, you begin to get the silhouette of a mountain range many miles to the south. As your train continues westward, you get an excellent view of the mountains and you are interested, for they are the first mountains you have seen in the great plains country.

The mountains are the Little Rockies, an isolated uplift standing out on the high plains plateau like an island. In fact, while the white man

Appendices

calls them the Little Rockies, the Indian has always known them as the Island mountains. They rise abruptly from the vast flat country surrounding them and the Indian in bestowing names on natural objects, permits nature to help in the selection of the name. They are more than 40 miles from the railway. Seen from the distance, they are beautiful; when you visit them you find one of the real scenic treats of all that wide flung plains region north of the Missouri river in Montana.

In a little basin-like beauty spot on the southwest slope of the Little Rockies is the mining and cow town of Landusky, a camp that came into being 40 years ago. It still exists and has flourished intermittently ever since it came into being. Mines of Landusky are producing gold today. Some very rich ore bodies have been uncovered in the district and a few have made comfortable fortunes in the mines there but the interest of this narrative rests in the fact that the name of this little mining town perpetuates the name of a turbulent, fighting frontier character whose counterpart has seldom been seen in any camp in all the western country.

Called Him "Pike"

He was baptized Powell Landusky. Out west they called him "Pike." He came to the mining camps around Last Chance and that region about 1872. That he was a Missourian was his boast. He was young when he reached Last Chance and became famous as one of the hard men and a tip top rough and tumble fighter before he had been there a year. He cleaned up on so many tough men around Last Chance that most of them concluded he was bad medicine.

Tall, rangy, with a frame like a cruiser of the first class and arms of extraordinary length, he had all the good things for a fighter as a beginning. These, with his prodigious strength and endurance, made him a formidable antagonist for any man. Besides, fear was not part of his makeup. He was a battler by nature. Brocky Gallagher had a name all over Montana as a great rough and tumble fighter. He whipped every man he met until, down at Rocky point, a lonely landing on the Missouri north of the Judith mountains, Brocky and Pike mixed and Pike gave Brocky such a beating his spirit was broken forever. That was after Pike had passed the 40-mile post. A man of such unusual physical prowess would naturally become widely known and Pike's fame reached far and to many borders.

Pike hadn't very attractive features when I first knew him. He might have been good looking at one time but a Blackfeet Indian had scrambled his facial exteriors all up with a buffalo gun in 1880 so it was hard to tell just how good looking he might have been. He was in the wild country along the Flatwillow creek, in what is now Petroleum country, trading with the Indians, the Blackfeet having pitched their camp near his trading post.

One evening Pike filled himself with whisky and, from pure cussedness, fired his rifle into the Indian camp. Unfortunately, he shot an Indian woman, White Calf's squaw, in the abdomen. A Blackfeet brave retaliated by taking a shot at Pike, the bullet striking him fair in the chin and tearing away the entire left lower jawbone. He lived 17 days on whisky while he was being taken on the overland journey east for a jawbone refitting. His fight with Gallagher was after he received the terrible wound.

He Hated Indians

I do not think Pike ever killed a white man; he just beat them with his hands so they didn't fight any more. His hatred for Indians was a mania—and no man knows how many of them he killed. He held no particular aversion for any tribe; to him they were all just Indians, and he hated them all. After the Indian shot him at Flatwillow, he was trapping one winter on the Lodgepole, a stream making into the Missouri from the south, a short distance down river below the mouth of the Musselshell. A band of Sioux caught him alone out in this isolated place, despoiled him of his furs, slapped him around to their hearts' content, kicked him all over the lot, took his provisions and traps and treated him to numerous other nameless indignities.

Pike and Flopping Bill were trading a lot of whisky to the Indians the next winter, their camp being about 20 miles down river from Rocky Point. Three Indians came to their camp, Pike recognizing two of them as having been in the party of his Sioux entertainers. He advised the Flopper that he was going to kill all three of them. After a brief consultation on the side, it was determined that the two white man should seize their guns and each shoot an Indian, which they did. The third unfortunate started to run, whereupon Pike told Bill to lay off with the gun—that he wanted to kill this Indian with an ax. He chased the Indian down to the ice on the river, caught him and chopped him to death with the ax. Not being content with that, he scalped them and, after that, shoved their bodies into a hole in the ice so the river would carry away all evidence of the crime. Recounting this affair later, Flopping Bill, a tough man himself, said that as soon as they returned to Rocky Point he dissolved his co-partnership in the trading concern.

Appendices

Indians Thought Him Crazy

At another time Pike and John Wert were camped near the mouth of the Musselshell river when a party of 22 Sioux came to their camp. Pike was cooking meat over the camp fire. One of the Sioux reached in and helped himself to a hot steak, whereupon Landusky knocked the Indian into the fire, seized his gun and began to punch every other Indian in reach with it, in the meantime kicking and striking at those he could approach. He scattered those Sioux like chaff. Wert said Pike would have opened fire if he had not interfered. Pike's unseemly conduct very likely saved the lives of both men as the Indians thought he was crazy, and an Indian avoids contact with a crazy person. After the Indians left camp one of them came back, leading two cayuses as a gift to placate the evil spirit they were sure controlled the wild white man.

Records of Chouteau county at Fort Benton tell that the miners and stockmen around the Little Rockies held a town meeting on Rock creek in June, 1894, and organized the town of Landusky. Ten years before then an itinerant prospector discovered placer gold in one of the gulches of the Little Rockies. Prospectors swarmed into the gulch, although the land at that time was a part of the Fort Belknap Indian reserve, but Indian reserves never stopped gold hungry prospectors. They called the gulch Little Alder, hoping it would be a miniature edition of that great gold producer at Virginia City. For a few weeks they came in flocks to dig in the gravel of Little Alder, Rock creek, Camp creek, Grouse gulch and every little stream bed in the mountains. The pay streak was lean, but they dug on for a while and then the placer boom died and the country passed back to its original soundless solitude, with the hunters of the Gros Ventres and Assiniboine tribes roaming its arid reaches for game and an occasional cow camp sending out its riders to look after stock grazing there.

A Lonesome Region

It was almost like Lewis and Clark found it, and left it. A cowpuncher got lost down in the breaks of the Missouri to the south, rode two days without finding a ranch or a camp and finally came to Bill McKain's cabin just at the edge of nowhere. As he rode up he said to McKain, "This is the damndest place I ever saw. You get lost in it and you're never found." Old brown Bill smilingly said, "Well, this place looks pretty good to you, don't it?" "Hell, no," said the cowpuncher, "I'm still lost." Nobody lived there then and nobody lived there ever until the second mining boom came and Landusky was created.

Pioneer Cattleman in Montana

In the summer of 1893 Bob Orman was prospecting in the Little Rockies. One day in August the heat and thirst drove him to the foot of the mountain where he worked in search of water. He found water and drank. Less than a hundred feet up hill on his way back, Orman picked up an odd looking piece of rock. Taking it home, he crushed and panned it that evening to behold a string of gold three or four inches long in his pan.

Further prospecting where the rich quartz came from disclosed an ore chute that yielded more than $100,000 from a hole less than 100 feet deep. Orman was a sort of son-in-law of Pike's, so Pike went in the mining business. He and Orman made a snug bunch of money working the August—they named the mine for the month in which it was found.

Again miners flocked to the hills. These were a different sort; they were hard rock miners this time. Then came the town of Landusky. A postoffice was established and the inevitable saloon or saloons—there never was just one saloon in a mining camp—came along to add to the fervor of a hunt for fortune.

Rustlers Arrive

May I digress for just a bit to tell you something of the sort of men who made up the body equestrian on the cow range in the Little Rockies region at this time? You know we are back in the year 1894, and it was just at this time that a red hot stockmen's war was raging down in Wyoming. Legitimate stockmen of our sister state started to clean up on the rustlers and, in consequence, there was a big exodus of the rustling element into Montana. It looked like the Wyoming bad boys all came to Montana when they moved and most of them came to the range north of the Missouri river.

These were gunmen. They were gunmen of sorts; the kind that had a Colt's .45 slung to each hip and tied down to the leg with a buckskin thong so there wouldn't be any accidents when they went to make the draw. Most of them were deadly sudden. Some of the lesser lights among them had only one notch on their guns; others had two, three, four; Long Henry had six. They were cowpunchers, too, the sort that knew how to rope and ride. Most of them would be top hands on any range. It may be said that the boys who were already on this range when the Wyoming lads got in were of the sort that were not timid, to say the least.

It was not long before Landusky became a favorite resort of these knights of the long rope and the quick draw. They made the little mining camp just like a good show—there was never a dull moment. One evening,

Appendices

after a particularly playful bunch had given the town a thorough shooting up, a rather modest little gambler remarked, "Fellers, she sure was hot, I say hot. I could a gone out there in the street anywheres and swung a pint cup around and caught a quart o' bullets in it." Evenings of this kind were the diversion of a town that had not yet known the law. It was just the setting where Pike would feel right at home.

Coming of Jew Jake

One character coming to Landusky when it was young was Jew Jake, at that time widely known in Montana. He signed his name Jake Harris. Jake had lost a leg in a gun fight with the city marshal of Great Falls some years before. As he was a gunman, he quickly became quite an addition to the social life of Landusky. He was a particular friend of Pike's. Pike erected a building for him and Jake engaged in the saloon business. In the rear part of the saloon he had a counter where customers might get overalls, cheap gloves and overshoes.

Jake walked with crutches, but when he was on shift at the bar he used only the left hand crutch, leaving the other hand free to use the No. 8 sawed off shotgun he always kept within reach. If it were an exceptionally lively night he used the sawed off as a crutch.

Jake hadn't been in Landusky very long until he sent to Anaconda and had Hogan come over. Hogan was a gunman; guaranteed to fit perfectly with his new environment. Small, frail and too evidently tubercular, Hogan looked anything but a gunman. Nobody ever knew just how good he was for he really never had a chance to display his wares.

Another group was the Curry brothers. They lived about five miles south of the town and raised cattle and horses. There were three of them, all known as proficient gunmen. Harvey, the eldest Curry, was known as the "Kid"; Johnny was a couple of years younger, the third of the trio being Loney, two years the junior of Johnny.

Harvey, or the Kid, was less than 30 at that time. The Curry brothers were doing well, making their stock venture a growing business, and were popular with most of the residents of the country.

Associated in business with the Currys was Jim Thornhill, rider and cowman, who worked on the D-S and Circle Bar ranges south of the river, and was well known among stockmen. The leader, though, was the Kid, a quiet, taciturn fellow, slow to make friends and careful to take no man into confidential relationship, save the immediate members of his house. All the Currys were dark and it was said they had a strain of Indian blood.

It was also said their true family name of Logan. I never got around to ask any of them about this.

Girl Caused Trouble

Pike and the Currys had lived as neighbors—in a real neighborly way—for five or six years and then there was a row. Some said it began over a plow one borrowed from the other. My observation was that it began from the same cause that has brought about more rows than any other in all this old troubled world—women.

Pike had married a widow woman, a Mrs. Dessery. She was the mother of four lusty girls. Two of these soon got married. Of the two remaining at home, one became very much enamored of Loney, the youngest of the Currys. Loney's reputation with women was not enviable and Pike objected. Between the girls and the plow and the tattle of helpful friends, they began to say things about each other and then to threaten. The countryside looked on and wondered how it would end. Pike had his partisans; the Currys had theirs. Everybody felt that some day there would be a showdown—and somebody would be hurt. Then, for some reason—a charge of changing a brand, or something of that kind—the Kid and Johnny Curry were arrested, the sheriff of Chouteau county leaving them in Pike's charge for a time. While Pike had these men in his custody, he took more than one occasion to threaten and grossly insult them, on one occasion threatening the Kid with a nameless indignity and calling him names that any self respecting man usually resents with violence. It seems that after this episode all the Currys began to drink more than they ever had done before. They were bad men when they were in liquor.

Landusky camp grew right along during the summer of 1894. Many new men came to the camp and into the mountains and the cowpunchers whooped it up plenty. One or two discoveries of new ore bodies kept up interest in the mines; the attractive environment kept others coming. A daily stage line was established between the camp and Harlem on the Great Northern railroad and there was much travel that way.

Along in November somebody suggested the camp ought to have a big community dance and dinner at Christmas time. So much favor this suggestion met that a big town meeting was held, where it was planned that the camp should let the world know it was a going concern and that the event should be the biggest social function the country had ever known. Everybody subscribed liberally so there should be nothing lacking. Then Warren Berry got up at the meeting and said they should have something extraordinary on the menu, that roast pigs and turkeys and chickens and baked hams were not novelties—there ought to be something folks would go home and talk about all winter. When asked what he would suggest, Warren said, oysters. Fresh oysters, not the old stereotyped, canned cove kind, but the massive old juicy Baltimore selects. So, oysters it was, and when the committee left it to Warren as to how many should be ordered, he said four dozen quarts ought to be enough and four dozen quarts it was. Orders were given to "Lousy," the stage driver, to wire for them when he went to the railroad. Lousy had never bought any but cove oysters before so he wired to Minneapolis for them, thinking the oyster beds were at the foot of the falls of Minnehaha. The express on them was more than the original cost of the oysters.

All Feverish Activity

From that time until the big day the camp was all feverish activity. The big time was all the topic of conversation and fully a barrel of bourbon was licked up in considering details and devising new features. Word had gone over all that sparsely settled country that Landusky was entertaining; they all heard it and they all came. And such people they were! They drifted in from the badlands 60 miles way, from grassy valleys in the foothills, from the alkali flats farther out, from remote places in the river breaks and from the gulches of far reaches of the mountains. They came in all the vehicles that were known to the time and they brought food enough to have fed the multitude in the wilderness, those who didn't get a break on the loaves and fishes.

There were more than 100, the biggest crowd of white folks that country had ever assembled. Everything was the best in the land, but the great achievement of it all was the four dozen quarts of oysters. It wouldn't do to let a novice monkey with these bivalves, they had to be prepared and served by a chef who knew how. So "Tie Up George," the most famous of all roundup cooks, was drafted into service and warned not to get cocked up until the feed was over. The writer's handsome new long bungalow, just completed, was donated for the preparation and serving of the evening and midnight meals; Johnnie Curry, second of the Curry brothers trio, loaned his big new log barn for the dance, while Loney Curry, a fiddler of no mean ability, volunteered to lead the home talent orchestra. No such thing as a piano was known in the country, but some folks on a ranch out 10 miles had one of those little portable Mason & Hamlin organs. A dead ax wagon was sent out to borrow the organ, and everything looked to be jake.

Pioneer Cattleman in Montana

A Frontier Jamboree

It was a real old-time frontier jamboree. For two days and nights they danced and ate, kept the drinking right up with the procession, and the harsh bark of the six-gun was heard many times, but it was all in good humor and noise was a part of the show. "Tie Up" made a masterpiece of culinary art of his oyster stew. They liked it so well that, after they had eaten one generous wash boiler of it, he made a second—and George wanted to make a third—but one gets enough even of oysters, to say nothing of four dozen quarts of them. Ranchers and stockmen stayed in town to enjoy the show. It was an outing for all hands, and folks then were not in such a hurry as they are now. Possibly there was not so much to hurry for.

Yet there was a tenseness through all of this apparent gaiety that seemed to forebode a tragic ending. When the gun fighters first came to town they all discarded their guns for the time being. If they wanted to wake the echoes for a moment they'd borrow a gun from the barkeep and have at it. The day following Christmas, in the evening, they all rearmed and everybody clung close to his arsenal. Every man there was watching, he didn't know just what for! The second morning after Christmas, Dec. 27, it came—as all had known it would come eventually.

A light fall of snow brought a chill to the air and the dreariness of the day encouraged the drinking men to hang close to the saloons. Jew Jake's had the smallest crowd of all. About 10:30 in the morning Pike and a friend dropped into Jake's to have a drink. There were seven or eight other men in the house, including Jake and his gunman, Hogan. Just before Pike entered, Loney Curry and Jim Thornhill came in but passed on to the little trade counter at the rear of the room, where they engaged Hogan in conversation.

Curry Started Fight

Pike was in the saloon less than three minutes and was in the act of filling his whisky glass when Kid Curry came in. The Kid walked up directly beside Pike, gave him a good stiff slap on the shoulder and, as Pike looked to see who it was, Curry landed a terrific blow on his jaw, knocking him down. Pike was wearing a very heavy fur-lined overcoat and had this handicap to contend with from the first. The moment the trouble started, Loney Curry and Thornhill drew their six-guns, admon-

Appendices

ished Gunman Hogan to attend to his own business as it was none of his fight. While one saw that Hogan obeyed, the other held up the house and warned all spectators that to interfere meant getting shot.

As soon as Pike fell, Curry was down on top of him with his knees on Pike's arms, holding them to the floor while he began to beat him without mercy. Curry would weigh scarcely 160, but he was a man of great strength, agile as a leopard and venting a spleen he had nursed and brooded over for months. Pike was then past 50, with the weight of that heavy overcoat to hinder him. The handicap of the smashing blow Curry delivered at first, the heavy garments and his age combined to make Pike fight a losing battle from the beginning. But he fought with everything he had. He fought until Curry had beaten him so that there is no question he would have died from the punishment he had taken. Not one whit did his courage weaken but human endurance may be strained just so far and human fortitude has its limitations, so that when Pike found he could fight no more and had suffered all the punishment a man could take, he called for help.

At this time Tommie Carter, a prospector, who had been a witness of it all, appealed to Loney Curry and Thornhill to have it stopped. These two were still holding their guns on the other men in the saloon, warning them not to interfere. Both young Curry and Thornhill refused to permit any interference. Then the Kid seemed to take new satisfaction in the work. He began in earnest to wreak all the vengeance he ever had stored up against his enemy. Pike called out no more and did the best he could while the Kid pounded and smashed his face and head until his brutal blood thirst was satisfied.

A Pitiful Sight

When the Kid finally finished Pike was a pitiful sight. The entire left side of his face and most of the rest of his face, and his head as well, had been beaten until they looked almost like a black eye. It seems, though, that when the Kid refused to quit when Pike called 'enough' that a new spirit of fight came back into the old battler, for when he was finally allowed to get up—he came with a gun. The gun had been in his overcoat pocket all the time of the fight but Pike had been unable to reach it. So quickly did he draw and hold his gun on the Kid that, for the moment, Curry stood and hesitated.

The drawing of that gun, however, was another bit of hard luck for

Pioneer Cattleman in Montana

Pike. It wouldn't work. It was one of the new fangled automatics that had just come out at that time and, either Pike didn't know how to use it or it went wrong, as most of those new ones did when they were wanted the most. Anyway, it didn't work. The Kid found himself in a moment, drew his .45, and it was all over. He shot Pike twice in the body—missed him the third time—and Pike battled no more.

Thus the fighter who had beaten so many men and had been so merciless when he confronted an enemy, came to his tragic end and was the first to lose his life in the town that had been named for him.

I have read many narratives of the killing of this widely known frontier character. With one exception, they have been hearsay stories, and have contained much that was imagination and much that was from truth. Few persons were in Jew Jake's saloon while the fight was going on. Of course Jew Jake and his gunman bartender, Hogan, were there; others being Tommie Carter, named before in this narrative; George Contway, a halfbreed; Loney Curry and Jim Thornhill, Jack Clark, George Allis and two or three others whose names are unknown—less than a dozen altogether.

About George Allis

George Allis was the first sheriff of Missoula county, the discoverer of Top Hand, one of the rich producers at Barker when that camp was booming, and one of the real old-timers in the state. Shortly after the battle started Allis walked out of the saloon and met the writer coming toward it. The uproar of the fight could be heard and I stopped to ask what was going on. He told me Pike and the Kid were having it, remarking, "Don't go in there. You are not interested and it's dangerous for there will be some shooting before it's over with."

Just then the first shot was fired and I distinctly recall seeing the other occupants of the place swarm out the back door. Jew Jake, being a cripple, fell out with his hands up in the air and I said to Allis, "They've got Jake, all right." It looked as if he were falling from a wound but the fact was he was so scared he didn't know just what he was doing. Thornhill and Loney Curry also came out the back way and Thornhill told Jake, as the latter sat on the ground, that they did not intend to harm him. Allis proceeded on his way and I entered the front door of the saloon just as Pike breathed his last. By this time the camp was a bedlam of excitement. In a very short time Johnnie Curry drove up the street in a spring wagon, into which all the Curry crowd loaded and drove out of the camp.

Appendices

I recall in particular that there were two men in Jake's saloon whom no one seemed to know. They must have been transients in town. I think, however, their names must have been "Legion" for I've talked, personally, to more than 100 men as the years have gone by who told me they saw it all—were eye witnesss. I couldn't dispute any of them as I didn't know the names of the two strangers.

Pike Was Ruthless

The true story of Pike Landusky would rival the best thriller Beadle ever published in his dime novel group. A life of strenuous battle on the frontier had been his for many years. The gun fight and the rough and tumble battle are incidents of a day to him. Hardships and adventure were his life from early manhood. His uncontrollable temper caused him much trouble and his vindictiveness toward those he disliked cost him plenty. His friendship was something worth while.

Pike would do as much for the person he liked as any man I ever knew. I had two material instances of this in my dealings with him. If he liked a man, he liked him if all the rest of the world were against him. If he disliked him that dislike grew into a dangerous, unreasonable hatred. There is no denying that he was merciless and implacable. And it is one of the just verdicts of fate that a man who lives by the gun, without either mercy or forgiveness, usually dies by the gun and by the same merciless violence he has dealt out to others.

Pike is buried on his old ranch holdings a mile down the valley from Landusky town. Just the place where he should lie and contemplate the changes as they come to a land with the passing of years. It is just 40 years since he engaged in his last battle and went on the long ride with the Rider on the Pale Horse. In all the years that come there will not be another like him.

The Daily River Press
February 5, 1896

THE CURRY SHOOTING

Under Sheriff Howell returned to-day (Wednesday) from Malta, accompanied by James Winters, who sought refuge at the Brown ranch after the Curry shooting. Mr. Winters states that after the affair was over he started on horseback for the railroad, intending to give himself up to the authorities; but his horse played out, and fearing trouble from

Pioneer Cattleman in Montana

Curry's friends he camped at the Brown ranch and sent word to Malta to telegraph for the sheriff. The officers had no trouble on arriving at their destination, none of the Curry element having put in an appearance.

It is a little singular that a deputy sheriff was hunting for John Curry at the time of the shooting. A bench warrant had been issued for his arrest on a charge of assault, and the deputy was making for Landusky by way of the Lansing ranch and along the Missouri river. He was due at Landusky on Sunday afternoon, the day after his man had been killed at the Winters ranch, so that part of his trip will be fruitless.

The Daily River Press
July 26, 1901

DASTARDLY ATTEMPT TO MURDER

One of the most cold-blooded and cowardly crimes ever committed in Montana is reported from the Little Rockies, which is maintaining its reputation as the resort of certain tough characters who are a menace to the peace and safety of law abiding citizens. A telegram was received by Sheriff Clary Thursday night from A. D. Gill of Landusky, who wired from Harlem, stating that his partner, Jas. Winters, had been shot from ambush at 6 o'clock that morning, at his ranch six miles from Landusky. It is learned that two bullets struck him, both in the abdomen, so that the wounds may prove fatal. It is fully 66 miles from the Gill & Winters' ranch to Harlem, where the nearest doctor is located. No particulars were given and, naturally, the would-be murderer is unknown.

Mr. Winters is known and respected throughout northern Montana as a good and reputable citizen, but has been feared and detested by the rough element that has succeeded in terrorizing that part of the country. He is so handy with a gun that his cowardly assailant preferred to shoot him from ambush when he was unarmed and did not suspect any danger. The Curry gang and their sympathizers have had it in for Winters ever since the latter killed John Curry about five years ago, an occurrence which was justified by Curry commencing to fire at him with a six-shooter. Curry claimed the Tressler ranch, which Winters had bought and tried to enforce his claim by ordering its owner out of the country.

During the recent hunt for train robbers the different posses made the Gill & Winters ranch their headquarters and this may have had something to do with the crime. Jailer Coatsworth and Stock Inspector Lund have gone to Landusky to investigate the shooting.

Appendices

The Sentinel
Knoxville, Tennessee
June 29, 1903

BANDIT LOGAN WAS LAST SEEN FIVE MILES FROM CITY SATURDAY

HE WAS RIDING LEISURELY ALONG A BYROAD HAVING LEFT THE PIKE—
SPOKE TO NO ONE HE MET

An empty cell, a puzzled corps of officers and possemen, a gossiping public and a voluminous court record, as reminders of his sojourn in this city, are today all there is of Harvey Logan, alias Charley Johnson, alias "Kid" Curry, etc., who since his capture at Jefferson City, December 15, 1901, has been confined in the Knox county jail, constantly under guard. The whereabouts of the bandit are still unknown. Latest reports received at the county jail today show no trace of the man, and there is no clue as to the course he took after he was last seen four miles south of the river. His tracery from the city leads to the Picken's Gap road, near Neubert Springs, where, in a long stretch of woodland on either side of the pike, the earth seemed to swallow him up.

Logan's escape was the enactment of another chapter in his checkered career, a repetition of former feats where nerve and cunning placed him beyond the ban of the law. Only this time he took no lives, but accomplished his escape with his wonted dexterity and craftiness.

First News in Sentinel.

As was detailed in *The Sentinel's* extra edition Saturday afternoon, the noted outlaw escaped from the county jail about 5:15 o'clock. So carefully had he planned his escape, that there was not a single break in its successful execution, and he rode to liberty as easily as he gained his liberty when he escaped from the Montana penitentiary, or the strong jail of Deadwood, South Dakota. It was about 4:15 o'clock when Logan coolly began his work Saturday afternoon that resulted in escape and placing him beyond official ken. He was sauntering up and down the corridor talking to Guard Frank Irwin, at random, when the guard, who frequently walked around the aisle between the wall and main cage, halted at the rear of the cage, where he had a fine vantage of the river. There was no one on the second floor of the jail save Logan and the guard. The guard made some remark about the river. Logan idly responded to the statement made by the guard and then advanced toward the guard

Pioneer Cattleman in Montana

and resumed the conversation, calling attention to some object in the river.

Caught the Guard.

The guard then started to resume his position in front of Logan's cell, on the west side of the cage, when the bandit threw a lasso or loop of twisted wire, about 3 feet in length, over his head and jerked him severely against the grating bars and said:

"Frank, I have got the advantage of you. I am going out of here, now, and if you do what I tell you I will not hurt you; don't and you are a dead man."

With other statements in accord with his previously laid plans, he forced the guard to thrust his hands through the bars of the main cage; and with his left hand still firmly grasping the wire loop, he made Irwin turn around, and tied the guard's hands together with strips of canvas torn from an old hammock, which he had previously prepared for the important purpose for which they now served. This was only the work of a few minutes, and as he completed the job, he said:

"I will now make Tom (Bell) let me out."

The guard added a few words, begging that Bell should not be hurt, and reminded Logan that Bell had nothing against him. The prisoner then ran into the bath room, where he had a number of pieces of moulding from a window facing, and which he then, or had previously, spliced, and went to the front of the cage. To the end of this timber he attached, or had previously attached, it is not known which, a hook made of the rusty bail of a bucket. He then began raking the floor in front of the corridor with a view of dragging within his reach the paste-board shoe box in which were a 45-calibre Colt's pistol and a 38-calibre Smith & Wesson pistol. In a few minutes he had them within his reach, and replaced the empty box in the same manner that he had drawn it to him. He returned to the guard, withdrew the watch of the guard, and said: have got."

Next the Jailer.

"I only want to see what time it is. I don't want anything that you

It was then 4:30 o'clock, by the guard's watch. He then repaired to the front of the cell, and began waiting for Jailer Bell, whom he thought would soon appear on the scene, as was his custom, but this was too slow for him, and he took his medicine bottle and began rapping the bars. The jailer appeared, thinking that he was needed, and Logan threw one of the pistols in the jailer's face, and said:

Appendices

"Open up, Tom, I am going out of here. I don't want to hurt you, but I will kill you if you do not open the door. I have nothing against you, but Fox had better stay out of my way. I am going out of here."

He then commanded the jailer to close the circular door leading from the steps to the second ward, and forced him to work the combination. The first time the combination failed to work, and Logan impatiently told the jailer not to "fool" him. The jailer was wholly in the man's power and the dramatic scene was soon changed by the door flying open after the opening click of the combination.

Logan Was Free.

He then marched the officer to the main office, down the basement steps and into the back yard of the jail where was found the sheriff's saddle mare. He commanded the officer to saddle the animal, and R. P. Swanee, an Italian helper and ex-prisoner who appeared, was forced to assist. About the time the saddle was placed on the animal, the sheriff appeared on the front porch above and was told by Bell, in reply to his question as to what was the matter, "that he would soon find out what was the matter if he did not get back into the house." The animal was saddled, but the bridle could not be found, and with his pistol in his right hand and the halter rein in his left hand Logan dashed out into Prince street, then into Hill avenue and into Gay and across the Tennessee river bridge and out the Martin Mill pike. He attracted much attention, but the general impression was that he was a livery stable employe taking a horse to a customer. Sheriff Fox had meanwhile rushed in to get his pistol, but before he could secure it, Logan had made good his escape. The sheriff had no rifle on the place. Jailer Bell returned to the jail and he and Jim, the colored cook, went to the second ward and there found Irwin and released him. Bud Woods, who resides on the corner opposite the jail, saw Logan leave, and noticed his watch at the same time and it was 5:05 o'clock. As Logan passed the old Adcock property on the opposite corner, he beckoned to a little girl, to whom he had often waved and called when a prisoner, as if to warn her to keep quiet. Sheriff Fox immediately came up town and gave the alarm.

Posse Sent Out.

He reached all of his deputies possible, and Deputies Hardin and Epps and Constable C. G. Gamble formed a posse that went out the Martin Mill pike and spent the night searching for the fugitive. The last they

Pioneer Cattleman in Montana

could hear of him was when he was near Neubert's Springs in the Pickens Gap road. Deputy Sheriff W. G. Lea, and Wm. McIntyre went to Sevier county, and did not return until Sunday morning. The only development Sunday in the case was the return of the Sheriff's mare, barebacked, lame in both legs and without a bridle. She was first seen on the Maryville pike two miles southwest of the city, grazing along the road. She showed evidence of hard riding.

Guard Irwin's Story of the Logan Escape.

"I can show you better than I can tell you how it happened," said Frank Irwin, the guard, when asked by a reporter for *The Sentinel* to describe how Logan came to get the advantage of him. He continued: "I frequently talked to Logan, and Saturday afternoon I walked to the south end of the walkway around the main caged section, and began talking with him about the river, saying, 'I think, Charley, that the river is rising slowly for so much rain,' and we then began to talk about it. I turned my back to him and was gazing out at the river from the second floor, when all of a sudden he threw the twisted wire over my head like it was a lariat, and said, 'I have got the advantage of you, Frank, and I am going out of here. If you move I will kill you; just do as I tell you and don't yell, and you are all right.' He then made me poke my hands into the main cage, and while he held one hand on the wire about my neck, he tied my hands securely with the strips of canvas, using his right hand and teeth to tie the knots. He then said, 'I am going out of here. Yell, and you are a dead man. I like you, Frank, and it may be that I will be stretched out here dead in a few minutes. I don't want to hurt Tom, but he has got to turn me out.' I then told him not to hurt Tom, as he had nothing against him. There he left me and went to work to get the pistols. I simply knew that he had me and that if I created any trouble he would cut my throat or kill me. He could have done that and accomplished his purpose in getting away as easy as not."

Jailer Tom Bell's Story of the Whole Affair.

When asked for a statement, Jailer Tom Bell said:

"I was so taken by surprise when he shoved the pistol in my face that I hardly realized what had happened. He would have killed me if I had not complied with his request, and I opened the door to save my life. I do not regret my action, and knew Logan would have shot me if I did not do what he asked me to do. He would have covered every

Appendices

man that came up until the door was unlocked. With those pistols, he had control of the situation. The details of how he forced me to go into the yard, saddle the horse, etc., are well known. I would not have had the escape happened for anything on earth, but Logan had me at his command, and to resist would have been death. I don't care what is said about the case. I knew the man, knew what he would do, and did his bidding to save my life."

Many have been heard to say that they did not blame Bell. Any sane man would have done just as he did.

STORY OF THE ITALIAN AS TO THE ESCAPE.

*Says He Was Ordered to Fall Into Line
With the Others and March.*

Swanee, the Italian, who saddled the horse for Logan, tells an amusing story. Swanee is a rather stout man and like most of his race talks excitedly and gesticulates freely.

He narrates how Logan came down the steps with Jailer Bell and met him. Neither of the men spoke as they approached, and as Swanee looked up he saw Logan, his slouch hat pulled down over his eyes with a pistol in each hand. If he had dropped out of the moon the Italian couldn't have been more surprised.

"Fall in line," said Logan, pointing a weapon in close proximity to the Italian's prominent abdomen development. Swanee was evidently of the opinion that the aim was perfect, so he obeyed without a word. Logan was cool and collected, he said, while the jailer naturally was not looking in his usual health.

"We wenta to de stable," said Swanee, "and he tola me to getta da saddle for da mare. Whena I could no find it, he swore and said 'Looka all roun.' I found de saddle, but not de bridle."

Logan rode off on the horse with only a halter.

ON LOOKOUT IN SEVIER COUNTY.

Special to *The Sentinel*.

Sevierville, June 29.—The report that Harvey Logan had escaped created some excitement here, but the sheriff did not go on a hunt as he could not do so at that time. Officers living in the southern portion of the county organized a posse and spent Saturday night and Sunday looking for him, but learned nothing of him. It was the impression here that he would make his way toward the Chilhowee mountains, going to the Tenth District, in the direction of Dupont Springs, but the officers who watched the mountain roads with this idea were disappointed, as the man was not heard from. The officers were heavily armed and prepared for the worst that might happen.

Did Not See Logan.

The report that has been circulated that Frank James and Cole Younger saw Logan when the show was here two weeks ago is untrue. Manager O'Neil called at the jail and asked to see Logan, but when the prisoner got a glimpse of the stranger coming into the jail, he hid in his cell and O'Neil did not get to see him.

Logan's Cell Left Just as It Was.

Logan's cell is in about the same condition he left it except possibly one or two articles have been moved in the investigation. He did not leave a scratch of a pencil as to his past or future. He took the two pistols, his razor, possibly a bar of soap and his shaving brush and one suit of clothing. He had only one good suit and he left the old clothing he sometimes wore when a prisoner. It is believed by Jailer Bell that Logan intended to make him ride away behind him if Sheriff Fox had offered to fire on him. He marched the jailer back to his cell and said, "Just keep quiet, I want to get my coat." The jailer asked Logan not to point the pistol at him, saying:

"That thing will go off accidentally, Charley, and you would shoot me."

"No, it will not. I am watching that. I won't hurt a hair of your head. I may take you a good piece with me, Tom, before I am done with you, so let's get out of here."

The jailer believes that Logan intended to make him mount behind him, but seeing that he had a clear field and knew that he would not be fired upon, he did not need the jailer to protect him.

Reward and Description.

As to the reward for Logan, Sheriff Fox on Saturday night offered $500 reward for his recapture, and the Great Northern railway and Express Company offers $500, and United States Marshal Austin offers $250. This makes $1,250, but the one who captures him, it is said, would do better to turn him back to Montana or Wyoming, where he can be

Appendices

disposed of at from $2,000 to $5,000. There are rewards ranging from $1,000 to $6,000 for his arrest alone.

The reward to Knoxville parties will, of course, not be paid, as his conviction was not completed. He was to have been resentenced July 10.

Following is the description of Logan sent out by the Pinkertons:

Age, 36 years (1901).
Height, 5 ft., 7 1-2 inches.
Build, medium.
Nose, prominent, large, long and straight.
Color of hair, dark brown.
Style of beard, clean shaven.
Eyes, dark.
Weight, 145 to 160 lbs.
Complexion, dark, swarthy.
Marks, has gun-shot wound on wrist; talks slowly.

APPENDIX B

Original Account of Jerk-Line Freighting by Joseph M. Hartmann

FORGOTTEN MEN, MARKED FOR HISTORY

Over fifty years was required by the author to compile the authentic material necessary to present his unique freight-team pictures and his own handwritten historical notes to the public.

By doing so he has revealed many aspects of the work done by freighters during the late nineteenth and early part of this Century by transporting commodities with oxen, mule and horse team, lugging loaded wagons over prairie and mountain trails to army forts, trading posts, mining camps, and frontier communities.

This work was beset with trials and tribulations which were only overcome by the traditional devotion to duty of the early freighters, a class of men, typified by the author, all of whom risked their lives, livestock, and fortunes to play transportation's leading role in "Our Winning of the West."

So has the author been bent to this work with ardent hopes that it will meet with everyone's approval everywhere.

PICTURES AND HISTORICAL NOTES OF
EARLY TRANSPORTATION IN THE AMERICAN WEST
BY
JOSEPH M. HARTMANN
Freighters with their string-teams
Blazed the trails across our continent,
And opened the remotest sections (or far country)
To the commercial transportation of the future.

Pioneer Cattleman in Montana

A facsimile of "the Half Breed Cart of Frontier Days" made by Joe Dussome, President of the Homeless Indians, and Joseph M. Hartmann. This type of vehicle was the first mode of transportation used on wheels in the American West. Its framework consisted solely of wood with buffalo hide strips to bind the fellows, or rims, and spokes in the hubs tightly together. It was used extensively in the forepart of this century by the offspring of French explorers who married Aboriginal Women and later became known as the Metis People, all of whom were well adopted to survive in the territory that embraced the upper Missouri River basin area. This cart derived its first name from its founder, "Charette," French accent for the ancient "Chariot."

Appendices

An anonymous picture of an Emigrant Train. The men and women who directed these trains constituted the vanguard of our American westward movement over prairies, valleys, and mountains to build the empire beyond the Mississippi, the Missouri, and other navigable rivers that flow toward the Pacific Coast.

To overcome all resistances to their progress enroute they made use of the crudest means and methods at hand, as historical accounts of their movement between 1840–60 has been revealed by previous authors to the public.

Pioneer Cattleman in Montana

The Bill Phipp's Bull Team on Central Avenue, Great Falls, Montana, 1890. This mode of transportation was foremost in use on the overland trails of the United States and the Canadian West from 1860 to 1890. During that era, cattle could be purchased from Southern herds trailed to the north and they were more plentiful than horses and mules. Perhaps the term "Oxen" was derived from the yokes and bows used with them. No leather harness was used by bull-whacker freighters. Oxen required no hay or grain but could thrive throughout the year on the luscious native grass along the trails. But, after 1890, horses and railroads became available for freighting service. Consequently the bull whackers and their string-teams of oxen, who had pioneered early transportation withdrew and have vanished forever.

Appendices

The Murray Boys, Bob and Jim were two of the early freighters in the Judith Basin country. In 1902, when I began to freight, I had the good fortune to drive with them from Harlowtown to Lewistown. From this a lifelong friendship originated. They had a reputation, second to none, in that country and from them I learned many skills of the freighting business. The Murray Brothers were undisputed champions with the blacksnake. With a ten foot shot loaded whip, they could pop out the light of a standing candle, and could snap off a row of marbles on a board one after another without disturbing any of the others. I was so captivated by the marvelous coordination of their string-teams that I felt a distinct calling to live the life of a freighter. So attractive was the occupation that I followed the career of a freighter for fourteen years, and I have never regretted the choice.

Pioneer Cattleman in Montana

Joe Hartmann's sixteen horse freight outfit in Malta, Montana, November 1907, loaded with 28,500 pounds of supplies for the Ruby Gulch Gold Mining Company and the merchants at Zortman. The Zortman-Malta round trip of 110 miles was completed in ten days. Our freight hauling charges were $1.00 a hundred pounds.

The Montana range bred horses were superior to oxen and mules. They possessed the endurance so necessary for winter freighting. They traveled faster and their hooves gave them better footing than the cloven hoofed oxen. The small hoofed mules were unable to compete on muddy ground. They'd lie down and roll out of it. But alas, since motor power replaced the horses driven by the freighters on our early trails, only the memory remains of their colorful past life when the West was young and wild and hard to tame.

Appendices

Joe Hartmann driving his sixteen horse freight outfit near Zortman, November, 1907. When the photographer took this picture of my freight horses in pulling action, I said, "Twenty years from now, I may be glad I had this picture taken." He replied, "It will be one in a million." The picture shows the "Jerkline" method of driving a string-team with one line, also the "Jockey-stick" that held the leaders while they led the others. By jerking the line snappily, the bald face, near leader, "Old Prince," would turn to the right; by pulling steady on the line, he'd turn left. Thus by using the Jerk-line either way to pass around road turns, the other horse followed likewise. On this trip my lead wagon was loaded with 33 cases of Hamm's Beer for the Dewar Brothers Saloon in Zortman. My brother, Tim is riding the saddle horse. I drove the horses shown in this picture when Tim and I made our memorable 44 day round trip with two long string-team freight outfits during the Hard Winter, 1906–07.

Pioneer Cattleman in Montana

© WINTER SUPPLIES FOR A MINING CAMP

Joe Hartmann's twelve horse freight outfit in Zortman, Montana, December 23, 1907, loaded with 18,500 lbs. of supplies for the Ruby Gulch Mining Company and the merchants of Zortman. To slow our wagons, or to prevent them from running while passing down hills, we used hand lever brakes and roughlocks on the wheels. We fed our horses oats in nosebags in order to catch and to harness them more easily. I was anxious to succeed in the freighting business and I asked an elderly freighter, Frank Whitmore, this question: "What will help me most to become a successful freighter?" "Why," he chuckled, "Nothing else but good pulling horses driven by a level headed freighter." While I pondered the meaning of his answer, he continued. "If you get stuck in a bad place with your freight outfit, good pulling horses will make the second pull for you. They will also make the third and the fourth pull for you if you know how to do things to favor them instead of losing your head in a crisis."

Appendices

The teams of Tim and Joe Hartmann at the foot of the Alabama Hill two miles from Zortman, 1908. We hauled ore two miles, from the Alabama Mine to the Alder Gulch Mill for the Little Rocky Exploration Company. Weather permitting, we loaded about eleven tons on each two wagons and made two trips daily. As both the Bald Eagle and the Alabama Hills were long, steep, and dangerous to descend, roughlocks had to be used on at least three wheels of each two wagons for safety sake. Wagon brakes were used only in emergency cases because of the wheel tires heating, falling off the rims, and causing a breakdown. To ward off another danger, we drove our team with six reins for this reason: When our loaded wagons were hard to start from the brow of the hills for the downhill pull, quite often the collars pulled up on the horses necks, shut off their wind, whereas, they'd stagger and would have fallen had we not held them back with the reins until they regained their wind and normal stride.

Pioneer Cattleman in Montana

Numbers and names of ore haulers for the Little Rocky Exploration Company in 1908, near the Alder Gulch Mill, two miles above Zortman, Montana, were as follows: No. 1, Frank Whitmore; No. 2, Frank Howe; No. 3, Harry Keller; No. 4, Jim Campbell; No. 5, Tim Hartmann; No. 6, Joe Hartmann. If we delivered over 100 tons of ore to the mill daily, we received $1.25 a ton; if less than that amount $1.00 a ton. Considerable excitement was often caused by the freighters betting on the weight of the loads that were hauled. For instance, one evening in August, 1908, my two wagon loads of ore were last to be weighed and 23,000 lbs. was required for all of us to receive $1.25 a ton. Whether I'd have that amount or not, bets were wagered by others until both loads weighed and they tipped the scale beam at 23,100 lbs. The heaviest load of ore ever hauled from that mine to the mill, 24,400 lbs. was delivered by my brother, Tim. He and I hauled over 6,000 tons of ore for that company during their eight months run.

Appendices

TRANSPORTING POWER PLANT BOILERS

The most perilous freight trip ever undertaken by a freighter in the American West was accomplished by Joe Hartmann, from January 10 to April 4, 1916, with a sixteen horse string-team. He was assisted by two capable men, his cousin, Martin Hartmann, and Abe Smith. The freight consisted of two water tube boilers, each weighing 36,000 pounds. They were hauled part way on a large logging sleigh, and the remainder on a huge steel truck, over a dim trail that led from Winifred, Montana, northward and down through the Badlands of the Missouri River, across the river on a ferryboat, and on to the power plant and nearby coal mine of the Ruby Gulch Gold Mining Company. This winding trail led through some of the most awe inspiring and wildest looking country in the United States. This trip, the climax of his fourteen year freighting career, was so difficult that three of his most faithful freight horses lost their lives enroute.

This picture represents the manufactured iron truck that was used by Joe and Martin Hartmann to complete their boiler hauling trip. Since the purpose for which it served has been specified [on preceding illustration], not only does this vehicle help to reveal the growth of transportation with animal power during the past century, but its existence also helped to introduce the growth in stature of the Iron Age to the world.

A Tribute to Early American Freighters
BY
JOSEPH M. HARTMANN
*Once monarch of our early trails,
Lest your craft as a builder of empire
be forgotten,
We dedicate "The Freighter" to posterity.*

Pioneer Cattleman in Montana

Although others have often asked Joe Hartmann, "Did you drive your string-team of horses with only one line, called the Jerkline?" and as usual his answer was, "Yes," never could he describe the method clearly until he presented these two pictures of the Jerkline Headgear, once used on the leaders of the freight outfits driven by him during the fore-part of this century.

Thereafter, however, their comments on his work were to this effect: "The truth of things that it portrays is of the pioneer cast at which everything one who reviews its various phases will direct his respect with admiration."

Appendices

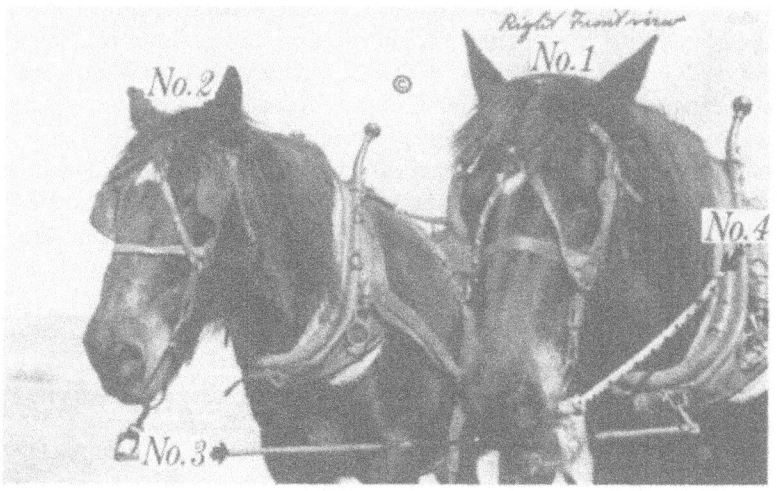

The Jerkline method of driving string-teams, used by most freighters in the early American West, was as follows: No. 1, Linehorse; No. 2, Off Leader; No. 3, Jockey-stick to space both leaders apart; No. 4, Left front view of Jerkline hookup to jaw-strap ring of Linehorse; No. 5, "Gee-strap," extending from Linehorse's (right side) bridle-bit ring to his lower, right side hame ring, was used by freighters to break lead horses to work with a Jerkline. To yank it and shout, "Gee," the linehorse would turn his head to the right and likewise, he'd lead the others working back of him. To pull it steadily and shout, "Haw," he'd turn and lead them to the left.

Pioneer Cattleman in Montana

This complete set of rare pictures and handwritten historical notes in parts constitute Joe Hartmann's contribution to the State of Montana, for the privilege that he has had to gain a career as a freighter on its open range domain. In that his work will reveal to the public, especially to the future students of history, the fundamental working features in connection with the most practical modes and methods of overland transportation with oxen, horses, and mules, once used by mankind in the early American West if not elsewhere, or during prehistoric times.

Appendices

APPENDIX C

Biography of Robert Coburn, from Progressive Men of Montana[1]

Robert Coburn, of Great Falls, is one of the best known stockmen in Montana. Of this extensive industry he is a pioneer of pioneers. While at times he has deviated from the strict line of this profitable business and turned his attention to the seductive interest of mining, his life work in the main has been connected with the cattle industry. In this he has found profit and achieved an enviable success. A complete biography of Mr. Coburn would constitute a most interesting and instructive work on Montana stock raising. Mr. Coburn was born at Smith Falls, Ontario, Canada, on October 12, 1837. His parents were Joseph and Anna (Holliday) Coburn, both natives of County Monahan, Ireland. They were married in that country, emigrated to Canada in the early 'thirties and subsequently their lives were passed on Canadian soil, Joseph Coburn being a lumberman and farmer. They had four sons and six daughters and both died when Robert was a child.

As far back as 1859 Robert Coburn came to Denver, making the trip across the plains by the Platte River. Here he mined with more or less success for three years. In 1863 he came to Montana, locating first at Alder Gulch, now Virginia City, and continued on Moody & Dixie's bars and also in Bevan's gulch. In 1864 Mr. Coburn was mining on Silver Creek when Cowan and his party came along and took up the first claim on Last Chance gulch. Mr. Coburn had learned of the presence of gold in the gulch from "Gold Tom," a squaw man, who panned out the first gold in the almost fabulously rich mining section in the fall of 1864. Mr. Coburn secured the ownership of discovery claim No. 4, and later purchased Nos. 7 and 8. In the spring of 1865, in company with George Cleveland and Jim Coburn, he began work on claims 7 and 8, having lost his claim No. 4 by being absent from it. On claims 7 and 8 the party averaged between three and four hundred dollars a day. In 1866 Mr. Coburn began ranching on Prickly Pear Creek. He had purchased cattle from Iowa and Minnesota, and his placer mining days being over he engaged in a new and even more profitable industry. Mr. Coburn followed stock raising here until 1869, when he moved to the mouth of the canyon on Prickly Pear Creek and continued ranching here until 1875 coming to what is now Cascade country. Here he took up government land and

[1] Page 200.

resided upon it until 1882, when he removed to White Sulphur Springs and in 1886 to the Little Rockies. He still holds that range of nearly 30,000 acres, which is well stocked with cattle, and he owns an interest in some mines near Castle and White Sulphur Springs.

Although having never been an officeseeker in any sense of the word, Mr. Coburn has been a life-long and faithful Democrat and is a valued Mason. Mr. Coburn enjoys the respect of all with whom he has ever been brought into business or social relations. In the welfare of Great Falls he has ever manifested a deep interest since he cast his lot with the citizens of the place.

In 1901 the Coburn Cattle Company was organized with a capital stock of $250,000 in 2500 shares, held by Mr. Coburn and four of his children, retaining 1619 shares. This corporation has practically taken in charge all of the Coburn cattle holdings in northern Montana.

Mr. Coburn was married in July, 1865, in Helena, to Mary Morrow, a native of Canada. They had seven children, Jessie (now Mrs. Maddox); William M., Robert J., Wallace D., Agnes M., Edna, and Warren, now deceased. Mrs. Coburn died in 1885, and in 1890[2] Mr. Coburn married with Mary Blessing, a native of Ohio. They have two children, Walter and Harold.

[2] This date should be 1887.

Appendices

APPENDIX D

About the Russell Watercolor

This Russell painting, *Roping a Cow,* shows my older half-brothers, Will, Bob, and Wallace Coburn, roping a cow and depicts a not uncommon incident explained to me when I was a kid. When I asked why the cow was being roped, I was told that when a cow loses her calf, probably killed by wolves or coyotes, the milk in her udder cakes and spoils unless she is roped and milked out.

A cow on the prod is a dangerous critter, as any old-time cowhand will readily confirm. This cow has charged Bob's horse, and Will has roped one hind leg. Wallace, on the black horse, is coming up to head-rope the cow.

The background for the painting was the sandstone rimrock country at the edge of the badlands between the Coburn Circle C home ranch and the north bank of the Missouri River in northeastern Montana.

The Bar L brand on the left ribs belonged to Will and Bob Coburn. My father, Robert Coburn, used a Half Circle C brand on the left ribs and thigh of his cattle and the Circle C brand on his horses. These brands were all registered in the brand book of the Montana Stockgrowers Association.

This Russell watercolor, dated 1897, was hung on the wall of what in that era was known as the "parlor" of my father's white three-story town house on the corner of Fourth Avenue and Tenth Street in Great Falls, Montana, three blocks from where Charlie Russell lived on Fourth Avenue and Thirteenth Street. There it hung from 1897 until about 1916 when the Circle C outfit was sold to the Matador Land and Cattle Company of Texas and our Great Falls home was sold.

At the time our Great Falls home was dismantled, Bob Coburn, for some unknown reason, took the Russell painting with him. Later when Bob died his widow Claire (Daisy) Coburn claimed the painting as part of his estate. Several years later Daisy sold the Russell watercolor, which is now owned by Mrs. David Hibbs of Tucson, Arizona.

I had completely lost track of the painting until one day about twenty years ago when I walked into the ranch home of the late David and Mrs. Hibbs and saw the watercolor on their wall. The size of the painting is $12\frac{1}{2}'' \times 19\frac{1}{2}''$.

—W. C.

Index

Adams, Jim: 126f.
Alder Gulch: 151, 228f.
Alford, Old Tex: 142, 191f., 198, 201, 203, 206
Allen, Julia: 168n., 170 & n., 174
Allen, William James: 160–62, 164, 167, 168 & n.; troublemaker, 160, 164; rumor about Coburns, 164, 170; meeting at Circle C, 165f., 169n.; killing of, 168n., 169n., 172, 192, 215, 251, 288f.;
American Fur Company: 6
Animas Valley (New Mexico): 116
Asher, Harry: 192–93, 197, 199ff., 202, 203; fight with Jim Brown, 194, 196, 214
Assiniboins: 4, 18, 19, 157, 163, 164, 168n., 169n., 172, 192, 215, 251, 288f.; sharing land with Gros Ventres, 163, 167

Badlands: 39, 102, 106, 124, 230; between the Missouri and Little Rockies, 37, 111, 184, 187, 236, 282
Baker, Aleck: 241, 245
Baker, Frank: 239–44, 245, 254f.
Baker, George: 102–104, 106
Ball, Bartholomew (Bart): 168n.
Ball, Cecilia: 167n.
Ball, Josephine: 169n.
Ball, Julia: 168n.; see also Julia Allen
Ball, May: 168n.
Ball, Tom: 199

Ball, William: 167n., 174
Bar L brand: 176, 179; selling of, 120; see also Bob Coburn and Will Coburn
Bar N Bar: 126
Bass, Sam: 108, 189
Bate's Point: 39, 41
Beard, Charlie: 32, 109f., 219, 268
Bear Paw Mountains: 126
Bear Paw Pool Ranch: 28, 108, 126, 135, 227
Beaver Creek: 161, 168n., 218, 236, 251, 253, 282f., 286
Bent, George: 167n.
Bickler, George L.: 183, 191f., 194, 197–98, 199, 201
Big Warm Creek: 161, 236f., 251, 282
Blackfoot Nation: 4, 163; see also Gros Ventres
Bracamonte, Mac: 257
Brewster, Charlie: 88, 127, 139, 142, 144, 179; handling horses, 140–41
Brewster, Horace: 8–9, 13, 39, 86, 88, 124, 127, 139, 142, 179, 180, 186, 204, 282; quits job as Circle C foreman, 175f.
Bridger, Jim: 6
Bronc rider: 82, 137–40, 143, 197, 202, 235, 279
Broncs: 139–44, 193, 235; outlaw, 141, 142; see also Wild Bunch (outlaw broncs)
Brown, Jim: 192–93, 197, 199f.; fight with Harry Asher, 194, 196, 214

331

Brown, Mary: 169n.
Bucket of Blood Saloon: 133ff.
Buenos Aires, So. America: 223, 225
Buffalo: 6, 7, 157, 251
"Buffalo Bill": see William F. Cody
Bullwhacker: 145f.
Bureau of Indian Affairs: 156–59, 161, 163
Butte College of Mines: 228f.

Cameron, Andy (Scotty): 249f., 258
Cantrell, Floppin' Bill: 39, 40
Carter, Charles: see Charlie Siringo
Cassidy, Butch: 68, 77f., 91, 99ff., 106, 119, 125, 225ff.; see also outlaw gangs and Wild Bunch
Castleberg, Phil: 259f.
Cattle: 163, 168n., 173f., 179, 185, 191, 215, 221, 264f., 282; longhorns, 7, 154, 156; industry, 7, 136, 223; disaster of 1886–87, 16, 18; Circle C, 19, 107, 126, 143, 146, 157, 159, 179, 180, 187, 203–204, 206, 210, 230, 235, 250f., 279, 281, 283, 287; branding, 90, 188f., 190, 191, 235; roundups, 126, 127f., 135, 180, 187, 191, 198, 225, 281, 287; cutting, 128, 188; roping, 128; Texas herds, 136, 156, 189; Robert Coburn's outfit, 154, 155, 176; Stockgrowers meetings, 155f.; tick fever, 156; Indian Department, 163, 164; brands, 176, 177ff.; loading steers, 207; butchering, 215–20; decline of industry, 221–24, 228, 230; free range, 221f., 282; outfits, 222, 223, 228; wars, 222; industry in So. America, 223, 225, 226; see also William James Allen, cattle rustling, Circle C Ranch, Robert Coburn, and cowpunchers
"Cattle baron": see cattlemen
Cattlemen: of Montana, 7, 16, 27, 28n., 39, 97, 155, 157, 164, 222f., 254; "cattle baron," 27, 221; domain of, 222
Cattle rustling: 37–44, 57, 168n., 170, 176; see also cattle and lawlessness
Cave-dwellers: see Indians
Charlie Collins' Saddle Shop: 136
Cherokee: 197, 199, 200, 203
Cherokee Strip: 179
Chief Joseph (Nez Percés): 7; encounter with Robert Coburn, 8–9, 12–13; surrender to General Miles, 13

Chouteau County: 28, 123n.
Circle C Ranch: 7, 8, 19, 54, 60, 68, 70, 82, 83, 84, 87, 88, 104, 106, 107, 108f., 122, 123, 126, 127, 135, 139, 146, 150, 153, 157, 161, 164, 166, 168n., 174, 179, 184, 215, 219f., 229, 230, 238, 250, 257, 164, 271f., 279f., 282ff., 287ff.; winter of 1886–87, 16; cattle, 19, 107, 126, 143, 155, 157, 159, 160, 187, 191, 203–204, 206, 210, 228, 235, 257; homesteaders, 29, 34; horses, 91, 190, 212; line camps, 125, 155, 231, 257, 279; outlaw broncs, 141; lawsuits, 160–61; meeting on, 165f., 168 & n., 170; roadhouse, 171, 173; selling of, to Matadors, 58, 176, 278, 280; brands, 176, 177ff., 230, 251, 257; roundup wagon, 184, 185, 190; roundup camp, 187, 191, 198, 281, 287; plan of mutiny, 212–14; talk of selling, 222, 224; sheep business, 228, 231, 232, 237, 247f., 251, 254, 257, 265, 269, 271, 275, 278; see also cattle, Robert Coburn, and cowpuncher
Circle Diamond: 28, 108, 126, 185, 197f., 204, 206, 229
Clay, Doc: 278f.
Coburn, Alta: 166, 172
Coburn, Bob: 69, 88, 93–101, 102–104, 106, 108, 123, 135, 155, 168n., 169n., 170, 200, 205f., 207–209, 210, 212, 222, 228, 280f., 283, 287f.; partnership with Will, 176, 177, 179, 230; medicine talk with Walt, 228–30; sheep business, 231; bet with Jake Myers, 245; see also Bar L. brand
Coburn Buttes: see Little Rockies
Coburn Cattle Company: 107, 121f., 123 & n., 174, 177, 230; formation of, 155, 176
Coburn, Florence: 166
Coburn, Harold: 230, 288
Coburn, Robert: 7, 18–19, 27, 39, 127, 154, 155, 161, 166, 176, 179, 206–209, 211, 224, 228, 230, 237, 248, 251ff., 273, 281, 284, 287ff.; ranch of, 7–8, 169n., 210; encounter with Chief Joseph, 8–9, 12–13; purchase of DHS Ranch, 15, 41; orphan, in Canada, 154; schooling, 154; entering U.S., 154; early life in Montana, 154; family

332

Index

of, 164, 167, 170, 280, 286; fire, 172; friendship with Horace Brewster, 175f.; loss of cattle, 176; cattle brand, 176; trouble with cowpunchers, 211–14; decline of cattle industry, 214–24, 230; talk with Walt, 229f.; home in Calif., 230, 288; return to Circle C., 250f.; selling of Circle C, 176, 278, 280; farewell to Circle C, 281–83, 287; rock monument to, 284; *see also* cattle, Circle C Ranch, *and* pioneers
Coburn, Vida: 166, 172, 211
Coburn, Wallace: 26, 88, 107, 124, 135, 155, 157, 164f., 166, 167 & n., 170, 172, 210, 212, 222, 224, 252, 258, 278, 280, 288; cattle brand of, 176ff., 179, 230; motion pictures, 288; *see also Rhymes From A Roundup Camp*
Coburn, Walt: 57, 85–86, 90–100, 107, 110, 125, 155, 157, 167, 168, 174, 175, 180, 182, 184, 189, 193f., 197f., 199f., 203ff., 206–209, 224, 251, 263, 266f., 270, 278–79, 280, 284–89; member of O.O.O. fraternity, 215; butchering cattle, 216, 220; schooling, 228; talk with Bob, 228–30; working with sheep, 230–31, 233–36, 249, 255, 257f., 269; encounters with Hansen's sheepherder, 237–39, 243; business with Grinnell, 271–74; car accident, 275–77; last ride with father, 281–83; "Ocksheebee," 288
Coburn, Will: 8, 88, 107, 119, 124, 135, 155, 164f., 166, 167 & n., 170, 171ff., 210f., 222, 228, 235, 280, 287f.; partnership with Bob, 176, 177, 179, 230; trouble with cowpunchers, 211–14; trip to So. Amer., 223ff.; *see also* Bar L brand
Cochrane, George: 169n.
Cody, William F. ("Buffalo Bill"): 7, 104, 143; Wild West Show, 143, 193, 253
Conley, Jack: 257
Contway, George: 170n., 174
Contway, Joe: 142, 144, 204, 233, 235
Contway, Pat: 170n.
Cowboy Detective, A: 124
Cowhands: *see* cowpunchers
Cow Island Crossing: 37, 123, 184, 257
Cowpunchers (cowhands): 62, 70, 82, 97, 107, 108, 118, 119, 120, 124, 126, 130–36, 137ff., 141, 147, 174, 180, 227, 229, 231, 234f., 281, 289; dress of, 122; Circle C, 127, 128, 166, 179, 180, 182, 188f., 197, 204, 207, 210, 212–14, 220, 232f., 235, 253, 266, 287; Montana and old-time dress, 130f., 133; equipment of, 131, 132, 137; horses of, 133, 137; Texas, 136f.; Southwestern, 222, 281; *see also* cattle *and* Circle C Ranch
Cowtowns: 20, 133, 146, 284
Crosby, John S.: 38 & n.
Cross L Ranch: 137
Curry, Bob: 133
Curry, Flatnose George: 77
Curry, Harvey (Kid): 36, 53–54, 68–71, 74, 75, 90ff., 95ff., 108, 109, 112, 116, 122, 125, 127, 225; feud with Pike Landusky, 56–58, 60–67; Wagner train robbery, 99–101, 175, 224n., 225; Hideaway of, 106, 107, 116, 122; hunt for, 106, 107, 111; friends of, 108, 116; gang of, 108, 125, 225; avenging death of Johnny Curry, 112, 114; Knoxville, Tenn., 117, 118; trial in Tenn., 117; getaway of, 117–18; accounts of death of, 118 & n., 119, 224n.; ranching in So. Amer., 119, 121, 224f., 226; *see also* lawlessness, outlaw gangs *and* train robbery
Curry, Johnny: 53–54, 56–58, 60–64, 67, 72–74, 96, 106, 108, 120, 127; death of, 74, 124; *see also* lawlessness
Curry, Loney: 53–54, 56–58, 60–67, 74, 96, 106, 108, 127, 133; *see also* lawlessness
Custer County: 136

Davenport, Beulah: 179
Davenport, Pete: 179
DHS Cattle Company: 161
DHS (Davis-Hauser-Stuart) Ranch: 8, 15, 18, 39, 108, 126, 206, 284
Davis, Jack: 85, 86, 87, 127, 190f., 194, 200
Dessery, Julia (Mrs. Pike Landusky): 56
Detectives: 40, 68, 78
Dodson, Montana: 30, 133
Donahue, Brian: 257
Dunbar, Angus: 231, 232

333

Duncan, Tap: 118
Dunlap, Margaret: 172
Dunlap, Miss (Mrs. Al Taylor): 214

Eyes-in-the-Water (Assiniboin): 19

Fallon County: 136
Farming, dry-land: 222, 254
Fires: 172; prairie, 173f.
Fort Assiniboine: 142, 164
Fort Belknap Indian Reservation: 15, 16, 18, 19, 84, 87, 155, 157, 159ff., 163f., 167, 168n., 169n., 170, 171, 184, 216, 280, 287f.
Fort Benton (on the Missouri): 6, 20, 28, 42, 76, 108, 126, 127, 167
Fort Benton River Press: 123
Fort Musselshell Crossing: 37, 123, 191, 279
Fortune, Vince: 210f., 213f.
Fort Whoop Up: 6
Four T brand: 176, 179; selling of, 230; *see also* Wallace Coburn
Fur trade: 6-7

Ganty, Joseph: 167 & n.
Garcia Saddle Company: 132
Gauchos: 223
General Miles: 13
Geronimo (Apache): 7
Gill, Abe: 81, 102, 111, 112, 115, 120ff., 225, 238; friends of, 112, 114; trip to So. Amer., 119, 223f.; selling of Winters-Gill Ranch, 121; disappearance of, 122, 123 & n., 124, 224
Gladeau, Rose: 172f., 210f.
Gold rush: 6-7
González, Nick: 265
Gordon, Tom: 233, 235, 243
Goslin, Louis: 171, 246
Graham-Tewksbury: sheep and cattle war, 222
Great Falls, Montana: 208f., 214, 228, 280, 284; selling of Coburn home, 230, 287
Great Northern Railroad: 20, 29, 54, 75, 95, 144, 146, 208; depot, 45, 191
Green Cattle Company: 127
Green, John: 127f.
Griffiths, Sheriff: 122
Grinnell (Idaho sheepman): 275, 278; sheep business with Circle C, 269, 271-74; car accident, 276-77
Gros Ventres: 4, 18, 19, 157, 163, 168n., 172, 288f.; sharing land with Assiniboins, 163, 167
Guerrero, José (Pepe): 259-62; sheepherding, 263-66; death of, 267f.

Half Circle C brand: 176-77, 179, 230
Hall, George: 122, 127, 179, 207, 219
Hanks, Camilla: 99-100
Hansen brothers: 238, 242ff., 255, 257, 265
Hansen Ranch: 240, 271; sheepherder of, 237-40, 242f., 265, 268; sheep of, 241-44
Harmon, Frank: 238ff., 241-43, 255, 257, 265f.
Harris, Jake (Jew Jake): 45-52, 125
Hartmann, Joe: 150, 152
Hartmann, Tim: 150, 152
Has-the-Whip (Assiniboin): 19
Helena, Montana: 161, 210, 212
Hilforts, Pete: 258
Hill, Clay: 258
Hill, Jim: 20, 28f., 32ff., 43, 144, 176, 208, 222
Hill, Walter: purchase of outlaw broncs, 142; Wild West Show, 142-43
Hog Ranch: 147, 244, 261
Hole-in-the-Wall country: 68, 77, 109, 112, 118, 122, 125
Holt, Joe: 233, 235, 243
Homesteaders: 27, 28, 32, 33, 34, 176, 221, 222, 234, 254f., 257, 277f.
Horner, Ruel: 29-30, 235, 250, 261
Horses: 35, 37, 84, 89, 126, 133, 137, 176, 221, 245, 279, 281, 283; reps, 126, 127, 138, 142, 146, 184, 188, 190f., 204, 207, 212, 280; Staple, 126; JHG, 127; breeders, 137; horsebackers, 206; locoweed, 221; *see also* bronc riders
Horse thieving: 37-42, 176; *see also* lawlessness
Howard, Joseph K.: 224
Howe, Frank: 32, 88, 127, 130, 135, 142, 143f., 179, 204-207, 233, 254-55, 257, 287; owner of Bucket of Blood Saloon, 133ff.; Charlie Russell portrait, 135f.
Hudson's Bay Company: 6, 133

Index

Hutchins, Mrs. Julia (Allen): 167n., 168 & n., 169n., 170 & n.

Indian Department: 18, 19, 161, 167, 174, 235, 271, 280, 287; brand of, 163
Indians: 4, 6ff., 9, 18, 145f., 164, 165f., 168n., 170, 172, 176, 203, 215, 265, 283; killing cattle, 156, 159; plight of, 156–57, 159–60, 163–64; agent of, 157, 159, 163; camps, 251
Iron Horn, Jesse (Assiniboin): 233, 251, 288
Island Mountains: *see* Little Rockies
IXL Ranch: 136

Jackson, "Dad" (Jim Thornhill): 108
Jackson, Frank: 108
J. C. Hyer Boot Company: 131
Jefferson City, Tenn.: 117
Jerk-line freighters: 145–46, 150–53, 249, 277; Hard Luck Smith, 29; equipment of, 147, 148
Johnson, Liver Eatin': 6
Jones, Fatty: 239, 254f.
Judith Basin: 7, 13, 15, 39, 126
Judith Basin Pool Ranch: 108

Kaufman, Louis: 26, 43n.
Kelley, Charles: 118
King Ranch: 190
Kingsbury, A. W.: 16, 43
Kingsbury, Wallace: 16
Knoxville, Tenn.: 117, 118; *see also* Harvey (Kid) Curry

Lamb lickers: 234, 253
Lambs: 232, 245f., 250, 252f.; *see also* sheep
Lampkin, Wash: 76, 127, 198f., 201
Landusky, Montana: 30, 32, 37, 54, 57, 77, 81, 109, 118, 119, 123n., 125, 146, 150f., 171, 239, 265
Landusky, Powell (Pike): 36, 44–52, 68, 70, 107; killing of, 36n., 67; feud with Kid Curry, 56–58, 60–67
Lankin, W. W.: *see* Wash Lampkin
Lawlessness: 36–44, 53–54, 56–58, 60–62, 68, 100–104, 106, 225; *see also* cattle rustling, Harvey (Kid) Curry, Johnny Curry, Loney Curry, horse thieving *and* outlaw gangs

Lee, Bob: 133; *see also* Bob Curry
Lemmon, Letch: 179
Lewis and Clark: exploration party, 6
Lewistown, Montana: 177, 230
Lincoln County, New Mexico: war of, 222
Little Rockies: 4, 6, 15–16, 34, 87, 100, 104, 108, 109, 116, 119, 122, 124, 125, 126, 147, 151, 171, 236, 239, 255, 281f., 287; location of, 3, 123, 124; lawless country, 36, 111; gold mines, 125, 170, 228
Little Warm Creek: 161, 236, 282
Llano Estacado: *see* Staked Plains
Lodge Pole subagency: 160f., 163, 164, 165, 168, 169n., 170 & n.
Logan, Harvey: *see* Harvey (Kid) Curry
Logan, Major W. R.: 88, 164, 167, 168n.
Longabaugh, Harry (Sundance Kid): 90–100, 119, 225ff.
Long Henry: 143
Long Knife, Roy (Assiniboin): 19, 233, 235, 288
Long S (Slaughter) Ranch: 136
Loughlin, Jim: 193, 199ff., 212, 214
Luneberg, John: 167n.

McClennar, Mac: 88
McDonald, Tom: 179
McGahn, Grant: 167n.
MacGilvra, E. E. (Boo): 168
Machine era: 35
McNeil, George: 184
Maddox, Fletcher: 280
Maddox, Jessie (Coburn): 8, 280
Malette, Joe: 150
Maloney, Tim: 88, 101f., 128
Malta Stockyards: 206
Matador Land and Cattle Company (Matadors): purchase of Circle C, 19, 58, 176, 278, 280; ranch of, 136, 280, 281
Matador Ranch: 136, 280, 281, 283; cattle of, 282
Matt, James: 167n.
Mayo Clinic: 279
Military forts: along the Missouri, 6
Milk River: 4, 20, 37, 126, 155, 231, 254
Miller, Scott: 179, 191, 198
Milner Square Ranch: 28, 108, 126, 229; wagon of, 184

335

Missouri River: 6, 37, 70, 111, 123, 126, 155, 184, 191, 230, 236, 257, 279, 282, 288
Mitchell, Jim (Mitch): 219
Mitch Field: 218
Montana Central Railroad: 20, 43
Montana: High, Wide, and Handsome: 224
Montana Stockgrowers Association: 26, 38 & n., 154f., 157, 176, 222
Mule skinner: 145f.
Murray, Jim: 150
Myers, Cecil: 179
Myers, Jake: 29, 31–32, 124, 128, 150–51, 171f., 191f., 197–202, 203, 205f., 207ff., 213f., 270, 279, 280; hired as Circle C foreman, 179, 182–86; family of, 179, 210; "Old Griz," 184; O.O.O. fraternity, 215; butchering cattle, 216, 219f.; sheep business, 229, 230, 232–35, 239–42, 251, 254–57, 259, 266, 271–74; sheepherding, 231; encounters with Frank Harmon, 243–44, 257, 265; foreman of Phillips' Ranch, 280, 287; bets, 245f.
Myers, Janie: 179

Neibaur, Ike: 179
Neihart, Montana: 214
Nester ranches: 185, 239, 257
Nez Percés: 9, 137
Night horses: 85
No Man's Land: 136
Northern Montana Roundup Association: 126, 155, 184; meeting about sheep and cattle wars, 223
Nunez, Frank: 232, 237, 241, 244, 246ff., 260–62; Circle C sheep boss, 231, 232, 234, 235, 241, 249, 254, 257ff., 263–66; docking lambs, 245; mourning death of Pepe, 267f.

"Ocksheebee": *see* Walt Coburn
Olathe, Kansas: 131
Old Black Dog (Assiniboin Indian Chief): 18–19, 215, 216, 218f., 251, 288f.
Olson, Pete: 88, 96f., 172, 210, 212f., 287
O'Neill, Mike: 100, 117
"One of Ourn" (O.O.O.): 215, 219

Outlaw gangs: 68, 76, 77, 81, 97, 107, 108, 109, 125, 189, 225; country of, 123, 225; passing of, 226–27; *see also* Butch Cassidy, Harvey (Kid) Curry, *and* lawlessness

Pampa land: 223f.
Panhandle (Texas): 136
Park Hotel: 280
Parrot Ranch: 237, 239, 282
Patagonia, So. Amer.: 224 & n.
Peralta (Mexican shearing crew boss): 248, 254, 259f.
Perry, Charles: 164, 165, 168, 170, 174; killing of William James Allen, 166–67, 169n., 170; trial of, 167–68
Perry, Dora: 170n.
Perry, Ella: 169n.
Perry, Jeanette: 170n.
Perry, Mary: 167n.
Perry, Tommy: 169n.
Phillips, B. D.: 58, 231, 233f., 239, 246, 254, 255, 271, 280, 287
Phillips' Ranch: 147, 244, 254, 278; sheep outfit of, 239, 254
Pinkerton detectives: 68, 77, 78, 80, 108, 109, 116, 118, 119, 124, 134, 225f.
Pioneers: of Montana, 6, 16, 185, 222, 287; Robert Coburn, 7, 176, 250, 282, 284
Place, Etta: 225
Pleasant Valley, Arizona: 222
Plott, Long Henry: 133
Pony Express: rider of, 145f.
Powell, Ed: 128, 133, 143
Powell, Puck: 128, 133, 143, 179
Pray, Charles H.: 167

Rafter T brand: 177, 230, 251, 280
Railroads: 29, 155, 176; St. Paul, Minneapolis and Manitoba, 20, 43; Montana Central, 20; Great Northern, 20, 29, 45, 54, 75, 95, 144, 146, 176, 208; Union Pacific, 77
Rainbow Hotel: 280
Ranches: 7, 8; owners of, 127; Texas, 136
Rattlesnake Jack: 257f., 262, 265
Rawhide Dan: 233, 244, 253
Reader (Robert Coburn's horse): 84, 251, 281, 283

Index

Red Barn Ranch: 230
Red River: 136
Remington, Frederic: 81, 122
Reynolds, Joe: 135, 190
Reynolds Long X Ranch: 135, 136, 188, 190, 229; wagon of, 184
Rhymes From A Roundup Camp: 288
Ritch, Johnny: 26, 36, 37, 44–52
Robbers' Roost: 116, 125
Robbins, Tommy: 279
Roberts, Fred: 179
Roberts, Lew: 179, 191, 198
Rochester, Minnesota: 279
Rocky Point Crossing: 37, 70, 123, 142, 184, 204, 230, 288
Rollin' M Lake: 240, 243
Roosevelt, Theodore: 38n., 157, 258
Ruby Gulch Mine: 88, 151, 228f.
Russell, Charles M.: 20, 26, 122, 135, 230

Saddle horses: 85, 137, 212, 281
Saddles: 132
St. Paul, Minneapolis and Manitoba Railroad: 20, 43
St. Paul's Mission: 184
Saloons: 133f., 152, 225, 271; keepers, 148, 207
San Carlos Apache Indian Reservation: 228, 287
San Diego, Calif.: 230
Schulke, Dr. Julius A.: 118n.
777 Ranch: 136
Sheep: 221f., 228, 229, 235, 238, 246f., 251, 257, 264, 266ff., 274, 278, 282; bands of, 221, 222, 230, 232, 234, 236, 237, 240, 244f., 253, 254f., 271, 274, 281; outfits, 58, 222, 238, 257, 265, 287; wars, 193, 222; herding, 231, 234, 236, 238, 241, 257, 265, 263; "sheepies," 231; lambing season, 232ff., 235, 236f., 245, 250, 253; camps, 236–37, 250, 255f., 262, 266, 273f.; dockers, 245; shearing, 247ff., 250, 252ff., 259; *see also* Circle C Ranch *and* lambs
Sheriff of Valley County: 95, 96, 98–104, 106f., 111; posse of, 101–104, 106f., 111, 114; trick on posse, 101–104, 106; hunt for Kid Curry, 100–104, 106f., 111, 115
Shod horses: 85
Shonkin Pool Ranch: 108, 126

Shufeldt Kid: 135
Sioux Nation: 4, 7, 163; *see also* Assiniboins
Siringo, Charlie: 78 & n., 108, 109; book of, 124
Sitting Bull (Sioux): 7, 168n.
Sizer, Walt: 233, 242f., 255, 257f.
Sklower, Joe: 252, 271ff.
Slaughter Ranch: 136
Smith, Hard Luck: 29–31, 150–53
Smith, Pryor: 166, 167 & n., 179
Staked Plains: 190
Stanford University: 228, 230
Stanton, George H.: 167
Star Cross Ranch: 190
Stevens, Oscar (Spud): outfit, 108; purchase of Half Circle C brand, 177, 230; purchase of Bar L brand, 230
Stranahan, F. E.: 167
Stuart, Charlie: 127, 128, 134, 179, 185, 191f., 193–94, 197ff., 203f.
Stuart, Granville: 18, 36, 41, 155, 185; trade with Robert Coburn, 15; meeting of cattlemen, 38 & n., 39, 157
Sturman, Big Foot: 150
Summers, Charlie: 179, 233, 235
Sun River: 126
Survant, John: 43n., 119, 223ff.
Surveying: 29, 32
Swain, Jim: 197–202, 203f., 214

Takes-the-Shield (Assiniboin): 19
Taylor, Al: 32, 84, 88, 92, 93, 96, 98ff., 172f., 210ff., 213, 214, 253f.; marriage of, 214
Texans: 136, 188, 281; outfits of, 136, 222
Thornhill, Bill: 90
Thornhill, Harvey (Man): 90, 91
Thornhill, Jim (Old Jimmer): 53–54, 57, 58, 60–71, 90, 106, 107, 108, 117, 122, 123, 127, 152, 226, 238, 283, 287; identifying Kid Curry's body, 118f.
Tracy, Dan: 280
Trading posts: 6–7
Train Robbers' Syndicate: *see* Wild Bunch
Train robbery: 77, 95, 99, 107, 111f., 118, 175, 225f.; *see also* Harvey (Kid) Curry *and* lawlessness
Travis, William: 167n.

337

Tressler, Dan: ranch of, 72, 108, 120, 124
Troop, John: 118
Turkey Track Ranch: 136
Two Dog Moore: 150f., 258

UL Ranch: 279
Union Pacific: 77

Visalia Saddle Company: 132

Wagner, Montana: 95, 100, 106, 107; train robbery, 106, 107, 111f., 117, 175
Walker, J. M. (Matt): 280f., 283, 287
Wallace, Norville: 190
Warrior, Rufus: 170n.
Watch-His-Walking (Assiniboin): 19, 251, 288
White Cloud (Abe Gill's horse): 122
White Horse (Assiniboin): 19
Whitmore, Frank (Whitty): 150, 152, 277f.

Whoop Up country: 6
Wild Bunch: 53, 68, 77, 78 & n., 91, 106, 109, 125, 225; *see also* Butch Cassidy *and* outlaw gangs
Wild Bunch (outlaw broncs): 141, 142f.; *see also* broncs
Wing, Peter: 167n.
Wingate, Charlie: 252
Winter of 1886–87: 16, 18
Winter-Gill Ranch: 104, 106, 111, 120, 124f., 262, 264, 268, 279
Winters, Jim: 72–77, 80, 102, 106, 107, 108, 111, 115f., 125; killing of Johnny Curry, 74, 124; death of, 112, 114, 120
Work horses: 85

XIT Ranch: 136, 190

Zortman, Montana: 30, 54, 77, 104, 106, 109, 119, 146, 171, 235, 239, 265f.

www.ingramcontent.com/pod-product-compliance
Lightning Source LLC
Chambersburg PA
CBHW020732160426
43192CB00006B/201